AMERICA'S

JEFFERSONIAN

EXPERIMENT

AMERICA'S

Jeffersonian

EXPERIMENT

Remaking State Constitutions
1820–1850

LAURA J. SCALIA

NORTHERN ILLINOIS
UNIVERSITY
PRESS

DeKalb 1999

© 1999 by Northern Illinois University Press
Published by the Northern Illinois University Press,
DeKalb, Illinois 60115
Manufactured in the United States using acid-free paper
All Rights Reserved
Design by Julia Fauci

Library of Congress Cataloging-in-Publication Data
Scalia, Laura J., 1959–
America's Jeffersonian experiment : remaking state constitutions, 1820–1850 /
Laura J. Scalia
p. cm.
Includes bibliographical references and index.
ISBN 0-87580-244-3 (alk. paper)
1. Constitutional history—United States—States.
2. Constitutional conventions—United States—States. I. Title.
KF4541.S32 1999
342.73'029—dc21 98-47535
CIP

To My Parents

Contents

Preface

I began this book in 1987, two hundred years after the writing of the U.S. Constitution. The anniversary date led many to continue in the footsteps of their predecessors and further investigate how that document helped shape American thought and practice. I too began with this intention, wanting to capture the ideological and legal development of America's allegiance to active popular sovereignty, one of the most distinctive features of American constitutionalism. Scholars such as Jack Pole and Edward Morgan have demonstrated how ingrained this commitment initially was.[1] Yet, scholars grasped the ideological impediments to popular sovereignty's development better than the rationale behind its subsequent growth. I soon discovered the source of this skewed understanding: the predominant focus on the national Constitution, a document whose primary concern was never to empower ordinary citizens. To understand why Americans expanded their constitutional commitments to popular rule over the generations, I would have to shift my research focus away from the misplaced national emphasis and toward the states, where the meaning and relative value of that ideal was not only debated but actually determined.

This book investigates America's constitutional commitment to popular sovereignty, at the state level. It looks to neither the theories underlying the U.S. Constitution nor the selected views of well-known national statesmen. Instead, it examines the ideas of local politicians and citizens, who joined together to rewrite their state constitutions and whose deliberations often led to the expansion of popular power. This research joins an emerging body of scholarship that stresses the independent intellectual and political significance of state foundational documents. However, the majority of state constitutional studies focus on developments leading up to the national founding.[2] This study examines the succeeding period, when states expanded the franchise and more than doubled the number of popularly elected officers.

At the same time, the contribution goes well beyond an emphasis on relatively unstudied materials. It also enriches our understanding of American constitutionalism then and today. Too often America's constitutional tradition is limited to the document produced in 1787, the views of *Publius* (the pen name for the authors of the *Federalist Papers*), and later U.S. Supreme Court justices.[3] As a result, we often think of constitutions as reflecting a particular liberal theory, one that channels man's inevitably selfish, acquisitive nature and that privileges personal and property rights above and beyond popular influence. A careful look at state constitutional designs and the rationale supporting them shows that the national emphasis on human fallibility and private rights has never constituted America's only model of constitutional government. For generations after the national founding, another equally liberal conception also existed, one that portrayed self-government as an inalienable right and constitutions as legitimate precisely because they condoned frequent popular input. This alternative view, developed at the state level, represents another ideological facet of America's constitutional tradition.

A methodological movement away from national-level analysis is especially necessary to understand America's commitment to popular sovereignty. The U.S. Constitution begins with "We the people" but contains no other declaratory statements emphasizing its commitment to or foundation on the populace. Although *Publius*, its iconoclastic defenders, occasionally touted the virtues of popular sovereignty, they strategically placed their emphasis elsewhere, namely, on the dangers of popular rule and the means by which the new document cleverly avoided them. Rather than reflect a national antipathy to the popular sovereignty ideal, these facts likely reflect the political reality of the time. Memories of parliamentary tyranny prevented the creators from designing a government whose authority rested anywhere but with the states. Too much direct popular control would have been seen as empowering a new England on the mainland. All this prevented defenders from stressing whatever direct democratic features existed, lest it buttress opponents' claim that the document really aimed to undermine state sovereignty.

Despite these obvious explanations for national silence on questions relating to the people's popular sovereignty, political scientists across subfields continue to evaluate America's commitment to this ideal by looking at national laws and debates among prominent statesmen. Vocal and well-known critics of America's democratic faith such as Benjamin Barber and Sheldon Wolin, for example, fault the U.S. tradition for not promoting active citizen participation, and they look specifically to the national Constitution as evidence of this dire situation.[4] Prominent scholars such as Joyce Appleby and Thomas Pangle portray the American system as one that values rights and economic prosperity above and beyond self-government. They and others depict this value hierarchy as the national founders' intentional response to people's known defects.[5] Finally, hundreds of scholars, like Richard Hofstadter and Neil Riemer, examine America's perspective on democracy and popular rule by focusing on national figures such as Jefferson, Madison, Jackson, or Webster, only to find weak instrumental arguments supporting popular sovereignty, both at the founding and over time.[6] In short, the U.S. Constitution, its initial defenders, and later spokesmen often speak on behalf of America's allegiance to popular sovereignty—and this, even though the nation's state builders consciously avoided questions of popular rule, deeming them the rightful providence of states.

Although the dominant level of analysis has been the nation, a growing number of scholars are paying serious attention to the theory and practice underlying state constitutions, especially how early documents reflect powerful commitments to popular sovereignty. Willi Paul Adams, Christian Fritz, Marc Kruman, Donald Lutz, and Gordon Wood have helped us understand how radically democratic and antigovernment initial state constitutions were. Many of these documents used language like that found in Delaware's 1792 constitution, which described political society as "derived from the people and established with their consent" (Poore 1878, pt. 1, 278).[7] They relied on legislative supremacy, not to indicate trust in government but to reflect faith in popular sovereignty, for lawmakers were supposed to be the voice of the people. Powerless and legislatively dependent executive and judicial officers would ensure that the people's governing control lay safely with themselves and their annually elected lawmakers.[8] Moreover, over half the initial state constitutions followed Virginia's lead and proclaimed that "the blessings of liberty" required a "frequent recurrence to fundamental principles" (Poore 1898, pt. 2, 1909). With this in mind, several states permitted citizens or specially selected representatives to reevaluate their constitution and its principles sometime in the near future. By 1790 eight original states had rewritten their constitutions.[9]

Scholars of the Revolutionary period and these early state constitutions generally agree that these initial commitments to popular sovereignty were part of a larger theory of constitutionalism and good government, one that included intellectual influences from classical and modern republicanism, British Common

Law, Lockean liberalism, the Scottish Enlightenment, and Protestantism.[10] Early constitutional concerns for protecting rights and avoiding arbitrary government reflect liberal influences, while demands for spiritual virtue and free conscience suggest religious sentiments, and desires for popular virtue and popular participation illustrate republican concerns. Thus, foundational documents from the Revolutionary period did not contain a unified vision of the good state but embodied values and concerns originating from various intellectual traditions.

Oddly enough, scholars of this early period readily accept that something radical occurred around 1787 and that a new vision of constitutionalism and good government took hold thereafter. For example, J. G. A. Pocock insists that the Revolution should be understood as the culminating influence of republicanism, yet he admits that this tradition had minimal sway by the turn of the century. Barry Shain, who traces the religious influences on intellectual thought during the Revolutionary period, sees Protestantism as strong and dominant until 1785 and then notes a remarkable disappearance of its political influence. Finally, state constitutional scholars such as Donald Lutz and Gordon Wood agree that initially strong commitments to popular sovereignty were permanently tamed by the realization that people were hopelessly selfish, unable to protect themselves against government abuse, and perhaps even capable of abuse themselves. All these studies strongly suggest that *Publius*'s new science of politics came to dominate political thought, such that a rights-centered liberal tradition now reigned.[11]

A quick examination of state constitutions written in the generation or two after the national founding readily shows that the passage of the national document did not radically alter state constitutional commitments to popular sovereignty. Instead, in the decades that followed, states expanded its application. By 1850, not only did 80 percent of the constitutions acknowledge that "political society is derived from the people and established with their consent," over half now also declared that "the people . . . have the inherent, sole, and exclusive right of regulating the internal government . . . and of altering and abolishing their constitution and form of government whenever it may be necessary to their safety and happiness."[12] Procedures changed to endorse this philosophy better. For example, as states increased the control enjoyed by governors and judges, they ensured that the newly empowered became subject to popular selection.[13] Though no women and few blacks were permitted to vote or hold office, states lifted pecuniary qualification on white political participation, allowing what many willingly called democracy and universal suffrage.[14] By the mid-nineteenth century, almost any constitutional change required popular approval, though not by a prohibitively high, super majority.

That the content of subsequent state documents did not reflect the same skepticism toward popular sovereignty as did the national Constitution does not necessarily mean local writers or supporters found this ideal a primary and essential feature of the good state. It does not necessarily mean that they rejected either *Publius*'s value hierarchy, which placed private rights and economic freedoms above self-government, or his theory of institutional design, which envisioned checks and balances as offsetting the dangerous effects of selfish human behavior. It only illustrates how narrow and potentially misleading our focus on the national Constitution has been. The question remains whether later designers of state constitutions agreed with their national forefathers that selfishness was acceptable when institutionally channeled and that rights were of primary importance while popular sovereignty was of mere instrumental value. Such liberal beliefs might still have led to expanded popular influence, on the pretext that the more people who participated, the less selfishness could harm rights. Only by looking at the ideas that drove changing provisions can such information be uncovered. Thus, this book examines the debates surrounding state constitutional proposals aimed at directly affecting the people's political sovereignty.

Throughout the first half of the nineteenth century, state politicians and citizens met at constitutional conventions to discuss the revision of various electoral laws, including those determining who could vote and run for office, on what basis legislative districts should be drawn, and which officers should be popularly elected. Their discussions centered on the overall purpose of foundational documents, the theory underlying constitutional design, and the role held by popular sovereignty in that theory. Speakers always agreed on two general points. First, regardless of how they thought their particular state should implement the ideal of popular sovereignty, they strongly averred that good constitutional government protected and preserved the people's lives, liberties, and properties. Second, speakers agreed that good citizenship helped prevent official and popular tyranny. However, they also recognized that well-designed constitutions must take individuals as they are and not try to transform them into selfless agents for the public good. The fact that state constitutional designers repeatedly found it necessary to acknowledge their commitment to these principles illustrates how prevalent the national science of politics had become. At the same time, a careful look at how these local state builders constructed the meaning and relative importance of these basic principles shows that behind broad liberal agreements lay important distinctions. If we tease out these distinctions we see the narrowness not just of our present understanding of America's commitment to popular sovereignty, but also of our understanding of the theoretical underpinnings of U.S. constitutionalism.

The chapters ahead discuss different nineteenth-century interpretations of what it meant to have a legal system committed to protecting rights and cognizant of an inability to alter human nature. Views on these matters clustered into two groups: one indifferent or perhaps hostile to greater popular empowerment, the other essentially democratic in its content. Politicians who argued against America's movement toward greater popular empowerment fall into this first group. They perpetually touted the importance of *private* rights, especially the right to acquire and dispose of one's possessions freely, while at the same time disavowing an equal status for popular rule. To these politicians there was a distinct difference between private rights and political voice and only the former deserved complete and unquestioned reverence. Although some conceded that these private rights were immutable precisely because they were freely enjoyed in nature, the vast majority argued that their inalienability relied on established laws, based on long-standing prior agreements (that is, the social contract). The defenders of restriction also agreed that, although popular government required its citizens to exhibit good character, well-designed governments must recognize every individual's selfish disposition. Some believed narrow interest in one's possessions established sufficient virtue among governors. All that was necessary was to install clever procedures and institutional designs that allowed this interest to cohere with the public good. Others believed that land acquisition transformed interest into virtue, for owners acquired such desirable attributes as frugality and moderation. Both cases entailed the same general assumption: all individuals were naturally acquisitive. The trick of state building was to manipulate selfish economic pursuits for positive gain. Although different in some important respects, these views look surprisingly similar to the so-called liberal, antidemocratic side of *Publius*'s vision of constitutionalism.

Those politicians who supported greater popular influence in and over government offered alternative interpretations of America's constitutional commitment to inalienable rights. They, too, argued that popularly governed states necessarily relied on naturally based behavior. However, these advocates of electoral reform adamantly repudiated the conception of human nature that their adversaries put forward. They noted that narrow self-interest did not naturally motivate citizens' behavior, for such single-mindedness undermined popularly governed states. Patriotism and a general interest in the good of the community—both seen as *natural* human sentiments—were necessary to protect the good state. In addition, these supporters of expanded popular rule usually included a voice in government among the inalienable natural rights. Whereas a few politicians agreed with those who fought reform and contended that rights took precedence in the good state as a result of an initial social contract, the vast majority saw government's commitment to life, liberty, property, *and* self-government as a priori. The good state derived its legitimacy from the state of nature and abstract principles. Prior agreements, whether unanimous or otherwise, were of human artifice and thus not the unshakable foundation upon which America's fundamental values and beliefs deserved to be based. Their views constitute a form of liberal constitutionalism currently ignored.

These findings give important insight into the development of nineteenth-century thinking about popular sovereignty. They illustrate that constitutional thought regarding the place of popular sovereignty in the good state was predominantly liberal, albeit liberal in a classical sense. Much of the language used to justify constitutional change or the status quo resembled what John Locke said in *The Second Treatise* about rights, self-government, and human nature. Although no constitutional writer of the time called himself a liberal and only a few referred directly to Locke as the source of their views regarding popular sovereignty, such parallels suggest strongly that his ideas were in the air. Whatever other liberal thinkers (such as Jeremy Bentham or John Stuart Mill) or other ideological constructs (such as republicanism or Protestantism) were available to state builders of that time, they were not considered a public language useful or persuasive enough to capture the essence of American state constitutionalism, particularly the place it gave to popular sovereignty.[15] That means American constitutions were not liberal in today's sense of the word. Designers neither praised the irreligious, freethinking, or wholly autonomous individual nor advocated a nurturing, diverse state, involved in engineering special economic and social outcomes.[16]

In addition, the above findings suggest that, although generally Lockean and liberal, the theories supporting state constitutions of the postfounding period did not constitute a unified liberal vision of the good state. Drafters of foundational documents regularly debated the particulars of government. They stressed different aspects of Locke's ideas and created different, competing interpretations of how and why America was committed to inalienable rights. Thus, the liberal foundations of America's state constitutionalism were multifaceted. They also appeared fluid and somewhat malleable. Which interpretation of Locke's teachings was stressed by the constitution writers depended completely on the writers' policy preferences. The pairings are unmistakable and suggest that America's early liberal allegiances were not purely ideologically based; they had political underpinnings too.

Aspects of these findings appear counterintuitive for several reasons. First, republican language seeks the development of citizen virtue and robustly defends popular participation. Since some like Lance Banning, Ralph Ketcham, and Drew McCoy have traced republicanism's ongoing influence up until the

1820s, one might expect that advocates of expanding the people's real sovereignty would readily use this participation-friendly, virtue-touting tradition to buttress their support for electoral reform.[17] There is also evidence that other intellectual traditions, such as the Scottish Enlightenment, British Common Law, and Protestantism influenced early views about rights and human nature, not just during America's formative years, but also in the early decades of the nineteenth century.[18] Furthermore, as discussed in the recent scholarship of Rogers Smith, other illiberal ideas influenced certain aspects of political inclusion debates, especially on questions of black empowerment and immigrant status.[19] With such different ideological traditions at their disposal, one would expect that a variety of values and ideals would have informed local state builders as they debated the meaning of rights, the limits of human nature, and the range of political influence to grant their inhabitants. However, this was generally not the case. Clashing intellectual traditions do not explain why some individuals endorsed expansion, while others did not.

Of course, numerous scholars, including John Diggins and Joyce Appleby, remain skeptical of recent "revisionism" and therefore would insist that of course liberalism was the dominant influence in America's ideological and legal development. Yet, the question remains what kind of liberalism prevailed in early nineteenth century, especially as related to the democratic developments of that period. Here, contemporaries tend to emphasize that strand of liberalism opposed to reform. Leading democratic theorists such as Benjamin Barber, C. B. Macpherson, and Carole Pateman admit that liberal values and beliefs were responsible for the actual growth in popular influence that took place during the late eighteenth and early nineteenth centuries, but they blame that connection for initial and continued half-hearted commitments to self-government. According to their account, the politicians who originally endorsed popular influence first and foremost embraced specific precepts of liberalism; that is, they recognized individuals as narrowly self-interested and wanted mainly to protect private rights and economic freedoms. The original endorsement of popular government was supposedly conditional on its ability to channel the interests of voters so that citizen rights and freedoms would be protected; popular sovereignty had no intrinsic worth.[20] Scholars discussing America's nineteenth-century suffrage expansion seem to support that historical account. For example, John Ashworth, Irving Howe, and Rush Welter look at national partisan debates on this issue and find similarly instrumental and conditional arguments for political influence. Advocates of reform supposedly stressed the presently ignored interests of the common man, whereas opponents worried about the negative consequences that his self-interested temperament would bring. Who should have the franchise is said to have hinged on who was capable of preventing corruption and protecting citizen rights and liberties, particularly those related to economic well-being. There is little sense that Jacksonian Democrats endorsed expansion because of the intrinsic value of active participation.[21]

Imbedded in the above arguments is the idea that advocates and opponents of popular rule justified their allegiance by using the same coherent, liberal sense of the good state, one that prized private rights and economic freedoms and saw self-government as an instrumental good, whose distribution depended on a simple empirical test, namely, what selfish individuals would do with the voting privilege. However, this characterization inaccurately captures the views of a large number of state politicians and citizens who designed constitutions during the first half of the nineteenth century. Many of these individuals wondered about the empirical consequences of expanding popular power, but it was just one of many aspects of their debate. Some relegated the ideal of popular sovereignty to secondary and instrumental status, but others did not. These others understood self-government to be an integral component of their commitment to rights. Not all constitution writers based their evaluation of popular sovereignty on the ground that citizens would regard only their narrow self-interest and that therefore all behavior needed to be institutionally channeled. Some took that position, but others acknowledged the existence of natural political sentiments. In all cases, ideological differences among nineteenth-century designers are best understood as differences within a liberal framework, though it is inaccurate to think of all facets of that framework as antidemocratic.

In itself, the idea that liberalism has many faces is nothing new. Other historians, such as David Greenstone and David Ericson, have also focused on nuanced ideological differences within the liberal tradition.[22] New in my study are the particular liberal contours uncovered by electoral debates, namely, that there existed a strand of American liberalism that supported democracy on theoretical as well as empirical grounds. Particularly interesting and useful is what the origin and content of these new contours tell us about the meaning of constitutionalism in America. The findings of this book stress that, throughout U.S. history, constitutions were not merely legal means to protect private rights and prevent human selfishness from taking the reins of government. They were documents whose purpose was also to empower the people. American constitutions were not documents with a singular intent or a coherent original meaning. Instead, as the product of debate, they hold together competing and infinitely contestable understandings of the good state.

Acknowledgments

nyone who has ever written a scholarly book knows that it is a lonely and laborious process. Many hours are spent alone, in a library searching through primary sources, in an office disentangling complex ideas, at a computer searching for appropriate words and phrases. But few really write a book alone; instead, there are always people who inform the process, introducing new sources, helping to unpack ideas, offering better means of expression. If one is especially lucky, there will be those who do more than enhance the book's content; there will be those who nourish the writer's soul, with friendship and faith.

I have been fortunate to have helpers of both kinds, those whose unselfish work improved the book's content and those whose giving hearts drove my spirit and fortified my integrity. Although none of these individuals are responsible for the problems that critics will uncover in my work, all deserve much of the credit for whatever brilliance there is. Thus, I now officially thank them for sharing their minds and of their selves, for selflessly offering intellectual guidance and spiritual nourishment.

I begin with recognizing the extraordinary help I received from Kristen Renwick Monroe, my mentor when I was in college, who has remained a trusted academic counsellor and who is now among my dearest friends. Her contribution to this book is unmeasurable; indeed, if I had never met her there would be no book. This project began as a dissertation, and it was her encouragement that persuaded me even to consider a graduate education. Her support and her constant reminders of the value of endurance helped me finish the dissertation (and, ultimately, the book). During my years of writing (and not), she believed in me as a scholar and gave me the courage to persevere. I thank Kristen Monroe for introducing me to the world of academia and the joys of research, for constantly nourishing me with the will to continue, and especially for her love and friendship.

While I was in graduate school and doing the initial research for this book, I was generously subsidized by a graduate opportunities grant funded by the U.S. government, together with a doctoral fellowship from Yale University. While writing the dissertation I had the privilege to work with three great minds: Rogers Smith, Ian Shapiro, and Joseph Hamburger. My greatest debt is to Rogers Smith, who during those years carefully read each draft. The pages he returned to me were always filled with copious helpful commentaries, often with suggestions for new avenues to pursue. Our conversations then and his writings today remind me constantly of America's rich and complicated intellectual tradition. To his greatest credit, Rogers has always let me develop my research as I, not he, felt best. I therefore thank him both for sharing with me his rich insights into American political thought and for generously respecting my own ideas (even when they conflict with his own).

Ian Shapiro was also helpful in the early stages of this project. While I was still in graduate school, we spent long hours debating the meaning of liberalism and democracy, forcing me to confront problems in my analytical accounts of both. I greatly benefited from our talks and am grateful to him for sharing his critical mind. With Joseph Hamburger, I again enjoyed many hours of intellectual discussion, concerning history, politics, and philosophy. He helped me see how deeply connected all three phenomena are. I am grateful to him for those many conversations as well as for the dignity and respect he gave me as an individual. I have never again met such a gentlemanly scholar.

While in graduate school, I became acquainted with Barry Shain, a fellow student traveler, who then and to this day not only influences my thinking but also nourishes my spiritedness. His great enthusiasm for knowledge and his desire for truth kept me alive in graduate school and today keep me honest in my intellectual pursuits. His careful reading and insightful criticisms of an earlier version of this manuscript were invaluable. His voracious love of ideas keeps him engaging others like myself in discussion and debate. These engagements have often made me realize how little I know. Because of them, I always want to know more. I thank Barry Shain for sharing his ideas and infecting me with his unabated curiosity. I also thank him for his friendship.

From Yale I became a faculty member at the University of Houston, where I spent several years revising the manuscript. The Political Science Department supported this endeavor by awarding me a paid junior faculty leave and by assigning me quality graduate students, such as Karen Baird, Sally Campbell, and Deborah Orth, who then helped collect valuable data. The greatest benefit of being at Houston was the interaction with faculty members, many of whom were interested in my research agenda. I especially benefited from the intellectual input of Mark Franklin, Donald Lutz, Susan Scarrow, and Alan Stone. Each of them read the manuscript in its entirety at some stage of its development. Each gave extensive, helpful, and encouraging comments. Of these four, I owe special thanks to Donald Lutz, an unassuming scholar and gracious man, who has taught me much about state constitutionalism. Without him, I would have written a different book, one less informed by America's legal and popular sovereignty tradition. Although I am grateful for the intellectual support of all of these four, I especially appreciate their friendship. They helped keep the project alive in my mind and heart, even when the burdens of heavy teaching and a commuter marriage got in the way. I thank them for making the university not just a place of employment but a supportive, collegial community.

During my tenure at Houston, I received financial and intellectual assistance also from outside the university. The Ford Foundation supported me with a postdoctoral fellowship and additional research money, which together allowed me to enjoy a year free of teaching, dedicated to research and writing. Northwestern School of Law graciously hosted me during this period. I am especially thankful to Stephen Presser who sponsored my stay there and to the school's librarians who every morning greeted me cheerfully and then left me to peruse their collection of rare books. I also feel indebted to the Liberty Fund, a nonprofit organization that regularly funds interdisciplinary seminars wherein scholars get together and discuss the meaning and value of liberty. I have learned much from these meetings. I especially profited from sponsored conferences on constitutionalism in the United States and Latin America.

I owe special thanks to people met there and elsewhere whose lively engagements helped me clarify muddled ideas. I hope all will forgive me for not acknowledging each of them specifically by name. I would no doubt omit more than I would include. Thus, let me extend my deepest gratitude to all those great minds who have talked with me about constitutionalism in America and elsewhere, who have discussed with me the meaning of liberty and liberalism. I have prospered from our conversations and from the written work subsequently sent me; both have influenced the ideas presented in this book. Also, let me thank here those anonymous readers who scrupulously reviewed the manuscript, as well as Martin Johnson who saw this project to completion. Each one's critical and helpful comments improved the argument and its ultimate presentation.

None of the help received was more special (or essential) than the sustenance given me by my parents, sister, and husband. They above all others nourish my soul. I am forever grateful for the way they gave from the heart. Without their unqualified encouragement and trust in my integrity, I would never have finished this book nor maintained my humane spirit. My husband, Torben Andersen, earns special recognition for always magically knowing when to encourage me to sit down and write and when to animate me to walk in the park. He supported my initial choice to live miles away and pursue an academic career and then compassionately endorsed my later decision to take a professional leave and raise a family. I am particularly appreciative of his unbounded understanding.

My sister, Lisa DesMoine, deserves credit for helping keep me and the drudgery of work in perspective. Her frequent phone calls about everything and anything keenly remind me that there is life outside my office walls, that in spirit my family is always with me. I thank her for those loving, useful distractions. Because of them, I never felt isolated. To my parents, I am especially grateful for their complete and unbounded devotion. My father, Joseph Scalia, who originally convinced me to go to college, saw the writing of this book as another comparable challenge, one I could easily accomplish. I greatly appreciate his unquestioned faith in my capabilities. My mother, Louise Scalia, always ensured I had a strong sense of self-worth. No matter how down or distracted I was, she was always there with a compassionate ear or a warm hug. Her unconditional love has always been an inspiration. I am especially grateful to her for reminding me how important love and friendship are above all things.

As I hope the above makes clear, most of those acknowledged did more than improve the book's content. They sustained my spirit and integrity, and this sustenance will be with me always. Long after the specific findings of this study are muted in my memory, I will recall and treasure the rich friendships the book-writing process fostered and deepened. In spirit, I dedicate this book to all those who, in contributing to this project, have challenged my mind and nourished my soul. In print, I dedicate this book to my parents, who have sacrificed so much so that I could come this far.

List of Abbreviations

The state conventions are noted in the text with the following abbreviations:

IA 1844 & IA 1846   **Iowa State Convention. 1900.** *Fragments of the Debates of the Iowa Constitutional Convention of 1844 and 1846.* Compiled and edited by Benjamin F. Shambough. Iowa City: State Historical Society of Iowa.

LA 1845   **Louisiana State Convention. 1845.** *Journal of Debates and Proceedings in the Convention of Delegates, 1845.* New Orleans: Besancon, Ferguson and Company.

MA 1820–1821   **Massachusetts State Convention. 1853.** *Journal of Debates and Proceedings in the Convention of Delegates Chosen to Revise the Constitution of Massachusetts, 1820–1821.* Boston: The Daily Advertiser.

NC 1835   **North Carolina State Convention. 1836.** *Proceedings and Debates of the Convention of North Caroling Called to Amend the Constitution of the State, 1835.* Raleigh: Joseph Gales and Son.

NY 1821   **New York State Convention. 1821.** *Report of the Proceedings and Debates of the New York Constitutional Convention of the State of New York of 1821.* Albany: E. and E. Hosford.

NY 1846   **New York State Convention. 1846.** *Report of the Debates and Proceedings of the Convention for Revision of the Constitution of the State of New York, 1846.* Albany: Office of the Evening Atlas.

OH 1850–1851   **Ohio State Convention. 1851.** *Report of the Debates and Proceedings of the Convention for Revision of the Constitution of the State of Ohio, 1850–1851.* Columbus: S. Medary.

VA 1829–1830   **Virginia State Convention. 1830.** *Proceedings and Debates of the Virginia State Convention of 1829–1830.* Richmond: Samuel Shepard and Company.

VA 1850–1851   **Virginia State Convention. 1851.** *Proceedings and Debates of the Virginia State Convention of 1850–1851.* Microfilm.

AMERICA'S

JEFFERSONIAN

EXPERIMENT

Introduction
Jeffersonian Constitutionalism

*C*onstitutions reflect a society's reasoned understanding of the good state. In America such documents are supposed to work through and balance inevitable tensions between the two primary concerns driving the political system, namely, a desire for an actively sovereign people and a wish to keep certain private rights privileged and inalienable. To achieve this balance, U.S. constitutions outline principles and procedures that embody these commitments. Inhabitants are expected to respect these concerns and their legal incarnations; they are expected to treat both as foundational goals, above the purview of ordinary law. Although in theory U.S. constitutions are supposed to pay homage to both primary allegiances, in practice the task is difficult. How does one prevent a sovereign people from undermining their constitutional protections or impinging upon rights security? How does one prevent a document, designed to keep certain rights inalienable, from destroying the people's freedom to live by laws of their own making? These are the same questions theorists ask as they contemplate the best way to understand liberal democracy.

The most common legal response to these difficult questions is to advocate a theory of constitutionalism that seeks to preserve document integrity and shield its contents from regular popular scrutiny. This was the view of James Madison, who contended that the living owe "a debt" and "a proportionate

obedience to the will of the [original] authors." He counseled future generations against seriously questioning the handiwork of initial designers, for a
"government so often revised become[s] too mutable and novel to retain that
share of prejudice" necessary to preserve the reverence and respect foundational laws deserve and require. For Madison tradition and stability gave foundational principles their force; periodic revision would "engender pernicious
factions" and "agitate the public mind more frequently and more violently than
might be expedient." In other words, the best-designed constitutions are created once and then avoid later public scrutiny. Madison endorsed this program
primarily because he worried that public tampering would affect the security of
rights, especially property rights. He feared that with frequent change and an
agitated public "all of the rights depending on positive laws, that is most of the
rights of property, would become absolutely defunct." Because Madison willingly admitted that "the first object of government" was "the protection . . . of
acquiring property," in praising constitutional stability, he apparently aimed to
preserve certain private rights, that is, to ensure liberalism's most fundamental
aim. Of course, Madison recognized that popular sovereignty was one of the
important principles constitutions aver, but he clearly gave it secondary status.
For him, the people's political input must be cautiously constrained in order to
preserve other, more valued constitutional ideals, particularly property rights.[1]
This Madisonian approach to constitutionalism leans toward a traditionally liberal understanding of good government, wherein rights and standing law take
precedence over popular sovereignty.

　　During America's formative years, not everyone wanted foundational documents to establish such an explicit value hierarchy. Thomas Jefferson opposed
Madison's ideal and spoke disparagingly of those who "look[ed] to constitutions
with sanctimonious reverence, and deem[ed] them like the ark of the covenant,
too sacred to be touched." Although Jefferson explicitly denied that he was "an
advocate for frequent and untried changes in laws and institutions," he explicitly recommended that constitutions and their imbedded principles be subject
to regular popular scrutiny, knowing full well that this would facilitate evolutionary change. He admitted, "Institutions must advance" to keep pace with the
"manners and opinions [that] change with the change of circumstances." Jefferson defended his position in part because he had great faith that human
progress would promote better political outcomes. However, the force of his
case derived from his simple belief that "each generation . . . has . . . a right to
choose for itself the form of government it believes most promotive of its own
happiness." For Jefferson, lawmaking—even the writing of constitutional
laws—belonged to the living. In a sense, he found only one principle immutable: the cause célèbre of democratic theory, the right of self-government.

All other constitutional features, including specially enumerated rights, could and should be subjected to regular reevaluation.[2] This Jeffersonian approach to constitutionalism endorses a far more populist sense of good government, wherein the people's reasoned understanding of the good state guides—and if necessary takes precedence over—rights and standing law.

Jefferson and Madison offered two different ways of balancing America's allegiance to private rights and popular sovereignty. Jefferson tipped the scales toward self-government whereas Madison tipped them toward rights. Although we usually think of Madison's vision as victorious and Jefferson's advice as unheeded, this myth is largely the result of our scholarly emphasis on the U.S. Constitution. This national document appears to applaud stability over popular sovereignty, for it retains most of its original structure and contains few declaratory or practical stipulations regarding popular rule.[3] The document and nine elite justices decide government limits. The people have limited influence over both ordinary and constitutional law. Moreover, by now, delineating inalienable rights and judiciously protecting them from popular and government tyranny are considered the U.S. Constitution's most treasured and important functions.[4] Given the character and predominance of this national document, it is no wonder that America's reasoned understanding of the good state is thought to be indebted to a traditional, rights-centered theory of liberalism, which makes self-government a secondary ideal.[5]

This conception is based on biased information. In the years following the exchange between Jefferson and Madison, state constitutions developed in a fashion different from their national counterpart. Local politicians and citizens blatantly ignored Madison's warnings and engaged in Jeffersonian practice, treating constitutions like mutable documents, subjecting them to the ongoing scrutiny of inhabitants and their elected representatives. From 1790 to 1850, states repeatedly tinkered with their foundational documents. While many constitutional changes occurred piecemeal, by amendments that politicians initiated and debated in legislative chambers, over forty-five special conventions were held, at which popularly chosen delegates met to consider revision from the bottom up.[6] Usually, voters validated both minor and major changes before they became binding, even when no constitutional stipulation required this procedure.[7] Though the level of scrutiny varied from state to state during this period of legal upheaval, every state reconsidered one or more aspects of its foundational document. Thus, nowhere were personal and property rights truly safe from reformulation. At the state level, the living determined which principles and procedures reflected society's reasoned understanding of the good state. As a result, constitutional content evolved in accordance with the manners, opinions, and circumstances of the postfounding generation.

That states followed Jefferson's constitutional advice suggests that these localities gave a prominent place to popular sovereignty, an ideal to which Madison gave only lip service. It did not necessarily mean that state constitution writers devalued the role that foundational documents should play in protecting rights or limiting government oppression. Nor did it necessarily mean that they deemed the will of inhabitants and their elected officials above the law of the land. Both of these were Madison's fears, not Jefferson's intents. However, because states allowed inhabitants and elected officials to decide exactly which rights, principles, and ideals deserved ongoing inalienable status, the consequences of this Jeffersonian experiment might well have been devastating. Unfortunately, we still have little sense how such a populist approach to constitutionalism can and does affect either the content of governing documents or the prevailing beliefs regarding their purpose. In an attempt to enhance our understanding of this dynamic, the chapters ahead focus on a dramatic constitutional change that resulted from America's first experiment with Jeffersonian constitutional practice, namely, the expansion of popular influence in and over government. These chapters outline the various conceptions of the good state that drove proponents and adversaries of this expansion, including prevailing views on the theoretical and legal relationship between popular sovereignty and inalienable rights. These views, even more so than the content of the changes constitution writers sought to support or undermine, help us understand how America's reasoned understanding of the good state evolved in the face of its first comprehensive scrutiny. They help us disentangle the extent to which constitutional reinvestigations lead to Madison's nightmare or Jefferson's evolutionary ideal.

ELECTORAL REFORM: AN IMPORTANT CONSEQUENCE OF AMERICA'S FIRST JEFFERSONIAN EXPERIMENT

During the postfounding period, when politicians and citizens repeatedly found themselves gathered to rewrite their foundational documents, the meaning of America's commitment to popular sovereignty was frequently the primary issue on their agenda. Their considerations led to several constitutional changes, but the most frequently discussed and highly contested were those proposals aimed at altering the people's direct political influence, particularly those that would affect their electoral influence in and over the three branches of government. This study focuses on these particular changes.

Perhaps the most studied and well-known of these reforms were those made to suffrage requirements. Before 1800 only New Hampshire and Vermont had no pecuniary qualifications for suffrage; three required only the payment of a

tax. Over the next thirty-five years, nearly every state rid itself of these requirements, granting nearly universal suffrage to white freemen, except those who
were paupers or criminals. Only a handful of states waited to do so until the
early 1850s.[8]

Most states marred this progress with new suffrage restrictions on blacks
and immigrants. During the eighteenth century, free blacks and whites were
subject to the same property qualifications; thus most freemen of African descent were prevented from voting. Nineteenth-century revisionists recognized
that the reforms would change this.[9] In response, many states introduced race
as a voting requirement, either by creating special, onerous property-holding
qualifications for freemen of color or by taking away black voting privileges entirely.[10] During this period immigrants also experienced voting setbacks. Initial
constitutions usually required that voters inhabit their state for one year prior
to any given election. By the 1850s several required that voters be citizens,
sometimes for several years. Others increased residency requirements, sometimes up to ten years. New restrictions help verify that the nineteenth-century
flirtation with a democratic suffrage was deliberatively qualified.[11] Moreover, as
states were now beginning to contemplate female suffrage, in some sense, even
gender-based restrictions were no longer innocent.[12]

In addition to suffrage reform, many states revised districting practices. According to most original constitutions, representatives served counties, whose
boundaries were drawn prior to or during the early years of independence. Migration patterns soon made these units grossly unequal, which in turn led to
constituent dissatisfaction and calls to reevaluate present practices.[13] During
the 1820s and 1830s, inequitable districting practices remained unchanged. By
the 1850s, some replaced counties with districts based on property, taxation, or
slaveholding. These schemes may have inadvertently given the underrepresented more say than they currently had, but proponents clearly intended to di-
lute the political power of city dwellers and to ensure majority control for agriculture interests and large landowners. Other states sought to equalize their
redistricting systems, allowing at least one house to be based on the actual or
voting population.[14] In most cases, the resulting policies were compromises,
with legislatures still granting disproportionate influence to sparsely populated
counties with large property holders. To the extent that one-person-one-vote
best approximates democratic representation, obviously nineteenth-century
provisions fell short of the ideal.[15]

Constitutional writers also discussed which government officers ought rightfully to be elected by the populace. Before 1800 only seven states popularly
elected their governors. By 1853 all directly selected their governors—as well
as previously appointed, low-level executive officers, such as the attorney

general and treasurer. Before 1800 only two states allowed popular election of any judicial officer. By 1850 most states permitted popular election of county judges, as well as justices of the peace and sheriffs. Although few states outside the West permitted the direct election of supreme or district court judges, many entertained the idea.[16] Wherever implemented, these reforms constituted an increase in direct popular influence; however, most states did not enact all proposed changes and thus their practices were probably not democratic by modern standards.[17]

These electoral reforms, along with the various other constitutional changes of the nineteenth century, were debated throughout the first half of the nineteenth century. The remaining records of these debates illustrate the great importance nineteenth-century Americans placed on these particular constitutional changes. In most cases, regardless of how many other issues were discussed, debates over electoral reform fill more than half the transcribed notes, indicating that either these issues were the most frequently discussed, or that contemporary recorders thought them the most worthy of later public interest. In addition, one does not have to read far to discover that designers across America understood electoral provisions to be their state's way of codifying its commitment to popular sovereignty. Deciding who should vote, with what proportionate influence, and for which officers were decisions that would affect the meaning and stability of the constitution and the values it reflected. The content of views put forward by document designers, together with the time and space allocated to recording those views, show that electoral reform— one of the legal consequences of this first experiment with Jeffersonian constitutional practice—was a matter of great salience, one that was part of America's core understanding of good government.

THE REMAINING RECORD OF THIS EXPERIMENT:
CONSTITUTIONAL CONVENTIONS AND THEIR PARTICIPANTS

Although electoral reforms were debated in legislative chambers and state constitutional conventions, there remain records only from deliberations in the latter.[18] The content of those debates, together with the changes resulting from them, show that despite the universal importance given to preserving popular sovereignty as an ideal, no two states responded to reform pressures in precisely the same manner. Some endorsed all the proposed electoral changes; others enacted the minimum. Some constitutional writers in these states saw change as an important step forward in the development of constitutional theory and practice; others saw it as a dangerous step backward. This diversity makes it extremely difficult, if not impossible, to depict a monolithic model regarding what Americans took to be the appropriate level of constitutional commitment to popular sovereignty or what they saw as the relationship between this ideal and their other, equally important, constitutional commitment to rights. Clearly all states were dedicated to the kind of legal evolution that Jefferson advocated. After all, every one revised its constitution during this first period of reform, and none escaped expanding popular sovereignty in some form or another. Yet, not all states were committed to the same level of day-to-day influence that certain electoral reforms would bring, not all members embraced change with Jeffersonian optimism. Thus, whatever generalities can be surmised about the effect of Jeffersonian practice on constitutionalism (that is, about America's understanding of the legal relationship between rights and self-government or the theoretical relationship between liberal and democratic ideals), those generalities must be based on a wide array of states.

With this in mind, the chapters ahead focus on the debates from ten state constitutional conventions held during the first half of the nineteenth century. Of the northeastern states, Massachusetts was chosen to represent the New England area, known for its stable constitutional tradition and strong moralistic character.[19] Here, Protestantism continued to influence many day-to-day institutions, and Puritanism still retained a legal stronghold. The state was largely Whig, with its most conservative elements living in the Boston area. Abolitionism was strong throughout the state.[20] Although the original constitution required electors to hold an estate, property restrictions were less stringent than elsewhere. Moreover, the document contained several democratically progressive features that other late eighteenth-century constitutions did not. Both legislative houses, as well as the governor and lieutenant governor, were annually elected by the people. Also, while senatorial districts were drawn according to how much taxes residents paid, representation in the house was explicitly founded on a "principle of equality," where every town had at least one representative and as many as its resident population proportionately required. Not only did the populace validate the original constitution, the document stipulated that a constitutional convention be considered in fifteen years and that this meeting as well as all subsequent constitutional changes rest on popular approval. Massachusetts's commitment to popular political influence in both ordinary and constitutional affairs is particularly notable, for its 1780 constitution still governs today.[21]

Not until Maine separated from the state in 1820 did inhabitants vote to convene a constitutional convention.[22] Rather than revise the entire document, participants at this meeting proposed fourteen amendments, nine of which gained popular approval. One of those allowed all taxpayers to vote. At the convention itself, few endorsed ongoing property requirements;[23] most debated whether a taxpaying qualification was even necessary. The issue of race never entered into discussions. Although no changes were made to the way senate districts were drawn, delegates considered a more egalitarian system based strictly on the population. Unlike other states, religious matters brought the most contention. Here, delegates came close to eliminating state funding for established local churches but ultimately failed to garner majority support. Delegates did manage to remove the requirement that civil and military officers swear allegiance to God and the Trinity prior to holding office, but even this was narrowly approved.[24] Like these examples, most amendments that became law dealt with procedural issues. For example one revised the selection procedure for notaries public, one expanded the electoral powers of military men, and another introduced an alternative means to introduce constitutional amendments.

All told, Massachusetts is a unique case. Its constitution, the most stable in the United States, escaped its first convention with only a few procedural changes. The state began with a democratically progressive constitution and stayed on the forefront, particularly regarding the unimpeded enfranchisement of freemen of color. In other words, the people of Massachusetts seemed to retain a reverence for their foundational document even though inhabitants had several ways to influence policy and constitutional law. In this sense, they managed to retain Madisonian reverence despite Jeffersonian democratic practices.

The state of New York was selected to typify the Mid-Atlantic, that part of the Northeast that had neither the constitutional stability nor the cultural and political homogeneity of the New England area.[25] Here, fragmented lines of power promoted local and sectional interests. The political power of Federalists, Whigs, and Republicans centered in the north and west parts of the state; abolitionists lived in the scarcely populated west. Unlike Massachusetts, New York's city center was controlled by the Democratic party and was generally enthusiastic toward suffrage reform, at least regarding white Americans. While the state housed the great organizer Martin Van Buren, prior to 1830 New York was known for its extremely fragmented party system. Even after the fortification of a two-party system, the state was always troubled by factions within the Democratic party and between Whig and fringe parties.[26] All told, New Yorkers lacked political, cultural, or economic cohesion and had few organizations or social mechanisms to foster ideological consensus, making compromise and expediency important forces in conflict resolution.

New Yorkers held two conventions during the first half of the nineteenth century. The first, held in 1821, convened to write the state's third constitution. The constitution then in force granted the people power to select legislators and the governor. Members of both houses came from districts containing roughly the same number of electors. Electoral debates primarily focused on the state's comparatively high property requirements for voting and officehold-ing. Through coalitions across party lines, these requirements were reduced to the payment of a tax. Unfortunately, to appease city Democrats, the new docu-ment retained the original, onerous property requirement for "men of color."[27] Convention delegates also considered whether to allow the people to elect jus-tices of the peace. However, this motion, which had bipartisan support, ulti-mately did not pass.[28] Finally, as was the trend for the period, the convention added a provision to the constitution stipulating that future amendments re-quired popular approval. In addition to these electoral reforms, the 1821 meet-ing also significantly altered various institutional features. For example, it elim-inated the council of revision and appointment, and granted the council's power of legislative veto and judicial appointment to the governor.

Soon after this constitution was passed, New York's population skyrocketed. This and other pressures led to calls for further democratization. In 1826 pecu-niary qualifications for white voters disappeared, and justices of the peace be-came popularly elected. In 1846 the newly enfranchised—together with other groups, such as supporters of the temperance, nativist, and abolition move-ments—helped bring about another constitutional convention.[29] Here, some is-sues like the question of a color-blind suffrage, and residency requirements for voting and officeholding, continued to split delegates according to their party affiliation. Other issues, like expanding the power of judges and subjecting them to popular election, had support from factions of both parties, in this case from the moderate wings of both. Still other issues, like restricting the legisla-ture's power to initiate internal improvements and accumulate new debt, en-joyed broad bipartisan support.[30]

Obviously, New York contrasts well with Massachusetts. Most obvious are its mixed signals regarding popular sovereignty. It had the only constitution in the North that did not contain an explicit declaration proclaiming the funda-mental importance of popular sovereignty in the good state. At the same time, inhabitants were more than willing to meet regularly to rethink and revise the document's purpose. With each meeting designers increased the political influ-ence of the vast majority of its people, although there were notable hesitations in the area of black enfranchisement. A difference of perhaps greater conse-quence is the evidence suggesting that New York would be less ideological and less principled than its northern counterpart. First, the state lacked the kind of homogeneity that might have helped members uncover widely accepted princi-ples or develop strong theoretical agreements on the importance of popular rule or on the meaning of constitutional government. Moreover, its legal tradi-tion was not a model of Madisonian stability, for by 1850, the state was being governed by its fourth constitution.

States from the South were also examined, with Virginia the most notewor-thy and important among them. What happened in Virginia influenced Amer-ica. For example, state builders across the United States quoted from and copied its original declaration of rights. Southerners came from neighboring states to listen each time Virginians met to change their foundational laws, for they knew inhabitants had carefully selected representatives from the highest political echelons.[31]

Despite this notoriety, in many ways Virginia is a typical southern state. It granted the bulk of governing power to slaveholders, making it virtually impos-sible for cattle farmers in the west to have consequential influence in any policy issue. Here, legislative districts were drawn so that the vast majority of lawmak-ers came from the less populated, eastern, slaveholding region. Onerous suf-frage requirements disenfranchised anyone east or west who lacked large plots of highly valued land.

The conventions of 1829–1830 and 1850–1851 were each called specifically with the hope of ending the impenetrable decision-making control held by wealthy landowners in the east. At both conventions, western farmers called for a more equitable representation system, one that accounted for the voting pop-ulation. Both times these reformers also aimed to give every free man the vote. At the convention of 1829–1830, some residents in the east joined their calls for an expanded suffrage, rejecting the idea of a universal suffrage and hoping to base qualifications on taxes paid or the value of the land, measures that would enfranchise more easterners, but not westerners whose land was relatively worthless. As these instances suggest, region and class—not party allegiance—divided delegates.[32]

The constitution produced by the convention of 1829–1830 was no victory for western reformers. New suffrage requirements, which granted the vote to anyone owning a freehold or renting land valued at $25, benefited only previ-ously disenfranchised easterners. Senate and assembly districts remained fixed according to county boundaries. A few additional seats went to western regions, but the majority remained in the slaveholding region. The judiciary system still left county courts extremely powerful. Finally, despite initial support for a pop-ularly elected governor, the provision was excised, leaving the east-controlled legislature to appoint every officer of significance. Not until the convention of 1850–1851 did western inhabitants see real gains. For example, the resulting constitution readjusted county appropriations and gave the west control of the house, while retaining the east's control of the senate.[33] It granted general white male suffrage and provided for the popular election of supreme court and appellate judges as well as the governor.[34]

For the above reasons, Virginia serves as an important case. Despite strong wording in its famous bill of rights on the importance of popular sovereignty and a community-controlled government, this was a hierarchical society with no pretenses about equality. Although there existed substantial and repeated political pressures outside the convention to enact reforms that granted power more broadly and equitably, elected constitution writers vigorously opposed them. Even after the 1850 reforms, inhabitants in the eastern part of the state still held disproportionate control. Of greater interest, Virginia's constitutional tradition appears to embody a complicated balance of tradition, stability, and popular sovereignty. On one hand, the fact that convention delegates met three times in a thirty-five-year period (a third convention was held in 1863) suggests that inhabitants did not highly revere the document's contents. On the other hand, the seriousness with which people took the selection of delegates and the state's long-standing reverence for its highly acclaimed 1776 bill of rights suggest that certain parts of the document were greatly respected by all.

Also included in this study is North Carolina, whose eastern slaveholding population held substantial political power despite its comparative population disadvantage to the rest of the state. Parties were fairly influential, but since they focused on issues of railroad construction and bank support, the state's electoral reform debates were left to follow regional and class divisions. North Carolina is of particular interest because of the unique tension underlying its constitutional tradition. North Carolinians were proud of their commitment to popular sovereignty and initially backed it with procedures not found elsewhere in the South. For example, even its 1776 constitution was drafted by popularly elected delegates. This document enfranchised freemen of African descent as well as anyone who paid public taxes. Despite such initial progressive features, North Carolina turned out to be one of the least amenable to electoral reform.[35]

The North Carolina 1835 convention was held largely in response to western calls for more political influence. The result, however, was a series of amendments that in several respects actually diminished the people's political power. One amendment abandoned annual elections, for example. Another removed the franchise from freed blacks, mulattoes, and persons of mixed blood. Yet another further restricted white voting by adding a new property requirement for senate electors. The basis of representation went from a county system to a senate districting system based on taxes paid and a house system mirroring the federal numbers system. While these new systems marginally increased the influence of the west, they did so on inegalitarian principles, which still left majority power with the eastern slaveholders. Consistent with this period, the convention adopted a few reforms of democratic consequence. The governor became popularly elected, and a new provision required popular approval for all future constitutional amendments. To these gains one might add that, whereas the original constitution allowed only Protestants to hold office, the new one extended the privilege to all Christians.

Given the above, North Carolina's practices represent a response to constitutional government and the role of popular sovereignty in the good state similar to—yet different from—its neighbor directly north. First, the document itself seemed more stable. The 1835 convention was the first time since 1776 that inhabitants had met to consider constitutional change, and their meeting produced only a series of amendments. Second, although delegates convened in response to democratic political pressures, they managed not only to prevent many of the proposed reforms, but to retract some of the powers citizens were originally given. Moreover, restrictions stayed in effect longer than elsewhere. Even its 1854 constitution still required all electors of the senate to pay public taxes prior to voting. This all occurred even though constitution writers here were working with a document that tradition had deemed principally committed to the people's sovereignty. If anything, it seems that here Jeffersonian practice led to a constitution more Madisonian than its original form, for members willingly curbed popular rule in the name of property rights.

Louisiana, the only southern state with a sizable commercial city, had a unique legal tradition. Its constitution, long and detailed, more closely resembled European civil codes than other U.S. constitutions. It lacked a separate list of rights or fundamental principles. Other features leave little reason to expect that an allegiance to popular rule supplanted this apparent disregard for basic guarantees. As in other southern states Louisiana's original constitution (of 1812) appointed its governor. It had high property qualifications for voters, and its scheme for drawing senate districts favored plantation owners. Most important, the document contained no specific declaration regarding the inherent value of popular sovereignty, perhaps suggesting an even less democratic tradition than its neighbors.[36]

The constitutional convention of 1845 was called largely to redistrict the legislature so that inhabitants from New Orleans and small farmers from the north and southwest of the state could have an influence proportionate to their population, though it considered several other electoral reforms, including a universal white male suffrage and the popular election of virtually all public offices. The victories were limited. The new constitution granted the franchise to every free white male citizen, residing in the state seven years, but only a few additional offices (of which the governor was one) became popularly elected. Who could run for this office was restricted by a fairly onerous residency requirement of fifteen years. In the end, most small farmers rejected districting reform—a fatal outcome for the inhabitants of New Orleans, who now constituted one-half the state's population but who held less than one-quarter of the legislative seats. With this bias in their convention representation as well, the result was a house districting system that was *less* proportional to the voting population than before, and a senate system just barely more proportional than it had been under the old constitution.[37] The city lost out again with regard to its large immigrant population, for the state instituted new high residency requirements for suffrage and officeholding. Finally, like many state constitutions that were revised during the antebellum period, the new document now included a proviso to make future constitutions popularly approved. It also severely restricted banking and put limits on the amount of debt the legislature could contract.[38]

Typical of the South, Louisiana retained majority control for its slaveholding population, doing so by franchise, officeholding, and districting provisions that kept commercial city dwellers in the minority. At the same time, Louisiana's unique constitutional tradition meant these features might be based on an entirely different rationale. Conceived of as a document of statutory laws and procedures, not of higher immutable principle, even its 1845 version neither contained a bill of rights nor declared itself a popular document. With no such parchment declarations to guide them, the delegates' allegiance to principle might have been noncommittal and their views about electoral reform void of theoretical values and concerns. Louisiana had the potential to be Madison's nightmare.

Other states with potentially unprincipled constitutional traditions were those in the West.[39] One of the two states examined from this region was Ohio, the oldest, most populated, and most developed in the area. Its original constitution, written in 1802, granted more power to the people than was customary back in the East. For example, the people selected not just legislators and the governor but also low-level executive officers such as the treasurer. Payers of a state or county tax together with laborers on state roads were eligible to vote. Elected lawmakers crafted districts. Soon after Ohio's first constitution was passed, things changed to make this last issue especially problematic. Migration from the North and the South greatly expanded the population. What began as a stronghold for party Democrats soon became a state evenly matched with Democrats and Whigs, as well as a significant number of Free Soilers. This partisan realignment left legislative districts subject to regular gerrymandering. The strength of the Free Soilers worried politicians, especially as the black population grew in the state.[40] Finally, the state had accumulated a fair amount of debt with its investments in canals and railroads.

In 1851 a constitutional convention was called in Ohio to respond to these problems, thought to be the result of a poorly designed foundational document.

One of the biggest debates at this meeting centered on how to base legislative districts. Many wanted to take away the general assembly's discretionary power and specify a representation basis in the constitution itself. No supporters of this change advocated using taxation or property as the basis. Some argued for population-determined districts so that lawmakers would speak for men, women, and children. Others supported voter-population districts in order to decrease the influence of those purposefully disenfranchised. Debate on this issue mainly focused on whether a fixed constitutional basis was desirable, and whether an explicit constitutional provision would cause the representative body to become too large for meaningful deliberation.

In addition, delegates debated questions of suffrage. There was little opposition for universal white suffrage, thus the change occurred easily. However, extending this privilege to freemen of African descent engendered heated discussion, and here restrictionist forces won. Of further note, Ohio constitution writers considered enfranchising women, but the proposal had few supporters and garnered only one impassioned speech on its behalf. Delegates also discussed which officers should be popularly elected. They ultimately approved a wide array, from local officials such as the state's attorney general and auditor to high-level officers such as supreme court judges subject to popular election. Where debate ensued, it was over implementation, for example, not whether judges should be elected but whether they should be elected at large or at the district level. Finally, like other states across America, the constitution created at this convention included new limitations on lawmakers' ability to contract debt and legislate internal improvements. Even the incorporation of banks became subject to popular referenda. In addition, the new document required popular majority approval for future constitutional reform.

All told, circumstances in Ohio meant that constitution writers there would view constitutionalism differently from their neighbors back east. Flanked by an individualist culture and a population that had tripled over a fifty-year period, there was no entrenched power hierarchy. Moreover, Ohio's convention delegates met with the view that much of their existing constitution needed a substantial overhaul, especially in the area of electoral reform. Giving citizens new and extensive opportunities to influence ordinary and constitutional affairs was a widely shared, unquestioned ideal. Although progress was marred by the designers' widespread antiblack sentiments, the general tenor and purpose of the convention suggest that, compared to their eastern counterparts, participants might have been more dismissive of foundational laws and institutions as containing immutable ideals and more sensitive to popular opinion as the ultimate force of good government. Thus, one might expect Ohio's Jeffersonian experiment to result in a document that reflected the people's will and prevailing circumstances;

one might expect a theory of constitutionalism that relied primarily on a principled commitment to popular sovereignty and made rights of secondary import.

Iowa represents an even more extreme case. Here, writers had hardly any established legal tradition, let alone a constitutional one. During the early nineteenth century, this area was considered real frontier territory, where drinking, gambling, and pistol-carrying lawlessness was said to abound.[41] Whether inhabitants were truly of this character is probably a matter of opinion, for there exist almost no written accounts of its territorial period. What is known is that the state's mining opportunities as well as its fertile lands attracted Americans from both North and South, and even Ohio. As a result of its promising economic opportunities, the territory grew rapidly and sought statehood in the 1840s.[42]

To join the union Iowa needed to have a written constitution, and in 1844 inhabitants called a convention to draft one. The resulting document prohibited slavery and greatly restricted public banking. Like its neighbors, Iowa hoped to lure easterners with promises of substantial political influence. Thus, its proposed constitution contained numerous democratic provisions, including universal suffrage and popularly elected judicial officials, as well as short terms of office for all three branches of government. The resulting constitution failed to garner majority support, not because of its economic stipulations or democratic features but largely because of a last minute U.S. mandate regarding acceptable statehood boundaries. A second convention, held in 1846, basically reproduced the same document, with appropriately revised territorial boundaries. This time the people approved it.

Little record remains from either of the constitutional conventions, although several speeches survive from debates over how to select judges.[43] These debates are examined in order to form a contrast with those in Ohio. With no inherent constitutional tradition and a pressing need to expand its population, Iowa's constitution writers had more reason to extol the virtues of popular sovereignty and to follow the precepts of public opinion over the dictates of any abstract principle or legal tradition. The result might have been the kind of document Madison feared.

As should be obvious from this discussion, states varied significantly. The samples examined here were indeed selected to maximize diversity, not just regarding the kind of legal choices about electoral policy but also regarding the kind of theoretical rationale that might have underlain those choices. With this issue in mind, the sample includes states with and without well-organized and powerful political party structures, for strong party control might have stifled or predetermined the range of intellectual debate. The sample includes states both with and without large immigrant populations, with and without bipolar interests, with and without divisive sectional conflicts, with and without large urban centers. These factors might have caused convention participants to worry about factions and narrow special interests and to forget the more fundamental theoretical concerns normally associated with foundational documents. The sample includes states with different political cultures, that is, those with varying combinations of traditionalism, moralism, and individualism, for each might have led to a different understanding of how and why government operates as it does. In addition, with legal diversity in mind, the sample includes states with alternative constitutional frameworks, including those that reinforced hierarchical relationships and those with egalitarian stipulations, those that were extremely legalistic and those with only vague government directives. Also, although every state engaged in Jeffersonian practice, the constitutional consequences varied. Thus, the sample includes states that became radically democratic and those that became less so, states that retained their basic revolutionary format throughout the antebellum period and those that radically restructured it two or three times during that period.[44]

In addition to cultural, political, and economic diversity within and across states, there existed a range of important differences among participants. Although all delegates were popularly elected, some were wealthy landowners while others were ordinary working Americans. Some were local politicians or even mere citizens whereas others were important state leaders or national representatives. New York's 1821 convention included such prestigious Federalists as Supreme Court Justices Ambrose Spencer, William Van Ness, and Chancellor James Kent. Also present were some noted Democrats holding state offices, such as General Erastus Root and James Tallmadge, as well as others holding national office, such as then U.S. Senator Martin Van Buren. Alongside these well-known individuals were ordinary businessmen, farmers, doctors, and lawyers (at the New York 1846 convention, the vast majority of convention participants were lawyers).

Virginia is an especially interesting case. Citizens seemingly cared deeply about the quality of individuals who were sent to redesign their foundational document, for at both conventions held during the first half of the century voters went out of their way to overlook a candidate's place of residence and to elect the very best statesmen. As a result, the Virginia constitutional convention of 1829–1830 included a large number of national statesmen, such as Federalist Supreme Court Justice John Marshall and Democratic Presidents James Madison and James Monroe. Also present were House Representative Philip Doddridge, a brilliant speaker and vocal advocate of reform; Philip Barbour, the Speaker of the U.S. House of Representatives; John Tyler, who later became president; John Randolph, former member of the U.S. House of Representatives and present ambassador for Andrew Jackson; and Abel Upshur, a highly respected Virginia judge.

The inclusion of such a broad array of states together with a wide assortment of participant backgrounds might well have translated into a motley
group of particularized, perhaps self-interested rationales for and against electoral reform. In fact, the expectation was that politicians would be responsive to
the social, economic, and political climates within their respective states and to
the demands of their particular professions. The expectation was that the
rhetoric of state builders would vary according to the peculiar political pressures impinging upon them and the overall cultural and constitutional traditions in which they found themselves. After all, their speeches were a public activity. As speakers realized, what they said would be reproduced in newspapers
and ultimately recorded for posterity. Surely delegates did not want to seem in-
sensitive to their fellow constituents, to their state's interest, or to its general
constitutional needs. As it turns out, however, these differences played a minimal role in the overall understandings of constitutional government that were
put forward by conventioneers across America. Because the study encompasses
such a diverse assortment of states and speakers, the similarities found are significant and extremely relevant.

A Look beyond Regional Diversity

A cursory reading of the electoral reform debates certainly illustrates the importance of such factors as a participant's career and his party allegiance as well
as a state's political, economic, and cultural peculiarities. The most vocal speakers were men of political stature, for example. So-called ordinary citizens spoke
less frequently and usually with less exuberance and less theoretical content.
Party identification sometimes mattered, as it did for Democrats in the issue of
black enfranchisement. Moreover, the issues that politicians raised varied from
state to state and region to region. For example, nowhere in the West were
there serious concerns about the dangers of democracy.[45] Delegates representing agricultural regions often extolled the virtues of farming. Only in Massachusetts was good citizenship intricately tied to religious faith. However, to focus on these particularities alone would be to ignore an essential feature of the
Jeffersonian revolution sweeping America in the postfounding era. State representatives across the United States were seriously evaluating their current conception of the good state, particularly how and why their specific constitution
endorsed the particular balance of popular sovereignty and rights inherent in it.
The chapters ahead focus on these careful considerations, by examining hundreds of speeches for and against electoral reform and then fleshing out the
extraordinary similarities that existed within and across states.

With this in mind, throughout this book, speakers have been identified according to their position on electoral reform, for it is their policy predilection that best encapsulates their views on the role of popular sovereignty in the good state and most meaningfully distinguishes them from each other.[46] On one side stood those wanting to expand the boundaries of popular power. These individuals—often called reformers or expansionists—proposed extending the franchise, reducing qualifications for officeholding, basing districts on voter population, and/or increasing the number of popularly elected officials. On the other side stood those who wanted to retain the present system of government, with suffrage restricted to the propertied, with electoral influence limited to the legislative branch and with even that influence disproportionately held by the wealthy and propertied. These delegates—often called restrictionists and antireformers—wanted to restrain the pressures for democratic reform that were sweeping across the states during the first half of the century. Although at times individuals spoke in favor of one reform and then against another, the vast majority of expansionist arguments resemble each other and differ starkly from any position against any reform issue.

Separating delegates and their ideas according to electoral reform preferences rather than, say, partisanship or political stature is perfectly consistent with convention practices. State records generally ignored most participant characteristics, listing only names and regional affiliation. For example, Virginia depicted Monroe, Marshall, and Madison as they did every other participant: according to the county that elected them. About half the states noted a delegate's profession but these listings said nothing about the person's political career. New York described law as the occupation of both Van Buren and Spencer. Louisiana did not even iterate the people who participated at its convention.[47] Consistent with this practice is how delegates treated one another. Although individuals brought their economic, political, and social stature with them, they almost never overtly deferred to speakers of high station; few were dismissive of another because of his partisan sympathies or personal profession. Moreover, when delegates disagreed with their colleagues regarding how to interpret specific constitutional principles or general American values, they did not group themselves with others of similar stature or merely agree with their fellow partisans. Only in Virginia did some delegates go on record to endorse an opinion precisely because of its advocate's stature or to belittle an associate's view as partisan rhetoric. For the most part, members interacted as peers who had joined together to debate the merits of electoral reform. They echoed the views of those on the same side of the electoral divide, not of those sharing stature or party affinities.[48]

In order to emphasize shared ideological sentiments and the relevant differences behind them, chapters are organized thematically and often by state to enrich the context of speakers' positions. Of course, most individual speeches are not as ideologically coherent as the presentation might suggest. Rather than give prepared texts, delegates usually responded ad hoc to the views and proposals offered daily on the floor. Speeches usually cannot be read in isolation, for politicians were trying to speak *to* each other, to build upon the arguments of their colleagues and counter the positions of their adversaries. Some offered detailed cases to support their points of view, but most of them selected bits and pieces of arguments already given, echoing the conclusions of their more articulate peers. This means that expositions were usually scattered and disorganized, not categorically broken into specific, disparate themes. For example, one moment a delegate emphasized the importance of popular character in preserving the good state; next he offered a detailed description of the state of nature; next he discussed the importance of history; finally he went back to questions of good citizenship, this time introducing his theory of human nature. Somewhere in the middle might be a long discussion of the problems of ancient Rome or the legal systems in alternate states. To reproduce full speeches might give a fuller picture of how particular individuals argued for or against electoral reform, but it would lead the reader in many directions simultaneously. Thus, in order to achieve coherence and emphasize the relevant theoretical issues underlying electoral reform debate, the book presents only snippets of selected speeches. No significant debate features are omitted, and (unless otherwise indicated) the issues described are those that were raised repeatedly, across states and over time.[49]

The chapters ahead use this form of presentation to illustrate the postfounding generation's preoccupation with how and why constitutions should balance their ongoing joint commitment to rights and popular government. No matter from which region delegates came, no matter how religious state inhabitants were, no matter why the convention was called, when debating questions of how much power the people should have, delegates raised the same fundamental concerns; they voiced the same worries and relied on the same principles to make their case. Over half the delegate speeches proclaimed that the most important constitutional concern was to preserve the inalienability of certain key rights, rights that belonged to everyone in nature and that had been granted immunity by their ancestors by being placed in foundational documents. Moreover, three-quarters of the speakers agreed that, while republican government could only be secure if good, virtuous citizens governed, constitutions must be realistically designed and must depend only on natural human behavior. Such views are clearly part of the language of liberalism. Their prominence illustrates how important this theoretical tradition is for understanding American constitutionalism in the nineteenth century.

A careful look at these liberal views and the divergent document provisions they supported will illustrate the complicated consequences of America's first Jeffersonian experiment. In one sense, they show that Jefferson's hope was fulfilled, for frequent reevaluation led to new constitutional practices. Conventions allowed states to find new and different ways to implement their foundational commitments. Laws and institutions evolved with changing circumstances. At the same time, this says little about how the revision process affected constitutional theory, the issue that concerned Madison. Here, the answer is less straightforward. On one hand, prevailing agreements regarding the importance of understanding human nature and protecting rights suggest that Madison probably overstated the ideological upheaval that would accompany popular scrutiny. Frequent reform had yet to destroy society's views of constitutional government as the legal backing for its reasoned theory of the good state. State builders still recognized that the document they crafted could not resolve questions of self-government in a vacuum. Instead, the document had to ensure that society's commitment to popular sovereignty was delicately balanced with its highly valued commitment to rights. On the other hand, because these basic agreements were really quite general, frequent reevaluation would not leave constitutional theory unmarred. State builders would have to decide what rights were essential and which, if any, could be sacrificed in the name of popular sovereignty. They would have to determine what kind of political behavior was natural and when natural proclivities would dictate curtailing rights and/or popular sovereignty. In fact, convention delegates discussed these very matters at every convention, which suggests that Madison was right to suppose that frequent constitutional scrutiny would likely transform the meaning and relative value of treasured ideals.

The rest of this book attempts to unpack these two facets, outlining the effect that Jefferson's experiment had on America's theoretical understanding of the good state. In an attempt to preserve America's dual commitment to rights and popular sovereignty, constitutional writers across the United States found themselves uncovering the same subtleties embedded in their valued ideals. They discovered that underlying America's understanding of the good state were at least two reasonable constructions of it, both of which endorsed the same general liberal principles, but each of which saw those principles as balanced with popular sovereignty in a different manner. These same two constructions existed in every state. In that sense, constitutional evaluations solidified these differences; they did not resolve them. All told, then, though Jeffersonian constitutionalism brought about different legal outcomes in each state, it reinforced theoretical agreements throughout the nation. However, as it reinforced shared concerns, it also solidified ideological differences.

Part One

Liberal ideology is founded on the belief that good government delimits and protects certain inalienable rights. These rights are immutable and belong to everyone not because government deems them worthy but because there exist higher laws, beyond the purview of ordinary will, that mandate their status. John Locke's teachings in the *Second Treatise* exemplify this view. For many, so does America's constitutional tradition. In this case, the first ten amendments to the U.S. Constitution are widely cited as the best example of the nation's liberal commitment to rights. America's states, however, hold equally good examples. Their written foundational documents reflect this allegiance, for they too constitute a set of higher laws that enumerate goals and aim to guide citizens and lawmakers.

In many ways state constitutions better exemplify America's revered commitment to rights as sacred and above the purview of ordinary lawmaking. For one, it was these local documents that inspired Madison to propose to Congress the specific list of amendments he did.[1] Although only half of the initial state constitutions contained a separate rights enumeration, all explicitly granted their inhabitants certain freedoms, including the right of conscience, free assembly, free speech, and trial by jury. Within fifty years after Independence, all but Louisiana had included a separate detailed list of prohibitive government acts and important citizen rights. With such lists, states prominently display their strongly held commitment to rights.

In addition, the state approach to the enumeration of its principled ideals and commitments differs from the national one in notable ways. Most of the states incorporated at least one provision to parallel each nationally protected right. In some cases the wording was nearly identical in state and national documents; in other cases state documents asserted positively the national taboo. Most notable is how the states declared the right of free conscience. Whereas the national constitution prohibits government interference, every state constitution was set positively—like New Hampshire's 1784 document, which declared "every individual has a natural and unalienable right to worship God according to the dictates of his own conscience and reason" (Poore 1898, pt. 2, 1281). Whereas the U.S. Constitution lumped several national prohibitions together, the state constitutions often separated the concepts, even devoting two or three separate declarations to particularly important rights. The New Hampshire constitution took eight separate positive provisions and declarations to cover the same freedoms negatively outlined in the first amendment to the national document. It also contained eight provisions regarding trial procedures.

State documents contained other declared freedoms and rights that were absent from the national constitution. Nearly all states included provisions, such as the prohibition against imprisonment for debt, and specific guidelines regarding penalties for criminal offenses. Many states asserted that the military was subordinate to civil authority, and that the bill of rights was above government manipulation.[2] Just how many additional rights were incorporated depended in part on the state, its regional location, and its constitutional tradition. Many New England states retained a tradition of short constitutions with general principles, whereas most southern states included several limiting declarations, many protecting the rights of slaveholders. Other factors such as the flow of European immigrants to a state, the amount of internal improvements necessary, the concentration of large city commercial development, or the size of the black population also influenced the kinds of rights and limitations that were incorporated into various state documents.

One of the most striking differences between state and national constitutions was how the former treated the rights of life, liberty, and property. The national constitution notes that none of these may be taken "without due process of law," and that property cannot be taken "without just compensation." State constitutions are far more explicit in describing the importance of these goods and the limits on the government's taking them. Half the state constitutions declared life, liberty, and property were inalienable rights, which individuals possessed *before* government, and which were therefore not grants or privileges of citizenship to be arbitrarily taken away.

These constitutional features express a liberal commitment to rights.[3] That these features survived—and were indeed enhanced as state constitutions underwent frequent political and popular scrutiny—suggests how firm these convictions were, but their survival says little of their relative value vis-à-vis the importance of the people's political influence. After all, often included in the separately enumerated rights declarations were Jefferson's ideals: an absolute allegiance to popular sovereignty and a call to recur frequently to fundamental principles. By 1850 not only did 80 percent of the constitutions acknowledge that "political society is derived from the people and established with their consent" (Delaware 1792 constitution, Poore 1898, pt. 1, 278), over half also declared that "the people . . . have the inherent, sole, and exclusive right of regulating the internal government . . . and of altering and abolishing their constitution and form of government whenever it may be necessary to their safety and happiness" (Missouri 1820 constitution, Poore 1898, pt. 2, 1104). A total of twenty-one states contained a proclamation of this sort, and nineteen also contained a proclamation similar to Delaware's.

That both private rights and popular sovereignty were given declaratory prominence in state constitutions raises two simple questions. How did constitution writers balance these concerns? When revising electoral laws, did they consider the effect that expanding the people's political influence would have on the security and inalienable status of personal rights? Rights and the ongoing security of the rights were among the most important issues concerning the designers of electoral laws. In gatherings called specifically to determine who should vote, for which representatives, and why, constitution writers asked themselves repeatedly how they could best preserve their state's most important constitutional commitments: which general precepts should guide them; which rights, if any, deserved to sway designers' deliberations on how to implement and limit the nation's commitment to popular sovereignty; and what bases should impart these important determinations. Close to two-thirds of the speakers for and against electoral reform tried to answer one or more of these specific questions. Given that they were discussing how much power to grant citizens, their obsession with rights shows that they saw their jobs as preserving a kind of liberal state, namely, one committed to preserving certain fundamental inalienable rights from the purview of ordinary will.

At the same time, many constitution writers disagreed over how the good state builder should understand the nature and origin of America's rights commitment. Their views on the subject showed how far they were willing to extend the people's political influence. Thus, examining their debates on electoral reform reveals both the nuanced character of America's liberal embrace of rights and the role played by political preferences.

The Origin of Rights

A quick glance at the recorded debates of any state's constitutional convention readily demonstrates that delegates found it essential to consider the impact that electoral reform would have on their constitutional commitment to private rights and on the rights' protection. At every convention, whenever the question of electoral reform arose, delegates on both sides of the issue illustrated the great importance they placed on rights. They assured their colleagues that the policy they supported would not harm fundamental and inherent rights. Some described rights as the essential aim of good government. Others described their mission as crafting a document to secure these ends. Across the states examined in this study, two-thirds of the speeches included statements that connected the delegates' support or opposition for electoral reform to their belief that constitutions must protect rights, the state's primary responsibility.

This was the case even in Louisiana, where the constitution contained no declaratory commitment to inalienable rights. At this state's 1845 convention, delegates considered electoral issues such as whether only native-born citizens should be allowed to hold office, whether a long period of residency was appropriate before a foreign-born citizen could vote, whether voters should be required to demonstrate a proficiency in the English language before casting their ballot.[1] Although nativist sentiments won out (the new constitution greatly narrowed the political privileges of the foreign-born), these issues generated much reflection and debate. Despite Louisiana's constitutional silence regarding rights, delegates found it necessary to remind each other frequently of the great importance they and the state placed on protected rights. Every delegate speaking in favor of allowing both native and foreign-born citizens to run for governor took the position of Christian Roselius, a Whig lawyer who had served the state as both legislator and attorney general. He reminded his fellow delegates, "The first and paramount object of this convention in framing an organic law should be to extend and secure to all citizens of the state, without distinction, equal rights" (LA, 1845, 233).[2]

At least two opponents of this generous stipulation (a quarter of those speaking on the subject) similarly declared their allegiance to universally enjoyed rights. Judah Benjamin, a fellow Whig who served alongside Roselius in the state legislature, explained to his colleagues that having stricter requirements for foreign-born citizens neither reduced them to "second class" inhabitants nor implied they had no rights. Although he recognized his proposed restriction meant that both groups did not enjoy all the same "political rights," he strongly believed that restricting these individuals from holding office actually ensured that all equally enjoyed "the primary rights with which all American citizens are vested" (LA 1845, 221).[3]

In most cases the context of discussion makes clear that, when delegates talked about the need to secure rights, they meant something particular and were not just affirming a general commitment to limited constitutional government. Instead, state delegates were usually declaring their allegiance to the ongoing security of three specific rights, namely, life, liberty, and property. Whether they endorsed more or less property qualifications for electors, whether they favored executive or popular selection of judges, whether they argued for a basis of property or population for representation to the house or senate, delegates designated these three private rights as important and worthy of serious, independent consideration. Questions of popular rule could not be addressed in a vacuum but were closely tied to issues of life, liberty, property, and their security. In certain states (Virginia and New York), nearly every speaker explicitly discussed these particular rights and the importance of their protection. In other states (Louisiana and Ohio), many speakers did not mention these three goods specifically as the rights at the foundation of their argument. Nonetheless, some speakers did so. That no one disputed their narrow interpretation suggests agreement was probably still widespread. In still other states (most particularly North Carolina), the specific list was not enumerated; instead delegates referred to the "rights of citizenship." Yet, even there, the general widespread commitment to private rights is obvious.[4]

The special bias toward the triumvirate rights of life, liberty, and property may usually be apparent, but the same cannot be said of any of the other civil rights and liberties normally associated with America's liberal tradition. Nor can it be said of the other concerns declared above ordinary government purview. When discussing electoral reform in the state constitutions, for example, delegates fretted mostly over the fate of one or more of the same inalienable rights: life, liberty, property, happiness, or security. Only two speeches out of hundreds offered for or against various electoral proposals included a specific reference to any of the rights associated with legal due process, such as trial by jury or habeas corpus. Religious freedom did not evoke widespread concern. If we exclude debates concerning the necessity of having elected officials swear allegiance to God, there were only eight unsolicited proclamations regarding the importance of religious freedom. In each of these eight instances, delegates simply added religious liberty to the standard list of life, liberty, and property. Although speakers found it unnecessary to affirm their commitment to religious freedom or other constitutionally stipulated rights, their silence in no way suggests they did not value these ideals. On the contrary, every constitution has always included a proclamation of the sacred inalienability of free conscience, and procedural protections for the accused were staples of every nineteenth-century state constitution. Together, such provisions attest to the importance of these other rights.[5]

Nevertheless, delegates' silence on these issues during electoral reform debates does say something. It suggests that participants saw little connection between questions of self-government and freedom of conscience, or between questions of popular rule and legal due process. Americans may have found trial by jury, habeas corpus, freedom of conscience, and the like important, even unalienable, but these concerns did not form part of delegates' essential language as they considered electoral reform. Only life, liberty, and property were deemed intricately connected to self-government.

Delegates' constant declarations regarding the importance of life, liberty, property, and their security as inalienable rights show clearly the constitution writers' preoccupation with these issues. Perhaps this last group were now considered above popular purview. Repeated unfaltering declarations about these concerns were an essential component of the public language of early nineteenth-century Americans. The declarations constitute a facet of that general liberal agreement that placed gentlemanly limits on how far reform could ever go.[6]

Delegates expressed their allegiance to life, liberty, and property in various ways. Not every delegate gave a long speech in their favor, and sometimes allegiance was implied rather than expressed directly.[7] Most often speakers discussing these rights and their protection spoke with evident reverence. Sometimes delegates declared their allegiance with a simple statement proclaiming these three goods as government's greatest object. When explaining the merits of property qualifications for voters a New York state supreme court judge, Federalist William Van Ness, reminded his colleagues, "life, liberty and property . . . are the three great objects for which all governments are instituted and to which all minor considerations should bend. If the security of these primary objects required, that a class of the community should be excluded from a participation in the affairs of government, they had no just ground of complaint" (NY 1821, 265). The judge did not explain why these three rights were great objects; he merely declared them so. He and many of the delegates at the New York convention and elsewhere explained why questions of popular influence could not be divorced from the importance of these inalienable rights. For him there were conflicts in the state. One day "the state will be convulsed with civil commotions." By extending the franchise beyond property holders there would be no security against the danger of these "commotions" (268). He feared extension because it would disturb the security of personal rights. In his case, as was the case with many delegates against electoral reform, not only was the protection of life, liberty, and property one of the primary aims of government: *before* advocating any change at all, wise delegates must first consider the effects that electoral reform would have on this protection. Although such cautionary declarations are found especially in speeches against electoral reform, both sides remained aware of the importance of rights and the need to declare their inalienable status. Convention participants recognized that they must pay due deference to life, liberty, and property, and that their public language must constantly allude to this deference.

These examples are simple declaratory statements. If all expressions of early nineteenth-century commitment to rights were phrased this simply, we might dismiss the words as mere rhetorical flourishes and intellectually shallow assertions. The delegates' declarations would not offer much insight into the philosophy driving nineteenth-century Americans toward or away from a more democratic understanding of popular sovereignty. Their words would not necessarily signify the influence of liberalism in general, or the influence of any potential liberal spokesman in particular. However, almost three-quarters of those who discussed the importance of rights in the good state gave some indication of what they saw as the origin of that importance. Some even offered elaborate theories explaining and justifying America's commitment to rights. The numerous explanations strongly suggest that the delegates' commitment to rights fell squarely in the language and tradition of liberalism; that is, the

speakers saw their commitment as inalienable, derived from higher-order principles and laws, and beyond the purview of ordinary legislation. At the same
time, they did not always agree on the origin of their allegiance to life, liberty,
and property; that is, whether rights derived their inalienability from abstract
natural law or from foundational agreements and the resulting documents. The
delegates' differences on this subject of origins represent one of the fractures in
nineteenth-century American liberalism.

ON THE ORIGINS OF ALLEGIANCE TO RIGHTS

Liberal ideology holds that forces worthy of reverence and above the
purview of ordinary legislators authorize the inalienability of certain fundamental rights. Most scholars studying the founding period stress the important
roles played by Locke and natural law in the way Americans understood the
origin of their commitment to rights. Locke declared life, liberty, and property
to be inalienable because of natural law, given by God, discovered by human
reason, and endorsed by compact. So did early Americans. In this view, ongoing active consent is more important as a tool—to protect rights and to limit
governmental abuse—than as a good in itself.[8] Scholars have also demonstrated
other authorities accounting for the range of America's rights commitment. In
the view of some, utilitarians and Scottish Enlightenment thinkers convinced
Revolutionary Americans that the pursuit of happiness was an inalienable
right.[9] Other scholars emphasize the importance of common law practices, including those derived from the Magna Carta, for these forbid the taking of
property without consent and recognize the inherent value of political representation, trial by jury, and prompt accusation of an offense.[10]

Each of these authorities influenced initial state builders in writing constitutional stipulations regarding rights. The question here is which authorities survived in the generations following. Delegates debating how to implement their
allegiance to popular sovereignty not only reminded each other of America's
inexorable commitment to life, liberty, and property but also frequently explained the origins of and reasons for that commitment. State builders argued
that both nature and tradition were legitimate authorities for constitutional
doctrines to rest on, but they differed slightly from their forefathers in the way
they described those authorities. They no longer considered Locke or any
other seventeenth- or eighteenth-century writer the authority on natural law.
They increasingly stressed rights rather than responsibilities in describing the
lessons derived from nature.[11] The traditions they emphasized were no longer
attributed to the British and their common law. Instead, by the nineteenth

century America's state builders saw their allegiances as being the product of their own legal tradition, embodied in their written foundational laws, that is, in their national and state constitutions.[12]

THE ROLE OF NATURE AND CONTRACT IN EXONERATING RIGHTS

A common practice among late eighteenth-century pamphleteers in America was to derive the origin and legitimacy of rights and responsibilities from nature. The understanding of nature usually included a theory of human rationality and the importance of God's divine law. Nature also signified a realm where individuals lived prior to the institution of government, from which people fled so as to secure "vulnerable" rights. This last aspect has long been considered characteristic of Locke. It is also often associated with late eighteenth-century American liberalism, since writers and supporters of the national constitution sometimes emphasized the natural origin of rights or specifically quoted Locke.[13] When nineteenth-century politicians referred to nature and natural rights, they usually relied on this narrow liberal interpretation.[14]

The hypothetical return to such a pregovernmental state was considered useful for discovering appropriate constitutional boundaries only by those who wanted to expand the people's political power. Other delegates—mostly antireformers—explicitly refused to base actual laws on natural principles. Many of these skeptics, however, did accept that life, liberty, and property were "rights of nature," insecure before individuals joined together into societies, and protected after the formation of government. For such skeptics, the signers of the social compact had chosen to secure these rights but had knowingly forfeited other equally natural rights. Thus, constitutions were not mere reflections of nature; they were documents that made immutable those particular rights which individuals had unanimously agreed to protect.[15]

Despite this difference, references to nature and compact resemble important aspects of Locke's teachings in the *Second Treatise*. Scholars today still debate whether Locke based legitimate government on consent or on nature. Nineteenth-century state builders also debated which foundation legitimate government was based on, and this shows that the ambiguity existed even then, if not specifically in the appropriate interpretation of Locke then certainly in what view accurately depicted the origin of good government. There is no evidence that the constitution writers saw themselves as deciding the appropriate reading of Locke; they probably did not even read his work. Yet, given the language they used to express their understanding of constitutionalism, nineteenth-century delegates were obviously familiar with Locke's language and the content of his teaching. His ideas, or the ideas upon which he built, were clearly still in the air and considered useful to explain the basis of American foundational law.

Records from the State of Virginia help illustrate how delegates envisioned nature and its connection to rights.[16] The existing records show Virginia's state representatives to be extraordinarily articulate and well versed in the state-of-nature theory. Over half the speakers discussed how individuals lived prior to the institution of government. They relied on descriptions of nature resembling Locke's—as well as alternative, rather imaginative, "natural" states. Often the views of one speaker filled pages of text. Both the breadth of discussion and the variety of styles demonstrate the delegates' meaning when they invoked the concept of natural rights. Virginia was an unusual case; it is only there (at both the 1829–1830 and 1850–1851 conventions) that we find so many and so detailed discussions of how individuals lived prior to the institution of government. Nonetheless, the views put forward offer insight into the philosophy underlying speeches made elsewhere.

Whereas Virginians may have been more articulate, in their understanding of state-of-nature theories they probably did not differ significantly from delegates representing other states. All these politicians would have been educated in the previous century, when schools across America taught boys in their teens theories of natural rights, discussing them as the foundation of America's civil society and its constitution.[17] There is evidence to suggest that Virginians held views of the good state resembling those of their peers, especially in the South.[18] The only unusual aspect of Virginia's debates was the large number of especially articulate, learned, and well-known representatives present at the convention. Thus, the varied constructions of nature, natural rights, and the social compact offered by Virginians probably reflected similar intellectual influences as existed in other states, although not the same desire and ability to proclaim them. The difference is mainly one of style, not substance. Delegates in Virginia were articulate, verbose, and explicit whereas representatives elsewhere were terse and relied more on implicit understandings and agreements.

Virginia's 1829–1830 debates concerning the basis of representation uncover delegates' meaning when they referred to rights as "natural." Close to half the recorded speeches on this issue included detailed references to nature and natural rights. A good example is from a speech by William Naylor, who represented a county in the western region of the state, where free labor and independent farming constituted the basic economy. He began his argument for a more equitable basis of representation by asking how Americans might discover the essence of their commitment to rights and majority rule:

The answer is, that they are to be discovered in the same way as in all other sciences, that is by tracing back those sciences to their primary elements. We must . . . refer back to man in his primitive condition. I know that the idea of man ever having been in what is called a state of nature, is ridiculed as being imaginary only, and as being a state that never had an existence in fact. . . . But in reasoning upon the subject, we have a right, for the sake of the analogy, to presuppose it. . . . We cannot, indeed, divest ourselves of the idea of the state which man must have been in previous to the formation of the social compact. This was the treaty to which every member of the community became a party, by which they unanimously agreed to form one body, and become incorporated as such. (VA 1829–1830, 129)

Many of Virginia's advocates of reform agreed with Naylor's understanding of rights, nature, and the compact. Philip Doddridge, a politician holding a seat in the U.S. House of Representatives who was considered one of the great oratorical leaders of the western reform movement, explained that the state's "declaration speaks explicitly of *a priori rights,* which are supposed to exist in a state of nature and are retained by men in society so as to be social rights secured by the social compact" (83). A co-leader in the reform movement, Alexander Campbell, whose interests outside the convention were spiritual in nature (he was a founder of the Disciples of Christ) gave an even clearer exposition as to why the state was committed to rights. Individuals have "certain inherent rights, of which when they enter into a state of society, they cannot by any compact deprive or divest their posterity, namely the enjoyment of life and liberty, with the means of acquiring and *possessing property*" (119).

In these cases, as with over three-quarters of the speeches favoring legislative redistricting according to voter population instead of property holdings, nature was a real or imaginative "state," existing prior to the institution of government and useful for heuristic purposes. This heuristic tool helped Americans discover the inalienable rights of humankind. By discovering the rights enjoyed in nature, good constitutional designers could determine two things. First, they uncovered what constitution writers could never tamper with when revising foundational documents. Second, they discovered guides for all their constitutional actions, for they could not make any change that would allow rights later to become subject to government or popular abuse. To call an aim a right and then give it "natural" status was equivalent to insisting that it receive full security in well-designed government. (Delegates did debate what exactly happened in nature and thus what rights were to be retained by legitimate government.)

Not all delegates debating the appropriate basis of representation found this hypothetical return to nature to be instructive. A couple of expansionists questioned the heuristic power of a return to nature. Their criticisms were mild, implying only that discussions about nature had little *additional* use. Briscoe Baldwin, a judge on Virginia's supreme court of appeals, implored his fellow delegates to forget state-of-nature theories: "Let us leave . . . to the school-men and sophists all the theories concerning the origin and nature of government [and worry about applying our principles to practice]" (VA 1829–1830, 99). For him—and for Chapman Johnson, one of the few easterners who supported the western movement to reform the basis of representation—there was little to be gained from investigating nature and the origins of government.[19] Americans already agreed on the existence of inalienable rights, and these agreements had become part of law and convention. Knowing their origin did not enhance their importance. For these men, the state-of-nature theory was a superfluous—although not necessarily false—rationale for insisting on the protection of rights.

On the other hand, those who opposed using the voting population as the basis to draw legislative district boundaries were more severe in their criticism of the state-of-nature theory, considering this hypothetical state useless for determining the boundaries of good government.[20] Many contended that nature had little role in determining which rights were inalienable, because life before the contract differed fundamentally from life after the institution of government. Some made this case by arguing that in nature everyone was an individual, not yet "civilized"; only after the compact did people become members of society. What occurred in nature could not guide constitutional designers, for constitutions were made for citizens of a society, not for individuals or "savages" of nature. The principles that defined the good state were conventional ones, established after the institution of society.

This view was put forward by Benjamin Leigh, one of the most outspoken opponents of reform, who had already long served the state in the house of delegates and would later continue his public service in the U.S. Senate. He reminded his colleagues that they were "employed in forming a Government for civilized man, not for a horde of savages, just emerging from an imaginary state of nature. . . . The very word *right* is a word of relation and implies some society" (VA 1829–1830, 160). According to Mr. Leigh, this line of reasoning explained why American Indians were not members of the states. It explained why the rights Americans enjoyed were earned through reason and the ability to use them wisely. Three other opponents of a voter-based districtory system expressed nearly identical arguments.

Antireform delegates most commonly rejected using nature as the basis of good government for the simple reason that with government came sacrifice. When individuals left nature to join society, they necessarily forfeited certain freedoms previously enjoyed. Attorney William Giles, then governor of

Virginia who had spent the last thirty years serving as a state and national legislator, openly contended that "All the rights of Government are founded in the consent of men and that consent is ascertained through the social compact" (VA 1829–1830, 237). He made this case to refute the western position that good government laws reflected nature's principles. Philip P. Barbour, another attorney who was then Speaker of the U.S. House of Representatives, explained, "The very nature of the social compact [was] that all who enter into it surrender a portion of their natural rights, in exchange for . . . other rights derived from the compact" (91). It is worth noting that Mr. Barbour (known as a "strict constructionist" of the national constitution) and the five other restrictionists who made this particular case all agreed that life, liberty, and property were among those natural rights that had been retained *after* the compact. In other words their complaint with the state-of-nature theory was not that there were no rights in nature deserving of reverential status in government. They differed from their adversaries only in their opinion of what they as constitutional designers should make of the fact. They thought only those rights that reasoned individuals had once unanimously agreed to secure deserved ongoing and absolute protection. Constitutions were founded on previous agreement. Actual tradition was more important than imaginary nature.[21]

Underlying this second set of skeptical arguments put forward by those opposing reform was a vision of the state of nature resembling that of their adversaries. Nature was a world prior to government wherein life, liberty, property, and happiness were insecure. It was not a blissful state, prior to or after the fall, but a secular one, prior to government. Individuals initially formed government to avoid the dangers of nature, and therefore government's primary role was to secure those rights that individuals had joined to protect. Whether government protected all natural rights (as reformers believed) or just some of them (as their adversaries contended), natural rights were understood as rights coming from a pregovernment, Lockean-like state of nature. In the end, regardless of how they understood the origin of government's commitment to life, liberty, and property, both sides agreed that well-designed governments secured against the abuse of each right.[22]

The prepolitical conditions that Virginia delegates invoked were not always abstract worlds. Five of the delegates debating the basis of representation described their own unique "state of nature," of individuals living without security on a desert island or in the "wild" West. Two opponents of crafting legislative districts according to the number of enfranchised inhabitants referred to the story of Robinson Crusoe to suggest that the state of nature was an individualistic state, where the strongest reigned. Knowing what happened in nature would not help in creating a social state. In a sense, these arguments paralleled the position of Mr. Leigh cited above. In "nature" man was solitary. After the compact, he was a member of society. In both cases antireformers rejected nature as a good guide for government principle.[23]

Other delegates who used unconventional stories about how individuals lived prior to government were three in favor of reforming the state's representation system; each contended that looking at the way people lived prior to government would help constitutional designers discover important principles of good government. Alfred Powell discussed at length what would happen in an unsettled territory if one hundred men worth $200 each wanted to join together with ten men worth $2,000 each. According to him, the hundred men would say:

> It is true you have the most property; but our lives and our liberties are as dear to us as your lives and your liberties can be to you. As to property, we bring into common stock our all and you do no more. . . . The compact can only be durable as founded upon mutual confidence. . . . Besides, if you shall have by virtue of your property, the political power which *you* claim, you may exercise that power upon our lives and liberties as well as upon our property. If, by virtue of our numbers we are to be feared as to matters of property, why may we not equally fear for our liberties, if we give to *you*, who are the *minority*, the power to govern us, especially as you have the wealth which is power in itself? (VA 1829–1830, 106)

Here, Powell created an elaborate story that stressed the a priori nature of an individual's right to life, liberty, and property and the individual's perceived ongoing importance after the institution of government. The other two imaginative accounts offered by reformers contained the same general aspects. In each case, the delegate investigated, through a "reasoned thought experiment," why and to what extent legitimate government valued rights. In each case the goal was to determine what kind of government rational people would agree to form. These reform delegates were relying on an unspoken agreement they shared with fellow participants that the boundaries of legitimate government power were defined *before* government, when free individuals lived without the constraint and protection of written laws. Knowing which rights individuals enjoyed in nature would conclusively determine the true foundations of government. The assumptions and intentions in these examples were the same as those found behind Locke's state-of-nature theory.

Outside Virginia, delegates seldom offered elaborate speeches about how individuals lived prior to government, but it would be hard to maintain that these other constitution writers did not share the same basic understanding of nature, natural rights, and government's legitimate foundations. Not only were speakers in every state likely to have been taught theories of natural rights in schools, but at nearly every convention one or more delegates talked about nature and the contract with sufficient detail to make clear that their ideas matched those of their Virginia counterparts. At each state convention except in North Carolina, at least one speech (and sometimes as many as half the speeches) for or against a particular electoral reform offered some account of what was entailed in a reference to the compact or the state of nature. The context of these remarks suggests that the speakers endorsed theoretical arguments similar to those used by their Virginian cohorts.

Those who favored restricting the people's political influence usually disparaged direct parallels between nature and government. For example, in his explanation as to why Americans of African descent should not vote, a Democrat-Republican then serving in New York's senate, Erastus Root, explained that blacks were "little removed from their barbarous and rude state." They did not understand the "principles upon which people unite" and form government (NY 1821, 185).[24] His argument paralleled that of Virginia delegate Benjamin Leigh. Not all "natural" settings contained good models for state building. The appropriate model on which to base government principles was not savage individualism. Others made arguments similar to the ones of Governor Giles or Philip Barbour, that governments were founded on agreements, not nature. In an argument justifying the franchise for whites only, lawyer-trained Elisha Williams, a Federalist politician and reputed adversary of Martin Van Buren, described what he saw as the relationship between government and nature. "We have a government founded on social compact: a portion of our natural rights have been surrendered" (248). Any agreed-upon surrender, especially at the time when people initially formed government, was perfectly legitimate and just. Having said this, Williams still made it clear that he believed everyone was "entitled to civil and religious freedoms." These were originally natural rights; they were among those not forfeited when the contract was made (248–49).[25] Sometimes delegates did not refer explicitly to nature or to the compact, but the analogy was implicit. Leverett Saltonstall, a Federalist who wished to maintain Massachusetts's requirement that all officeholders swear allegiance to God, told his colleagues:

> "The great object of civil society is the protection of the life, liberty and property of the members," and "to furnish them with the means of enjoying in tranquility their natural rights and the blessings of life," and those entering into it have a right to agree upon such a system as in their opinion will best promote these great objects. . . . The people of this Commonwealth are a voluntary association. (MA 1820–1821, 205)

In his view, the voluntary association had agreed it would be governed by a constitution that would never renege on the commitment to life, liberty, and property. This meant making sure no other provisions were ever added that would threaten their inalienable status and freedom from legislative and popular will.

The common thread in all these examples is the general antireform depiction of why statesmen must be committed to the security of life, liberty, and property. These three personal rights may have been enjoyed in nature, but the reason they had become a staple of the good state was because government was formed with this purpose in mind. Not all the freedoms enjoyed in this pregovernment state were likewise to be freely enjoyed after the formation of government. Only those freedoms that individuals had initially agreed to protect rightfully concerned state builders.

In contrast, delegates favoring the expansion of the people's political power were more likely to describe nature as directly influencing government design. Federalist Peter Jay, in an impassioned speech favoring enfranchisement for white and black taxpayers, complained that behind the argument for a white-only franchise lay the implicit assumption that convention members "have a right to construct the government in the manner they think most conducive to the public good" (NY 1821, 200). He disagreed with this assumption. Delegates should "not consent to violate all those principles upon which our free institutions are founded or to contradict all the professions which we so profusely make concerning the natural equality of all men" (201). Similarly, when speaking against Ohio's plan to retain the word *white* in the section concerning voter qualifications, physician Norton Townshend adamantly contended, "All men must have the same natural rights. For the protection of these rights governments are instituted among men" (OH 1850–1851, 550).[26] In this last case, the argument was explicit: people joined together precisely to protect the inalienable rights enjoyed (with poor security) by individuals prior to the formation of government.

When delegates talked about inalienable rights, most would have been familiar with the state-of-nature theory as an explanation for what made those rights special. In addition to their schooling and the intellectual climate of the time, they had the views of at least one (and usually more) of their fellow delegates to remind them that "natural" rights were those belonging to everyone by birth and existing prior to the formation of government.[27] In most cases, there arose a dichotomy between the views of reformers and antireformers concerning how useful this theory was to the building of constitutions. Those who favored extending electoral privileges explained the origin of America's commitment to rights by tracing it directly back to the state of nature. Knowing what rights and privileges individuals enjoyed there determined the rights and privileges they should enjoy with government.

Restrictionists disagreed. Adversaries of reform saw the powers of and limits to government as the result of initial agreements made when people left nature. Nature was not the guide; the compact was. Popular agreements made prior to the convention determined the rights that government was responsible to protect. For antireformers the priority of rights was by now a fixed part of the American tradition. Delegates had convened merely to renew and reinforce that original agreement.

This dichotomy holds within it a paradoxical feature. On one hand, the advocates of restricting popular power based their concept of governments' entire legitimacy on the people themselves, albeit on views articulated some time in the past, usually dating back to the period when colonists decided to write their first foundational documents. Thus, whereas antireformers agreed that ordinary legislation and popular will were contemporary dangers to constitutional principle, they accepted that currently revered principles reflected nothing more than the will of earlier legislators and electors. A quasi-democratic understanding of the foundation and limits of government drove their present adversity to democratic change. On the other hand, the advocates of expanding popular power based their view of government's legitimacy not on what the people of the past or the present reasoned but on abstract immutable principles. Certain principles deserved constitutional reverence no matter what people en masse thought. These writers and revisionists of the original foundational documents had to follow innate immutable standards. That is, reformers found themselves dependent on extra or antidemocratic forces; they used an understanding of fundamental law that was completely divorced from the popular sovereignty ideal to promote democratic advances in legislative practice.

The Importance of Highly Regarded Man-Made Laws

Whatever the perceived source of the inalienability of rights, politicians and citizens debating electoral reform were keenly aware that if "foundational" documents declared certain rights inalienable, they were by now immutable and worthy of unquestioned reverence. Because their constitutions and similar founding documents declared life, liberty, property, happiness, and their security inalienable, so must right-minded politicians. That other important and revered documents such as the Declaration of Independence and the U.S. Constitution also contended that rights must be equally enjoyed by all only further obliged politicians and citizens to assure these aims. The sample excerpts show that delegates made this case in varied ways. The differences regarding the role of nature in government design should not be forgotten, for most of the documents on which delegates relied purported these very rights to be "natural."

Many of America's founding documents refer to a set of inalienable rights and freedoms that are traceable to nature, that is, to life before the institution of government. Few readers need to be reminded of the Declaration's monumental claim "that all men are created equal; that they are endowed by their Creator with certain unalienable rights; that among these are life, liberty, and the pursuit of happiness." Although in this passage rights are attributed to the Creator, not nature, the signers of the Declaration acknowledged that these rights belonged to Americans prior to the formation of government. In the sentence preceding, colonists explained that given "the course of human events" they must "dissolve the political bands which have connected them with another" and "assume . . . the separate and equal station to which the laws of nature and of nature's God entitle them." Signers of the Declaration explained the need to return to a kind of state of nature, a state in which men were free of the political bonds of government. The unalienable rights that the signers then listed were said to belong to every colonist, even after the bonds of government were dissolved. Rights were not government grants. They were derived from nature, and therefore beyond the purview of ordinary legislation.[28]

A number of state constitutions included proclamations alluding to the contractual nature of the document and the natural status of certain personal and property rights. Several constitutions contained declarations similar in intent to the renowned preamble of the 1780 Massachusetts constitution: "The Body Politic is formed by a voluntary association of individuals: It is a social compact, by which the whole people covenants with each citizen, and each citizen with the whole people" (Poore 1898, pt. 1, 956). In this case the document is considered the codified version of the compact that initially brought men together to form government. In most cases the reference was less explicit, as in New Jersey's 1776 constitution, which began by saying "all constitutional authority ever possessed was . . . , by compact, derived by the people" (Poore 1898, pt. 2, 1331). Then there were those connecting constitutions to nature and natural rights. Half the state constitutions shared Massachusetts's contention that "All men are born free and equal, and have certain natural, essential, and unalienable rights; among which may be reckoned the right of enjoying and defending their lives and liberties; that of acquiring, possessing, and protecting property; in fine, that of seeking and obtaining their safety and happiness" (Poore 1898, pt. 1, 957). According to passages of this type, individuals possessed rights *before* government. Rights were not government grants or privileges of citizenship.[29]

Both the Declaration and various state constitutions referred to natural rights, to rights belonging to individuals prior to government. Life, liberty, property, and their security were of this type; so always was the liberty of conscience and sometimes the pursuit of happiness. Speakers deriving the immutability of these rights from legal declarations in such foundational documents did not always discuss where or how these documents came to include the principles they contained. Some delegates discussed explicitly the direct correspondences among constitutions, the original compact, and nature, whereas many more remained silent on the sources of constitutional principle and therefore on the origin of its inalienable contents.[30]

Yet many of the documents the delegates relied on explicitly derived these rights from a pregovernmental state. Personal and property rights, like natural rights, belonged to everyone by birthright. Thus, many of the people who based the inalienability of rights on constitutional law were implicitly recognizing their original value in nature. However, for most restrictionists, written laws codified only certain natural rights, the ones agreed to at the initial compact. For these individuals a reliance on written laws might signal a reliance on natural rights (but only those natural rights retained because of agreed-upon conventions and explicit constitutional reference).

Something should be said about America's other notable foundational document: the Constitution of the United States. In the antebellum period the document was usually thought of as a set of guidelines for national limits, a document selectively applied to enhance America's developing economy and to resolve interstate and nation-state disputes. It was almost never described as a document used to preserve individual rights from state abuses. This function is thought to have come later, after the passage of the Fourteenth Amendment, and then only selectively until the twentieth century.

Yet, contained in the national constitution is a clause that some nineteenth-century delegates understood as protecting the inalienable rights of every American citizen, as protecting the same rights that both the Declaration of Independence and most state constitutions noted as immutable. This was article 4, section 2, which states: "The Citizens of each State shall be entitled to all Privileges and Immunities of Citizens in the several States." Given that a significant number of delegates interpreted this clause as exemplifying the nation's allegiance to preserving certain rights for all citizens, across state lines, it should be said that even the national constitution can be construed as one of the many foundational documents referring to and verifying America's inalienable commitment to rights. However, although designers of this national document may have believed in the natural origin of rights, the document itself is silent on the matter.

Speeches from various conventions help illustrate both the importance of America's own legal tradition and how far this tradition relied on the belief that government's legitimacy derived from nature. Embedded in many of the speakers' descriptions of their job as convention delegates was the view that conventions took place in lieu of a popular assembly.[31] Delegates gathered at conventions because the people had voted to dissolve the existing government and to form a new one. The people had voted to revoke their existing system of rule, which meant they had returned themselves to a state similar to nature. Citizens had asked representatives to create a new agreement to protect rights and reasonably limit government power. State representatives now had a specific well-defined task to perform: to construct a constitution best approximating the original, legitimate compact. Despite differences between reformers and antireformers, both sides agreed that the rights to life, liberty, and property must be kept immune from tinkering by constitution writers, lawmakers, or ordinary citizens.

The constitutions of Virginia, Iowa, Massachusetts, and Ohio all contained declarations concerning the natural status of life, liberty, and property. Delegates from these states often reminded each other that, as constitutional reformers, they must secure the fundamental principles inherent in their founding document. Since their constitutions explicitly noted the inalienable importance of life, liberty, property, and security, delegates must also respect those concerns. There was often a subtle difference in these discussions between reform and restriction arguments. When Daniel Webster, the great orator and defender of property rights, spoke in favor of maintaining the religious oath for Massachusetts state officers, he declared: "there are certain rights . . . which the whole people—or the government . . . —owe to each individual. . . . These rights are stated with sufficient accuracy in the tenth article of the Bill of Rights in this constitution. Each individual in society has a right to be protected by it, in the enjoyment of his life, liberty and property" (MA 1820–1821, 161).[32] Philip Nicholas, a supporter of Jackson who nonetheless consistently voted against reform, reminded his fellow delegates that Virginia's bill of rights "speaks of inherent rights of which men, when they enter into society, 'cannot by any compact deprive or divest their posterity'." The inherent rights enumerated in the constitution included "the enjoyment of life, liberty, with the means of acquiring and possessing property, and pursuing and obtaining happiness and safety" (VA 1829–1830, 364).[33] When one of Ohio's lawyers, E. B. Woodbury, advocated enfranchising blacks, he first explained that "all men are by nature free and independent and have certain inalienable rights, among which are those of enjoying and defending life and liberty, acquiring, possessing and protecting property, and seeking and obtaining happiness and safety" (OH 1850–1851, 553). Ohio's constitution, he noted, explicitly granted everyone these rights.

Both Webster and Nicholas were restrictionists. Webster just stated the constitutional rights; Nicholas described them as ones kept upon entering society. But when Woodbury, an expansionist, made his case, he connected constitutional principles with nature, *without* qualification. Despite their differences these delegates shared the common perception that state constitutions were authoritative sources mandating the continued and unadulterated importance of personal rights. For them, these documents exalted life, liberty, property, happiness, and security above ordinary decision making. Because of this, it was their duty as constitutional designers to preserve and protect these essential concerns.

Even in Louisiana, North Carolina, and New York, where state constitutions did not contain explicit declarations proclaiming the inalienable importance of rights, delegates still found ways to refer to foundational documents within the American tradition to justify the exalted status of personal rights. One way to do this was to invoke article 4, section 2, of the national constitution. Although this section is usually not associated with a mandate regarding individual rights across state lines, delegates from New York, North Carolina, Louisiana, and Ohio maintained that this nationally sanctioned clause demonstrated America's fundamental commitment to ensuring everyone equal rights.

For the delegates who invoked this article, it showed that every citizen in their state was entitled to the rights enjoyed by citizens in other states. These delegates contended that accepting the authority of the national constitution obliged state constitutional designers to acknowledge and preserve this equality. When speaking in favor of a color-blind voter requirement, attorney Steven Humphreyville explained that, according to "the Constitution of the United States, whatever rights are conferred upon a class of citizens should be conferred upon all belonging to that class" (OH 1850–1851, 552). In his view, this clause meant it was "unconstitutional" to deny Americans of African ancestry their fundamental rights. In response to a similar claim made by individuals favoring less strict requirements on who might run for office, Whig Judah Benjamin from Louisiana explained that while the U.S. Constitution admitted all should be protected in "the primary rights, with which all Americans are vested," the article in question did not admit that any citizen "shall be vested thereby with the right of an elector in every state" (LA 1845, 222). In other words, the national constitution guaranteed some rights—private rights—but not political voice. (This national provision was most frequently utilized by New York. Here both restrictionists and expansionists agreed that the national constitution mandated equal rights to all citizens; they just disagreed whether self-government was one of the rights deserving constitutional reverence [see Chapter 2].)

A number of delegates found the Declaration of Independence useful in supporting the inalienability of rights. Physician Norton Townshend bolstered his argument for extending the franchise to women by quoting from the Declaration: "I believe that '*all* men are created equal,' that they are equally 'endowed by their creator with certain inherent rights'" (OH 1850–1851, 550). (Obviously for him, the reference to men meant men and women.) In his argument to extend the franchise to all taxpayers Daniel Tompkins, a lawyer and Democratic party leader involved in New York state politics, found it necessary to remind his colleagues that "'Life, liberty and *the pursuit of happiness*'" were essential aims of American states. What made these essential? For him they gained this stature in great part because they "are set forth in the declaration of independence as cardinal objects" (NY 1821, 235). In both these later instances, reform delegates did not stress the natural origin of America's rights commitment as they explained its legal origin. Nonetheless, in each instance, they relied on a document that itself proclaimed these rights natural.

Although not necessarily explicit in the above arguments, behind them existed two alternative interpretations about the relationship between constitutional provisions for rights and nature and the compact. For those who endorsed nature as the basis of good government, state constitutions were the embodiment of natural principles. Constitutional legitimacy came from nature, and American constitutions were legitimate because they followed this ground. For those who rejected nature as the sole foundation of society's reasoned understanding of the good state, constitutions embodied only those principles that were agreed to by the signers of the compact, not all aspects of natural life. Constitutions were sets of human laws—albeit laws above citizen caprice and legislative whim. In one case principles were derived from nature; in the other case from prior agreements, historical successes, and standing conventions.

An important agreement underlay both positions: constitutions were practical documents, which had incorporated America's fundamental ideals. Any right whose immutability was documented in America's well-established, highly regarded, long-standing fundamental laws should not be harmed, either at the convention itself or later, as a result of acts now taken and by the consequence of subsequent unexpected offenses. This meant constitutional rights must instead always be carefully protected against possible citizen or leader abuse. These documents had successfully limited governments for over a generation and therefore should not be lightly disregarded.

With such arguments delegates across America demonstrated their commitment to an important feature of Madison's constitutional vision, wanting to retain private rights above legislative whim and delegate fancy. The delegates' positions show the influence of liberalism, aiming to limit government through laws that rest above the purview of ordinary legislative activity. They particularly aimed to restrict government's ability to interfere with the lives, liberties, and property of its citizens.

THE POINT OF DEPARTURE FROM BASIC LIBERAL AGREEMENTS

Questions of rights clearly were of great concern to politicians and citizens as they revised their foundational documents. It is worth remembering, however, that the snippets sampled were not observations by constitution writers revising rights declarations or redefining power limits of particular government branches. These snippets were from speakers in the process of revising electoral provisions. Why, then, did so many of the speakers make at least passing reference to the origin and ongoing importance of rights and their protection? The answer seems obvious. The speakers thought these were aims of the good state, most intricately tied to questions of popular rule. They believed these were the aims sanctioned by nature and foundational laws.[34] Furthermore, these three aims were seen as so important that publicly declared pledges to them were commonplace and necessary for any political representative seeking to establish the legitimacy of his arguments. Anyone who did not align himself with preserving the life, liberty, and property of every U.S. citizen was not a good American. (This was public rhetoric, not the reality.)

Scholars of liberalism may debate why rights should be placed above ordinary legislation; they may debate the best design to ensure these aims; but none denies that a fundamental aspect of liberal rhetoric is the undaunted commitment to certain birthrights—rights that belong to everyone and forever remain above the purview of ordinary legislation. All would concede that a government designed with these aims in mind signified an attempt to create a liberal state. Thus, given the discussions that took place at state constitutional conventions, it is safe to say that participating delegates were strongly influenced by liberal values when deciding how to frame the representative features of constitutional government.

This is not the whole story, however. Behind the delegates' general agreement to keep certain private rights above ordinary law lay a disagreement that would have ramifications for how delegates viewed electoral reform. Delegates chose different sources to explain America's commitment to rights. Expansionists relied on nature's principles: as they saw it, each right that originated in nature deserved protection after the compact, that is, in America's constitutional law and practice. The logical consequence of their view was that no human intermediaries—neither the signers of the contract nor delegates selected to revise it—could rightfully alter government's commitment to certain aims. Neither necessity nor goodwill justified any restriction of natural or God-given rights. On the other hand, restrictionists believed they had little to gain from studying nature, since rights gained their status from another source—from prior mutual agreement among members. Life, liberty, and property deserved special consideration in the good state because of America's foundational laws and its tradition of following the original compact.

The skeptical arguments of antireformers were significant, for their views constituted a fracture in America's liberal consensus. Restrictionists posited that rights derived their legitimacy from agreements, traditions, and constitutions. In doing so, they were deriving the legitimacy of government from America's own historical tradition rather than from abstract principles or from a strictly prepolitical state. In this sense, they denied that principles existed above and beyond man and his limited reason. They posited instead only that consent determined which principles were fundamental. This appeared to constitute a movement away from the Revolutionary endorsement that higher principles (not man-made law) determined the limits of government toward a more modern notion that consensus (not abstract principle) makes governments legitimate.[35] Restrictionists agreed that written constitutions were necessary to emboss "higher" laws onto paper, but they noted that these very documents derived their original legitimacy from an earlier human agreement, which had then been perpetually enforced. This meant that constitutional authority and the status of rights relied on the actions of men.

That restrictionists' view had such widespread support may imply that Americans never fully embraced the Revolutionary idea that fundamental guiding principles derived their legitimacy strictly from abstract reason. Whether a reintroduction of an old idea or a long-standing parallel justification, the view put forward by antireformers constituted a subtle shift in the grounding of the good state. Both sides advocated retaining the status quo, namely, keeping life, liberty, and property both inalienable and well protected from capricious invasion. Changing rationale without changing purpose is hardly noticeable. Nonetheless, the logical consequence of the antireformers' position was potentially radical. It was what Madison feared. According to restrictionists, the initial signers of the compact—ordinary men—originally determined which rights would become inalienable in the state. Since they, as constitution writers, were redesigning the compact, did they not also have the legitimate power to determine which rights should remain inalienable? Restrictionists would have said both no and yes—no regarding life, liberty, and property, and yes regarding any other issue.

The prevailing dispute over what constituted the appropriate basis for legitimate government had substantive significance and explicit consequence even during the first half of the nineteenth century. Reformers wanted to radicalize government to change existing practices to fit more closely with an abstract ideal. Antireformers wanted to justify the legitimacy of present provisions regarding popular rule. By replacing abstract principles with earlier agreements, they could restrict government's aims to life, liberty, and private property, the "consensus" rights. They could consistently argue against any attempts to change government's existing commitments, for change was precisely what traditionalists fight against. This was a necessary and important strategy, for their adversaries claimed that self-government was a right of nature. To the extent that reformers had accurately described the natural state, restrictionists had to respond cleverly. They did so by reducing the power of natural law over government design.

Reformers and Popular Sovereignty

he rhetoric surrounding early nineteenth-century electoral reform reflects America's widespread and devoted commitment to certain private rights and liberties, most particularly Locke's triumvirate of life, liberty, and property. Delegates may have debated the source of government's commitment to these aims but they never wavered on the state's responsibility to ensure them. Behind their dispute over the source of government's obligation to rights lay another important point of contention, as to which constitutional concerns should be considered rights of inalienable status. Convention delegates discussed whether life, liberty, and property were the only immutable aims of the good state. They contemplated the relationships among these three rights, as well as with the other constitutional ideal they had met to reformulate, namely, popular sovereignty.

Delegates used theories of nature, the original compact, and the role of foundational documents not just to discover why Americans were committed to rights but also to understand the relationship between this general commitment and Americans' responsibility toward property and self-government. Advocates of reform often described political voice as an inherent right, which derived its importance from those same authorities officially approving private rights. Opponents of reform looked at the same authorities but came to different conclusions. Antireformers thought the compact granted political power selectively and conditionally. Many believed not only that private rights were the sole rights granted immutable status but also that, among these revered rights, property held a superior status. Both sides shared a common liberal language regarding rights as authoritative ends of the good state; they differed in their interpretation as to what this liberal conviction entailed.

Expansionists, for the most part, rejected what they saw as a false distinction between political privileges and personal rights. In Virginia, advocates of an extended suffrage and a representation system based on voter population insisted that everyone enjoyed equal political influence in the state of nature. Before formal society, individuals governed themselves and no person had more voice than another. The just compact and its resultant laws should secure general suffrage and equal representation. In New York and Massachusetts, advocates of an extended suffrage agreed. They referred to nature and various foundational laws to demonstrate how political power belonged by right to everyone. In these states and in these contexts, reformers repeated that life, liberty, property, *and* a voice in government were all inalienable rights; that each belonged to every individual; that each derived importance from the same revered sources. Although it was only in these three states that discussions were dominated by this issue, throughout the thirty-year period in all states, advocates of reform blurred the distinction between public and private rights, insisting that the immutable ends of the good state included widespread enjoyment of both personal rights and political voice.

At later conventions, nature was hardly ever emphasized as the source of the equation. Yet, at least some advocates of reform tried to convince their colleagues that the same authorities that mandated a commitment to life, liberty, and property also mandated an unfailing commitment to political voice. In this sense, reformers had an understanding of rights that went beyond the standard liberal conception. They viewed self-government as an immutable right and spoke of it as no different from the other three.

Over the entire thirty-year period of this study, restrictionists disagreed strongly with what they saw as their adversaries' conflation of rights with privileges. Restrictionists contended that no individual had an a priori right to self-government. Even if people once enjoyed political power in nature, this had no bearing in present-day society. Good government reflected initial agreements made upon forming society. Initial agreements had granted inalienable protection to life, liberty, and property only. The people never consented to grant popular influence over officials the same status as those other three personal concerns. Indeed, people had voluntarily agreed to restrict their influence in the name of protecting private rights, especially property rights. No matter what reform issue was being discussed, opponents contended that the very source that exonerated personal and private rights undercut the independent value of sovereignty. Political power was a *privilege* that government granted carefully and selectively. Life, liberty, and especially private property were the inalienable rights of man, and it was for these—especially for property—that governments were formed. This view resembled what has now been termed the traditional liberal view.[1]

Delegates debated which rights were enjoyed in nature and which rights were dutifully preserved by a just compact. They debated whether good government naturally included self-government, and whether ongoing popular influence was a privilege granted to the propertied by an earlier compact. In many ways, arguments both for and against electoral reform resemble aspects of Locke's *Second Treatise*. If one stresses Locke's views about the people's powers—including the naturalness of everyone's right to self-preservation, the obligation of the community to consent to the majority, and the legislature's sovereignty as originating from the people's grant—one may conclude that the true Locke is a radical democrat.[2] If one stresses other views, one may conclude that Locke endorsed popular rule only as one among many government alternatives.[3]

State builders did not see themselves as battling to find the true meaning of Locke's *Second Treatise*. They rarely quoted Locke or any other natural rights theorist. They sought instead to understand which rights limited government and best suited America's political tradition. Their discussions led to different interpretations of what was meant by an inalienable commitment to rights. The point is that both views are liberal and Lockean. Any extent to which nineteenth-century views resemble plausible interpretations of the *Second Treatise* only goes to show that Locke's ideas were in general circulation at that time and were considered appropriate for understanding the essential features of constitutional government and society's reasoned understanding of the good state.

POLITICAL VOICE AND INALIENABLE RIGHTS

Both reformers and antireformers considered the possibility that self-government was an end comparable to private rights. The evaluation given depended on the speaker's policy preference. Antireformers argued consistently that popular power as an aim was distinct from and less important than private rights. They never described political voice and personal rights as ends of equal or comparable worth. When they discussed popular influence they usually avoided using the word *right* and instead referred to *privilege*.

Most expansionists who spoke on the subject, especially when speaking in favor of extending the franchise, refused to distinguish between political influence and the other inalienable rights of nature and constitutional government.

To have a voice in the selection of lawmakers was no less an inalienable right than life, liberty, or property. These arguments constitute an interpretation of American liberalism that has been generally ignored. Because of this, expansionist views on the issue are discussed in some detail in the selections ahead, whereas antireform positions are mentioned only briefly.

Over time expansionists became less likely to justify their commitment to political voice solely on its character as an inherent human right. After 1830 reformers relied more on America's legal tradition and less on abstract principles and nature to explain government's inalienable commitment to popular rule. However, time may not be the primary cause of this trend. The issue to be debated and the locale of the convention partially determined which power of authority the delegates were to use to make their case for expansion. Debates at Virginia's 1850–1851 convention, for example, were as intensely philosophical as at their earlier meeting. In New York, the Second Great Awakening appeared to have influenced political rhetoric at the 1846 convention, for delegates talked mainly about God's will and less about natural law.[4] Other debates at the convention and across the states concerned black enfranchisement and the selection of judges. At conventions held in the 1820s, even discussions on how to best select nonlegislative officials did not illicit many comparisons between rights and political voice. In the case of black enfranchisement, delegates at earlier conventions were slightly more conversant in natural rights theory than they were later, when racial tensions were growing and fears of riots and rebellions had surfaced. Part of the changing equation between inalienable rights and the vote may be because of the issue discussed or the context for the debate. But the decline no doubt results partially from a temporal decline in the perceived merit of the language of rights, especially natural rights.[5]

The Vote

A common point of contention in questions of suffrage was whether the vote was a right or a privilege; whether everyone, by his birthright, deserved to exercise the vote; or whether it was something to be granted by government representatives according to their discretion. In every state examined where franchise questions emerged, proponents of expanding the franchise for whites referred to the vote as a right; restrictionists referred to it as a privilege, granted only to those recognized as able to use it safely. Many of the expansion delegates explained that individuals had exercised the right of voting in nature and that this right continued after the compact. They claimed that America's founding documents—individual state constitutions as well as the Declaration of Independence and the U.S. Constitution—sanctioned the continued inalienable importance of this great right. A few saw the vote as the crowning right of freedom: they claimed that without its exercise a man was no different from a machine or a slave. In all expansionist cases voting was a right, no different from life, liberty, or property, deriving its legitimacy from the same sources. It therefore was a value that constitution writers should unhesitatingly emboss in foundational documents.

Restrictionists, on the other hand, denied that rights and the vote could have equivalent stature in the good state. A few admitted that both might have been enjoyed in nature, but none believed that this equality survived the original compact or America's later written rendition of it—that is, in constitutional law. As these constitution writers saw it, society had made a clear distinction between private rights and economic liberty on one hand, and political privileges on the other.

A few expansionists differentiated between political voice and private rights in a manner similar to restrictionists. No argument in favor of expansion, however, rested on the explicit claim that political voice was separate and secondary to personal rights. By far the overwhelming majority of expansionists who discussed the role of rights in the good state refused to distinguish between the political and the personal, thereby offering an alternative interpretation of America's liberal commitment to rights.[6]

At Virginia's 1829–1830 constitutional convention, every delegate who favored extending the franchise discussed the issue in terms of rights and the protection of rights. Two-thirds of the delegates referred to the vote as a fundamental and inalienable right, indistinguishable from the other so-called essential rights of mankind. These reformers verified the importance of the vote *exactly* as they and their adversaries legitimated the importance of personal rights. Philosophers, foundational law, and nature made immutable the rights of selecting legislative officers. Charles Morgan of Monongalia began his argument in favor of extending the franchise to all taxpayers by noting, "Able writers [say] . . . that the right of voting . . . is a sovereign right and one of first importance in free Governments." Since "Government is, or ought to be instituted, not for the restraint of . . . rights, but for their security and enlargement," the suffrage should be expanded (VA 1829–1830, 377). Morgan later expanded on what he meant when he said voting was a sovereign right, of first importance. Some contended that the essential rights of man were only those that "Governments please to bestow upon him," but Morgan believed man "has . . . certain inherent and inalienable rights of which he cannot be divested with impunity. Amongst those is the right of a voice in Government to which he is to submit" (388). For Morgan, and others who shared his view, suffrage rights belonged to all; no just government could legitimately deny them to anyone (at

least not to any white male citizen).[7] Other speakers alluded to nature as the
origin of the vote's immutable status. The argument was that, because everyone
had political voice prior to joining together formerly, government had no right
to take it away. Eugenius Wilson, who represented the same district as Morgan,
noted that suffrage was

> the most honorable and precious of . . . natural rights. . . . Not withstanding all
> the ridicule which has been cast upon the natural rights of man, not withstanding
> the repeated denial of their existence, . . . I believe that Nature . . . has conferred
> certain original rights upon men; and among these, none appears to me more
> clear and undeniable, than the right of appointing our own agents. And this right
> may exist apart from and anterior to any regular social compact. (351)

Lucas Thompson made a similar case, declaring suffrage a right, deriving its
roots from nature. This speaker, like many proclaiming the inalienable status of
popular power, embraced self-government for both instrumental and inherent
reasons. For Thompson exercising the suffrage was not just

> a vote for public functionaries. . . . It is the right by which man first signifies his
> will to become a member of Government of the social compact, his consent to, or
> his veto upon measures of the Government. . . . This being its definition, then is it
> a natural right? [Man] has natural rights, life, liberty, the pursuit of happiness and
> the means of acquiring and enjoying property. Suffrage is the substratum, the para-
> mount right upon which all these rest for protection, preservation and safety. This
> right . . . has its origin in every human being. . . . it is inherent and appertains to
> him in the right of his existence; his person is the title deed. . . . All our important
> rights, whether civil, social, or political are properly speaking, natural rights. (412)

Thompson explained that extension was sustainable "by reason and common
sense and is expressed in our Bill of Rights, which says—all men are equal, with
certain natural rights, with right of suffrage a right inestimable to freemen,
with all power derived from the people" (413). The vote derived its inalienable
status from both nature and Virginia's foundational law. The right to vote was
so important that "a man that has no voice in government . . . is already half a
slave" (418).[8]

Underlying each of these speeches was a simple claim, found in every state
examined: the vote was a right, no different from the personal rights. The
same documents and scenarios that gave high priority to personal rights legitimated the high priority of political voice. As John Rogers Cooke made explicit
toward the end of Virginia's suffrage debate, those who say there is a difference

between "rights" on the one hand and "privileges and immunities" on the other may be accurate but "the elective franchise was included in the former term" (VA 1829–1830, 440).

Elected delegates in Virginia used Locke's exact language more than at any other convention, yet expansionists gave his political teachings a radical interpretation, as these few examples show. When looking back to life before government, rather than a struggle over protecting one's life and possessions, expansionists saw a world where individuals had the power to make important decisions for themselves. They depicted the state of nature as a kind of democratic state. Knowing that at least some of their colleagues found a return to state's origins important for understanding the limits and directives of good government, they crafted their positions so that they gave a plausible account of those beginnings. They appealed to the agreed-upon importance of nature, as the first stepping stone to the contract and constitutional government. Then they not so quietly introduced self-government as one of the goods of value in that important state. Here (as with reformer arguments at every convention examined), delegates cleverly worked *within* liberal language and agreements, and they expanded meanings. They did not speak about the value of self-government in the language of other traditions. Self-government was not a means to produce virtue; it was not a means to keep the community free from corruption. It was something individuals held as their own, prior to the existence of government. Both times the vote was compared to liberty, it was done on an individualistic basis. The nonvoter was a slave; the repercussions for the independence of society as a whole were not discussed.[9]

At this same convention, and others, restrictionists recognized and refuted this radical teaching. In Virginia, the majority speaking against suffrage reform vociferously maintained there existed a fundamental distinction between personal rights and political privileges. Philip Nicholas illustrated the adamancy of their retort:

> One of the fallacious [arguments for extending suffrage] is that which attempts to found the right upon the principle of natural equality. This pre-supposes that suffrage is derived from nature. Now, nothing can be clearer than that suffrage is a conventional and not a natural right. In a state of nature (if such state ever existed . . .) every man acts for himself. . . . When he enters into the social state, . . . he gives up to the society the powers of Government.
>
> . . . .
>
> [R]epresentation and suffrage are social institutions.
>
> . . . .
>
> [The framers of our constitution] were wise and practical statesmen, and they knew and felt they had established a rule which was perfectly compatible with re-

publican institutions. . . . [The Bill of Rights] speaks of inherent rights, of which men, when they enter into society "cannot by any compact deprive or divest their posterity," "namely the enjoyment of life and liberty, with the means of acquiring and possessing property, and pursuing and obtaining happiness and safety." . . . This last clause does not comprehend suffrage, or representation, or any fancied rights growing out of them; first because these are not natural rights; and next, if they were, [they could be surrendered] to the regulation of society. (VA 1829–1830, 363, 364, 364)

These selections demonstrate three usual restrictionist responses to the rights-based expansionist argument. First, Nicholas denied that individuals enjoyed the power of self-government in nature. Second, he introduced differences between man's condition before and after nature. Third, he explained that government represents the outcome of the compact, and that people agreed to protect personal rights, not political voice.

Thus, the original status of self-government ultimately should not matter to nineteenth-century constitutional designers. All three excerpts explain why voting was not an inalienable concern of the good state. Governments were not based on nature; therefore it did not matter whether self-government once had natural status.[10] Only personal and property rights were among the essential concerns of the good state; only these rights were due each and every American citizen.

At the 1820–1821 Massachusetts convention, delegates discussed how far to alter existing qualifications for the franchise. There were few proponents of the status quo (for continued property requirements), unlike in other states. Instead, delegates debated whether voters should be taxpayers (not a very onerous requirement given the situation within the state).[11] As was suggested by constitutional tradition, the question whether to drop all requirements mostly centered on questions of principle, not on practical consequences of either choice. Nearly every delegate who mentioned the importance of rights and their protection also contemplated whether the franchise was among the inalienable rights. Those who preferred a tax requirement maintained there was a fundamental difference between political power and rights. For example, after explaining the great inalienable importance of property rights, lawyer-trained Warren Dutton of Boston (most opponents of reform lived in or near Boston) went on to say that the question of whom to enfranchise "was no question of right; it was wholly a question of expediency. . . . It was in the nature of a privilege" (MA 1820–1821, 247).

Over half the advocates of lifting all pecuniary restrictions countered this distinction by explaining that voting was among the inalienable rights—

enjoyed in nature, preserved in the original contract, and now embedded in America's foundational laws and principles. Some speakers also elevated political voice to the height of liberty, comparing its loss to slavery.[12] The words of lawyer-trained James Baldwin exemplify the reform response. Baldwin believed that voting should be extended without qualification: "it is asserted in the bill of rights . . . [that] all men are born free and equal. . . . Property cannot give them a right of voting; because the right belongs to all persons, who are born equal, and should be equally entitled to all the privileges of freeman" (MA 1820–1821, 255). For Baldwin and over half the speakers advocating universal male suffrage, the vote was an essential component of the good state, equal in value to the personal rights.

The only notable difference between the arguments put forward by Massachusetts's delegates and by Virginians was that the northern representatives rarely gave elaborate descriptions of nature and man's right to self-govern within it. Instead, they stressed voting as a right embedded in their constitution, a constitution described in the preamble as a voluntary association and compact and whose declaration connected many citizen rights to nature. Again, agreed-upon principles about the origin and superiority of rights and the inexorable responsibility of constitutions to ensure that citizens enjoyed these rights were coopted to justify the original and ongoing importance of voting.

At New York's 1821 convention, delegates debated whether to extend the franchise beyond the propertied and to include all taxpayers, laborers, and military men. Delegates also debated whether the word *white* should be added. As in Massachusetts and Virginia, delegates favoring extension often denied any difference between political voice and the other inalienable rights. Only Martin Van Buren, then U.S. senator and soon to be president of the nation, alluded to a hierarchy between private rights and political voice. He claimed that if "calamitous consequences could result, . . . he would be the last man in society who would vote for [extending the franchise]" (NY 1821, 264). The only New York reformer who made extension conditional on security, thereby intimating that self-government was not an inalienable right of its own merit, was a Democrat, President Jackson's immediate successor. This was not the rationale of most expansionists.

When Van Buren's colleagues compared personal rights to political voice, they declared that the very same high sources that legitimized the inalienability of one also sanctioned the other. Seven of the eight speaking out against a white-only franchise described the vote as a fundamental right whose restriction violated basic principles found in nature, preserved in the compact, and presently sanctioned in the nation's foundational documents. Some speakers favoring the extension of black suffrage tied the right of voting to the principles embedded not just in existing laws, but in nature itself—thereby blurring any distinction between political and personal rights. Federalist Peter Jay argued that blacks "were born as free as ourselves, natives of the same country, and deriving from nature and our political institutions, the same rights and privileges which we have" (NY 1821, 183). For Jay equal rights meant equal right to life, liberty, property, and political voice.[13]

New York delegates at the 1821 convention (unlike those in Virginia and Massachusetts) claimed that national documents supported their case. The Declaration of Independence and its portrayal of man's initial and natural equality and of government's original contractual nature mandated general suffrage. Physician Robert Clarke of Delaware declared that retaining the word *white* was "repugnant to all the principles and notions of liberty, to which we have heretofore professed to adhere, and to our Declaration of Independence, which is a concise and just exposé of those principles" (NY 1821, 186). In explaining how the Declaration was applicable he told his colleagues, "the great fundamental principle that 'all men were equal in their rights' was settled." Thus "it ought to be the invariable object of the framers of our civil compact, to render all men equal in their political enjoyment" (236). Dr. Clarke wished to bring his colleagues to the logical conclusion that equal in rights meant equal in voting rights, not just equal in personal rights. He quietly assumed that voting was an established legal right since the Declaration was signed. The problem thus far was that New Yorkers and others had not yet understood and applied this document correctly. Of course this was by no means a settled interpretation of the Declaration's meaning, but by imploring delegates to base their decisions on this document (a democratic document, as he saw it), he hoped to make his adversaries look like critics of the very origin of America's independence and its principled commitment to rights, instead of merely critics of general suffrage.

New Yorkers frequently used the national constitution to explain why suffrage was a right that state constitutions could not legitimately restrict. Abraham Van Vechten, known for his legal work in landholdings and also for his state service as attorney general, explained that the color of an individual did not "justify us in taking . . . any of the common rights which every free citizen enjoys." The national constitution made this clear in its contention that "citizens of each state are entitled to all privileges and immunities of citizens in the several states. The effect of this provision is to secure to the citizens . . . equal privileges and immunities." Just as "we cannot withhold [rights] from . . . citizens of other states when they migrate into this state," we cannot remove rights from free citizens of color who already reside there (NY 1821, 194).[14] Van Vechten's view represents a broad interpretation of article 4, section 2, of the U.S. Constitution and of national government responsibility. He not only included self-government among the inalienable rights, he also claimed that the nation denied state discretion on how to define rights and to implement their security. In a narrow sense, he was claiming that the government system of the union was truly national, not federal.[15]

By the 1830s most states lifted all property-holding and taxpaying requirements for voter eligibility. In most cases the implicit intent of these reforms was to effect universal white male suffrage.[16] States had few freemen of African descent. As demographic patterns changed, however, certain states were forced to face the question already debated at the New York 1821 convention: how should laws treat free Americans of African decent? Should requirements for the franchise be color-blind? If they were, free blacks—a group previously kept silent when property requirements were in place—would suddenly gain political power. After the pecuniary requirements were lifted, some states with sizable black populations focused on whether race should be a qualification for voting.

Around the same time, great numbers of Catholics began migrating from Europe, and this too raised questions regarding the wisdom of erasing all pecuniary qualifications. Was it safe to grant poor, newly arrived immigrants the power to influence political decisions? Should citizenship be required prior to exercising such control? Most states yielded to nativists' pressures and at least increased residency requirements, but often this was done without heated debate.[17]

In general, discussions on black suffrage focused less on questions of rights and more on questions of competence. Were free men of color competent to share as full members in the political society?[18] Although this other issue was the dominant topic, the same dichotomy between expansionists and restrictionists—regarding political voice, rights, and privileges—remained clearly present. No restrictionist equated political voice and private rights, whereas expansionists usually blurred any distinction between them. Reformers usually relied on the same authorities to applaud suffrage that they and their adversaries used to acclaim personal rights. The main difference from earlier debates was the frequency of these claims and analogies.

At the 1835 North Carolina convention, delegates who had gathered to discuss black enfranchisement mostly debated whether Americans of African descent were citizens of the United States. In a sense both sides agreed that, at least for full citizens, rights and powers were equal partners. The underlying assumption for most speakers was that with citizenship came personal rights and a guaranteed voice in government. If blacks were not full citizens, then, like aliens they should enjoy personal rights without political influence. Both sides blurred the distinction between private rights and political voice, at least for male citizens. Although the citizenship status of blacks was the focus of debate, some speakers ignored this issue and instead examined the relationship between private rights and political voice and their necessary constitutional commitment to each.

Two antireformers explicitly distinguished the vote from other rights, denying any inherent connection between voting and freedom in any sense. Hugh McQueen asked his colleagues to contemplate whether the "negro" would refuse his freedom if he knew it did not include the franchise. He thought not: "suffrage never enters his head when he is struggling to obtain his freedom" (NC 1835, 77). The issue hinged on whether blacks had "a right to vote." It was McQueen's opinion "that they had no *right*, and that good policy requires that the *privilege* should be withheld from them" (356, emphases added). A little over a third of the delegates who spoke in favor of black enfranchisement indirectly equated the vote with the other rights. When describing why he favored enfranchising blacks, John Kelly argued that to deny free blacks "the right of voting" was an "injustice," for it went against "the broad principle that all men are entitled to equal rights and privileges, that nothing but arbitrary power can forbid their free exercise." Disenfranchisement was "contrary to all principles of free government" (356). Kelly and his colleagues who wanted to allow property-owning blacks the right to vote certainly did not claim that blacks had this right by nature (North Carolina was a slave state), but most of them saw their suffrage as nonetheless sanctioned by higher law, namely, state constitutional law. Since the prior constitution of North Carolina did not specify race as a qualification to vote, they saw the present proposition as undermining the authority of the state's most important document. Although these reformers did not explain the inalienability of voting as forcefully and explicitly as earlier reformers from the other states had, at least some recognized that the authorities they and their colleagues agreed mandated the inalienability of private rights also granted equal enjoyment of the right to vote.[19]

At the 1846 New York convention, debates favoring an expanded black franchise moved away from secular justifications for the right of suffrage. At the previous convention delegates relied mostly on natural law, the Declaration, and the U.S. Constitution to mandate the enfranchisement of free men of African descent. Now, probably as a result of the religious revival that took place in New York in the early 1830s, "the Creator" was the most often cited legitimizer of state principles. He was the primary reason that states were immutably committed to rights in general, and to the vote in particular. Nonetheless, two delegates—both Whig lawyers involved in state politics—compared the vote to freedom, and its absence to slavery. George Simmons argued that to deny someone the vote was to take away his liberty. He contended that restrictions according to race would "enslave a portion of our citizens" (NY 1846, 790). Alvah Worden argued that, by extending the franchise to blacks, delegates would be "extending the 'area of freedom'" (791).[20]

The restrictionist arguments suggest that advocates of giving blacks the vote were probably still contending that inalienable rights included the vote. First, prior to the secularization of political rhetoric, God and nature were equivalent sources of authority. Second, although the record contains no expansionist reference to nature, restrictionists referred to it as a common myth. Democrat John Kennedy, for example, devoted most of his speech to explaining that the elective franchise was "not a right, emanating from nature, born with [the individual] and alienable only for offenses against society." On the contrary, it was "a privilege, acquired by grant of the governing power." Kennedy rejected any proposition that assumed blacks and whites deserved the same political privileges. "Nature revolts at this proposal" (NY 1846, 783).[21] Horatio Stowe, one of the many lawyers present at the convention, adamantly proclaimed that despite arguments to the contrary "[t]he vote is not a right but a franchise, a privilege, a matter of policy and expediency" (787). That he and others found it necessary to distinguish political voice from personal rights suggests that people (either at the convention or elsewhere) still contended that voting was an inalienable right, deriving its legitimacy from sources higher than human fancy.

At the 1850–1851 Ohio convention, delegates mostly made scattered remarks regarding how American society should view blacks versus whites.[22] As in North Carolina, delegates debated whether Americans of African descent were citizens, but this question did not preoccupy them in their discussions quite as much. Moreover, although arguments at the Ohio convention lacked the theoretical cohesiveness one finds at earlier conventions, one can uncover echoes of the same pattern that existed elsewhere. Those favoring a policy granting propertied blacks the vote sometimes spoke about enfranchisement as if it were an inalienable right, whereas opponents responded with outright denial. Half the speakers favoring black enfranchisement commented indirectly on the relationships between political voice, inalienable rights, and government grants of privilege. High sources, they noted, dictated that all should equally enjoy the vote. E. B. Woodbury was against enfranchising only whites in part because the Ohio constitution says "'All political power is inherent in the people.' . . . and they have the right to alter or reform the [government] whenever they may deem it necessary." Then also, "It is part of our Declaration of Independence." To ask the disenfranchised to accept a government in which they were not active participants "is in violation of its principle" (OH 1850–1851, 554). Woodbury was giving a particular view of his state constitution and the Declaration; he was giving the abolitionist view. Of interest is not the validity of his interpretation of these documents, but that he took the documents used by his adversaries to authorize the immutability of private rights and instead used them to authorize a similar status for popular rule.[23]

Every time delegates considered who should vote, they debated whether the inalienable rights of mankind included the suffrage. Restrictionists remained consistently loud and emphatic regarding the secondary and instrumental role of political voice. In accordance with fundamental law and earlier contracts, constitutional designers must first and foremost ensure the preservation and protection of personal and civil rights, the very rights that people originally compacted to protect and that present constitutions embossed as immutable ideals. The franchise was a privilege, not guaranteed at the compact but selectively granted to some, for reasons of expediency and according to the evaluation of judicious constitution writers and legislators. None of the fundamental laws and principles upon which America was built mandated the widespread enjoyment of political voice. A few admitted voting was exercised in nature, but because they rejected the pregovernmental state as the basis for determining the limits and powers of good government, they had no problem denying the so-called natural right to vote to particular citizens after the formation of society. According to their conception of the good state, people agreed to codify the inalienability of private rights, but they never agreed to elevate political voice to the same high status. Voting was granted only on the basis of expediency, on its ability to protect personal rights. In this respect, their view resembles that attributed to *Publius* and the traditional Locke.

Expansionists almost always blurred the distinction between personal and political rights. When asked to consider the enfranchisement of Americans of European descent, reformers were fairly explicit regarding the nature of political voice: it was among the inalienable rights, enjoyed in nature, preserved in the original compact, and sanctioned by America's own foundational laws. The particular authority on which expansionists most relied usually paralleled the authority they and their adversaries most used to justify the inalienability of private rights. In Virginia, delegates commonly looked to nature as the grantor of political rights. In New York, expansionists looked to the national constitution and the Declaration of Independence. In Massachusetts, they looked to their own constitution and its famously worded preamble. In each case, the sources that sanctioned private rights also mandated political voice. By the 1830s, however, speakers favoring the enfranchisement of Americans of African descent were less emphatic about proclaiming voting an inalienable right. This resulted partly from their own racist prejudices, their inability to admit that blacks and whites were truly equal.[24] Yet, in spite of prejudices, whenever delegates discussed political voice versus private rights, they spoke as if these were of the same ilk, that is, comparable aims of the good state, deriving value from the same sources and traditions. Despite the rise of party power over this period, when discussing who should have the franchise, delegates rarely expressed worries that the "masses" would elect party stooges. Nor did they discuss the electoral realignments that the changes might engender.[25]

A study of suffrage debates over the thirty-year period suggests that, although the rhetoric of rights remained important and although many still found the existence of high-order, extraconstitutional principles useful to discover authoritatively whether the vote was a right or a privilege, the rhetoric of *natural* rights appears to have lost ground. State and national documents were increasingly cited as the authority on which good constitutional designers should rely when revising existing documents.[26] The decline may have something to do with the nature of the later suffrage issue, in that, as slavery became a more contentious and nation-splitting issue, to describe blacks as equal and worthy of natural birthrights might simply have become more difficult. Nonetheless, New Yorkers in the 1840s still made the case for a natural equality—albeit with God as the source, not the secular state of nature.

Regardless of who or what served as the basis of granting popular sovereignty the status of personal rights, at each convention in this study the expansionist argument was that selection procedures and government limits were defined by laws above the purview of ordinary legislatures. These higher laws demanded that individuals equally enjoyed private rights and political voice, at least a voice in the selection of legislative officials. Public and private rights were inescapably intertwined. Popular sovereignty—narrowly understood to mean electing lawmakers—was an inalienable goal of the good state. There was no hierarchy wherein it took second stage to personal rights. The liberal language of immutable principle and higher law that made personal rights inalienable dictated that the vote be treated the same way. For suffrage reformers, liberalism was the language of political inclusion.

Equal Representation and Majority Rule

Most states in the union initially drew legislative boundaries by county lines. By 1820 migration patterns within and across states made these original districts grossly unequal, with certain underpopulated areas controlling legislation. Who held the disproportionate legislative power varied from state to state. In both North Carolina and Virginia, all the slaveholding large plantation owners lived in the east where a majority of the legislative counties lay. In both states, the existing representation system granted this group control over decision making even though it constituted a minority of the real population. In Louisiana, the existing county system gave New Orleans (with half the state population) less than one-fifth of the total seats. It privileged farmers in general, especially large plantation owners in the southeastern part of the state. In all three states, reformers wanted a voter population basis, to take away the control slaveholders had on legislative decisions. In Massachusetts and Ohio, reformers fought for a population basis. In both states there appeared to be no special interest that would gain by this basis, although the change would upset the existing balance of power. Despite these significant disparities across states, advocates of greater representational equality often used the same type of language to make their case, whether they were from the North or South, East or West. They argued that majority rule and voter equality were essential and fundamental rights of freemen, found in nature, sanctioned in the contract, embedded in principled declarations in many of America's founding documents. In this sense—regardless of who advocated changes to the representation system, and why, and regardless of the practical political motivations for certain regions wanting more say—the same theoretical arguments were used across these states. They contained the same language that advocates of suffrage reform found appropriate to make their expansion case.

At each convention where the issue of districting arose, delegates were well aware that existing systems purposefully granted some individuals disproportionate influence in the legislative branch. Under present allocations, some legislators represented a populated area and therefore spoke for a large number of people; others spoke for areas with only a small population. This often meant that a majority of senators and house representatives were selected by, and therefore represented, a minority of the voter population. Even advocates of the status quo recognized this consequence and never refuted their embrace of minority rule. Instead, they and their adversaries—the proponents of a system more closely based on (voter) population—wondered whether America's fundamental laws and principles required constitution writers to endorse majority rule, in both branches of the legislature. Could the philosophical principles guiding America sustain a system of government that gave extra voice to a select portion of the population? The question of how much proportional power to give each voter was sometimes debated in terms of rights. Was majority rule an inalienable right or a government grant left to the discretion of the designers? A delegate's response to any of these questions depended on his political position.

Advocates of a voter population basis contended that, regardless of how districts were crafted, if these units gave additional voice to the propertied and taxed, it meant certain individuals would enjoy more rights than their less fortunate brethren. Behind this was an implicit and sometimes explicit argument: in America, rights were to be distributed equally. Political power was a right, not just a means to protect rights. The present system sanctioned inequality by claiming that some deserved more voice than others. Such inequality would be inconsistent with the theory of natural rights and good constitutional government. Despite the diverse situation across states, arguments against new or existing bases privileging certain voters and regions over others often contained the underpinnings of this argument. Speakers of this inclination collapsed or ignored distinctions between political and civil rights. They claimed that nature, American law, and principle all sanctioned both majority rule and personal rights.

Those who favored systems privileging areas and interests over disparate individuals took a consistently different approach. Like advocates of a restricted suffrage, these individuals distinguished private rights from political power. They claimed emphatically that the fundamental laws and principles guiding American government displayed an undaunted commitment to personal rights, especially property rights. But they contended that such guideposts remained silent on issues of political influence. Thus majority political power was not an inalienable concern of the good state. Self-government was to be understood only as an instrumental good, to be distributed cautiously, according to expediency. These parallels were prominent, even though speakers from different states often stood for radically different forms of representation and had radically different political motivations. In places like Virginia restrictionists were slaveholders, and in Massachusetts they were abolitionists.

In most states, however, delegates did not discuss the relationship between representation and rights with the same fervor and detail as they did in debates about the franchise. At the 1850–1851 Ohio convention, for example, delegates did not connect the question of representation and majority rule to an issue of fundamental rights. Instead, delegates debating apportionment worried that leaders, directly responsible to the people, would become tools of party corruption.[27]

In each state except Virginia, there was always another reason dominating the reform position. Most state delegates were not as wholly preoccupied with other issues as they were in Ohio. Usually at least two speakers contemplated whether majority rule was among the essential, inalienable rights. But this issue was neither the main nor the most frequent reason offered for endorsing the voter population basis. Representation was more frequently understood as a means to empower interests than it was seen as an inalienable right. That is, though self-government was an inherent right, for many, equal representation was an instrumental good, a means of giving each person's inalienable right a chance of influencing policy. In most of these cases, to the extent majority rule was considered a right, with the sanction of higher law, it was constitutions and written man-made documents that verified the importance of equal political voice. Again, equal representation was not revered because of human or mutable principle, but because of America's traditional interpretation of how the right of self-government should be enjoyed.

The difference between these debates and those above about suffrage suggests that arguments about the inalienable status of voting were not merely rhetorical ploys but a perspective reserved for the particular act of governing, for the particular act of influencing lawmaking.[28] No postagreement could purge someone of his voting birthright; but once someone had voice, how much voice was less essential and therefore more a matter of contractual agreement, perhaps even of expediency. Equal voice gained its legitimacy from human artifice, through original agreements and foundational written laws, for example; it had special value because of its consequence on the people's ability to influence legislation.

At the 1820–1821 Massachusetts convention, delegates who debated the basis of representation worried first and foremost about *protecting* rights. There was widespread agreement for maintaining a tax-based representation system in the senate, and so only three (one-sixth) of the speakers spoke in favor of a voter population basis in both houses. Republican lawyer Henry Dearborn was the only one who justified this position by describing political power as a right (Dearborn held no political offices but he was part of a prominent family). He began his speech by saying he "did not know whence the principle, by which the senate is apportioned by the present constitution, was derived." After evaluating various sources and finding it supported only by "the British House of Lords," he rejected the principle, for in the United States "all [are] freemen and have equal rights." At the close of his speech, he "appealed to the magnanimity of the rich to yield to the poor their equal portion of rights" (MA 1820–1821, 257).

Although Dearborn was not explicit, his argument contained two important assumptions. First, since he searched for high-order principles supporting the property bias, he indirectly implied that America's representation system must be grounded in some theory. Second, since he appealed for change on the ground that everyone had equal rights, he indirectly implied that an equal voice in legislation was a right in itself. Although only Dearborn made this case (and only indirectly), it appears that his opponents were familiar with his position and found it a dangerous one. Many who wanted to maintain the present system of allocating districts according to taxes paid by inhabitants found it necessary to explain that, even though they advocated a property basis for the senate, they supported rights' enjoyment for all.

For opponents of reform, unequal representation and equal rights were not incompatible goals, precisely because "rights" did not include political power. The words of Massachusetts's great orator Daniel Webster serve as a good example of this position. Throughout his speech, Webster praised personal rights, especially property rights: "Life and personal liberty are no doubt to be protected by law; but property is also to be protected by law" (MA 1820–1821, 312). "It would be monstrous to even give the name of government to any association in which the rights of property should not be completely secure" (312–13). Amid these praises, Webster found it necessary to repeat, four times, in slightly different ways, that *no* town had "any *right* to representation except as far as the Constitution creates such right" (318). "Representation of the People has heretofore been by towns because . . . [it] has been thought convenient" (319). Equal voice was not a right of nature or of citizenship. It was a privilege to be granted according to expediency, according to whether it would help protect potentially insecure rights.

In Louisiana, delegates also debated the appropriate basis of representation. Here they emphasized leaders' responsibility to interests. On the one side were those arguing to make each district represent as equal a portion of voting population as possible. Those favoring this basis did so on the grounds it would give the city and its commercial concerns a "fair" say. On the other side were various arguments to include considerations of slaves, property holdings, or tax payments when drawing districts. Those favoring these bases aimed to ensure that each and every county in the countryside had a separate representative. With this kind of arrangement, agricultural concerns would have majority power in the legislature. Despite this emphasis on representing interests, a couple of Louisiana delegates favoring electoral reform discussed whether this issue disturbed America's commitment to rights. One of them, Whig lawyer and state politician Christian Roselius, believed that both law and principle mandated the creation of districts by voter population. For him, only when each representative spoke for the same number of individuals did every voter have an equal voice. He noted that "the first and pervading principle of a representative democratic government is, that all citizens of the political community were entitled to an equal participation in the political rights conferred by the social compact." In his view, the compact granted majority rule and good government must retain that principle (LA 1845, 333).

Arguments like this one apparently had *no* influence on the other side, unlike in Massachusetts, for no restrictionist found it necessary to distinguish carefully between political voice and inalienable rights. This silence illustrates how marginal the rights argument was for Louisiana delegates seeking to expand representational power to a majority. As in Massachusetts and Ohio, expansionists did not see the level of influence as important as a voice, per se. This suggests that the rights language was carefully applied, and its use might not have been disingenuous. Although everyone had a right to influence government, how much influence was a different issue.

Only in Virginia, at both conventions, did the question of rights dominate the debate over the basis of representation. At the 1829–1830 convention, delegates engaged in a long discussion over how to base representation. Here all twenty-eight delegates speaking on the issue gave extended philosophical rationales to support their positions. Many spoke for days at a time. House delegate John Rogers Cooke, the first of thirteen delegates to speak in favor of the number basis, set the tone; his elaborate arguments were repeated by many who followed him. Cooke explained in great detail the principles supporting the construction of districts according to the size of the voting population. He referred to a whole list of authorities that sanctioned the right of majority rule: including nature, Virginia's constitutional declaration of rights, the fathers of the Revolution, Locke, Sydney, and Milton. He noted that "The deep foundations of our Republic [rested] on *the sovereignty of the people* and *the equality of men.*" Virginia's "Declaration of Rights . . . was made by an assembly of sages and patriots." These fighters of the Revolution risked their lives for "principles of eternal truth, . . . principles deep seated in the nature of man." These principles are "'that all power is vested in, and . . . derived from *the people*', 'that all men are by nature *equally free*', and 'that a *majority of the community* possesses by the law of nature and necessity, a right to control its concerns'." These principles constitute the "basis and foundation of Government" and were sanctioned by Locke, Sydney, and Milton (VA 1829–1830, 54). Cooke continued with the observation that all were by nature equally free, which meant that "no *one* man is born with a natural right to control any *other* man" (55). Thus no select portion of the population ever possessed the right to rule over the rest; everyone must have equal influence. Given this mandate for equal influence, he contended that "the essential character of a free Government" was majority rule (56). After discussing a number of other reasons why Virginia ought to embrace representation by population, Cooke ended his speech as he began, telling his colleagues that to make legislative districts based on property would be "to destroy the great landmark of natural right, established at the era of the revolution, [and] to repudiate all the principles of government which have been, until now, held sacred and inviolable" (62).

Throughout the debate that followed this opening speech, expansionists often recalled many of the same principled arguments laid out by Mr. Cooke. They described majority rule as a right sanctioned by great men like the revolutionaries and constitutional founders, by documents of higher law like the state constitution, and by nature itself.[29] Some equated the exercise of political voice with the release from bondage. For nearly all Virginians speaking in favor of a district system based on the voting population, there existed respected authorities who verified that majority rule was a right. These were the same respected authorities that mandated societal deference to life, liberty, and property.[30]

Virginia's politicians, meeting twenty years later, described the issue of representation in the same way as Cooke and his colleagues. Again, those favoring the number basis relied on natural right, fundamental documents, and revered men of the past to support representation by population and the inalienable status of majority rule. Again, some compared the lack of equal political power to chattel slavery. Waitman Willey, a prominent Whig from the western part of the state who had served the state in both its house and the senate, justified a number basis because it adhered to "the cardinal maxims in our Bill of Rights; that all men are by nature free and independent, that all power is vested in and consequently derivable from the people; and that a majority of the people is the only true basis of the legislative power of government" (VA 1850–1851, 15). As was the case with Willey, many of the Virginians who spoke on behalf of a voter population basis found innate value in majority rule and the population basis of representation. Because majority rule was a right, with the same theoretical backing as the other immutable personal rights of nature, procedures must approximate it. As in other states, Virginians trying to maintain a representation system that empowered a privileged minority rebelled against the contention that political power deserved the same inalienable status as personal rights.

Virginia's debates over the basis of representation constituted a special case. Only here was majority rule so often and so clearly defined not only as a right but as an *inalienable* right deriving its legitimacy from nature and the compact. In other states, advocates of a voter population basis talked about this issue as if it were a case of fundamental rights, but they did not do so as consistently, explicitly, forcefully, or frequently as they did in Virginia or as when they debated suffrage expansion. Certainly at each state some advocates of a more egalitarian system of representation talked about equal political voice as if majority rule were among the inalienable rights, to be revered as well as universally enjoyed and protected. In such cases, distinctions blurred between power and rights. Nonetheless, fewer delegates stressed the inalienable importance of equal voice.

Most of these debates took place in the 1830s, 1840s, and 1850s, so the authority most frequently mentioned as the reason majority rule deserved immutable status was the existing fundamental law, not a priori natural rights. Again, while the decline in the belief in the forcefulness of nature is partially because of the times, it is also a factor of the state's intellectual tradition. After all, in Virginia, home to so many of America's initial leaders, this issue remained the predominant reason for expanding the people's political power. At the same time, delegates may have purposely deemphasized the *right* of majority rule and its natural or immutable status for genuine reasons. Voting was the essential popular instrument for exercising sovereignty; in this sense, only it deserved the privileged title of an inalienable right of freedom. However, the question of how much voice to give voters was a separate question of a more practical bent that should, perhaps, therefore be determined by law and/or expedience.

Popular Control over Selecting Officials

Arguments equating political power and personal rights almost disappear in debates over how to best select executive and judicial officials. These arguments were absent, even in states where the records abound in discussions over other electoral issues. Those very individuals who made the case that citizens had the immutable right to control the selection of their legislative officers rarely applied this principle to the selection of other branches of government. Thus, it appears that the inalienable status of popular influence was largely reserved for popular leverage over those officers in charge of lawmaking.[31]

At the 1821 New York convention those favoring popular selection of justices of the peace and sheriffs never made reference to these choices as rights stemming from nature or foundational law. Instead, they and their adversaries debated the issue mainly in terms of what kind of leaders would be selected. Those favoring reform believed the people would make good, independent choices for these officers. Those against reform warned of the evils of party politics and the inevitable corruption that would occur in the judicial branch. Since so many New Yorkers saw the vote itself as an inalienable right, sanctioned by the state and the nation's most important foundational documents, and since the vote was exercised only to select legislators and the governor, one must conclude that they saw distinct limits in comparing political power to a right. The language of rights was reserved to areas of popular sovereignty that had traditionally been understood as essential for governing. Expanding the people's power to the selection of petty justices was an experiment that did not merit the same high status in America's set of principled beliefs. Expanding the people's power in this area was to be judged according to the outcome, that is, according to the kind of leaders they would select.

This general pattern exists in every state. For example, at the 1829–1830 Virginia convention, questions of rights permeated debates over the franchise and representation basis. In fact, nowhere was the discussion more rigorous and philosophically crafted. Yet delegates largely ignored the issue when discussing the reasons for selecting other officers. The contrast is startling. Here delegates debated whether the governor should be popularly elected. Those favoring elections described this procedure as a necessary application of popular sovereignty, but not as a fundamental right. They never looked to constitutional principles or the conditions of nature to justify the people's direct selection of executive officers. A few miscellaneous side comments concerning the selection of governors suggest that some reformers were willing to make this lead, but these were the exception rather than the rule. Richard Henderson remarked that although those against the popular election of governor believed that they were doing the people a favor by giving them one less office to worry about, in fact, contrary to this assumption, "the people will not thank gentlemen for consulting their *ease* by curtailing their *rights*" (VA 1829–1830, 473). Democrat and western reform leader Philip Doddridge relied on the authority of Jefferson, who (he believed) equated power and rights. Mr. Jefferson had supposedly said that "'the true foundation of republican Government is the equal rights of every citizen in his person and property and in their management.'" Since calls for representation by population, suffrage extension, and a popularly selected governor were calls for expanding rights, Jefferson's words supported each of these electoral reforms (476). For Doddridge, there should be no qualitative distinction between any of the electoral reforms. Beyond these two isolated remarks, which attempted to erase distinctions between political power and private rights, no other expansionist alluded to this connection.

Moreover, the only case where an authority was mentioned, it was a human voice, perhaps one seen as a bit more respectable and worthy of deference than any ordinary delegate, but one who himself questioned the ongoing legitimacy of constitutional laws and immutable principles without simultaneous popular consent. Given the liveliness and intellectual depth that characterized debates over other electoral reform issues, the relative silence here suggests that Virginians did *not* consider popular influence over the executive branch to be as important as an influence over lawmaking, a view perfectly consistent with their previous constitutional tradition.[32] As a result, those preferring an appointed executive branch did not have to explain carefully the difference between political and private rights. Instead they concentrated on questions of protection. They worried that popular election would increase the governor's power, make him impossible to control, and thereby threaten rights in general. In the end, these antireformers won, for a majority of delegates voted against a popularly elected governor.[33]

In 1835 North Carolinians also discussed how to select a governor, but the records are scanty. The available commentary centers on what the people want, not on principle; but even so the last antireform speech, by delegate Gatson, is of some interest. He attempted to characterize what he saw as the three main arguments put forward by his adversaries. The first was the claim that popular selection of the executive office was "an important extension of popular rights" (NC 1835, 337). Although he rejected this claim as wrongheaded, his listing of it among the three main positions taken by those in favor of gubernatorial reeligibility suggests that some people favoring unimpeded popular selection of the executive branch spoke about this power as a right. The evidence is weak, however.

By the time Virginia delegates met again in 1850–1851, the tide had changed and popularly elected governors were the norm throughout the United States. They quietly changed this aspect of the selection process and instead debated whether serving governors should be reeligible for office. Again, discussions centered on other issues, this time mainly on corruption and party politics. This stands in stark contrast to the way these same men discussed questions of representation. Only two speakers described political voice as an inalienable right. One of them, delegate Hoge, explained that "man, by entering the social compact, surrenders none—no not one particle—of either his sovereignty or his natural rights. On the contrary . . . they are both supported and strengthened by the compact." The right of selecting leaders should never have been revoked, since anyone who surrendered this right "ceases to be a man—he becomes a mere automaton—not a freeman . . . but a mere machine turned at the will of he who works the machinery by which he is governed" (VA 1850–1851, 171). For Hoge, by denying citizens the right to select the leader of their choice, one denied them their most fundamental, inalienable human power. Hoge's was a powerful argument, but almost no one echoed his sentiments. Most delegates seemed to agree that the right to select nonlegislative officers was really not a matter of rights, but a matter of expediency.[34]

In Louisiana in 1845, convention politicians discussed whether the people should directly select judicial officers. For the most part delegates debated whether the people had the competence to select good judges, and whether the electoral process itself would result in judges corruptly aligned to party dogma rather than to appropriate moral and legal principles. Only one speech in favor of elected judges proclaimed that the right to select *all* officers was among the inalienable rights of humankind. The argument was put forward by Read, the most vocal proponent of popularly elected judges, who believed that

> To deny the right of the people [to elect supreme court judges], is to deny at once, that truth asserted in the Declaration of Independence [and] . . . in the Bill of Rights that "all power is inherent in the people." This denial assails the first principles of a popular government. . . . I hereby hold the right of the people to elect their judges as indisputable and undisputed. (LA 1845, 745)

Appointing them is a "denial of the expediency of the exercise of popular rights" (746). Although other delegates here debated the question of how to select other, lower-level judges, no other speaker equated judicial selection to any of the inalienable personal rights that everyone deserved to enjoy. Again, as was the case in other state debates over how to select nonlegislative officers, the real issue was corruption in the electoral process. Delegates feared the growing power that political parties would have on an officer's actions; they feared elected leaders would merely follow the party line, ignoring state needs and the people's interests. They did not see selection of judicial officers as a clear inalienable right, but rather as a question to be determined by the consequential outcomes of its exercise.[35]

When debates arose over the extension of popular influence into nonlegislative areas, those favoring expansion rarely spoke of this kind of political influence as an inalienable right. Advocates of these reforms usually endorsed popular control over executive and judicial officials for other, less principled reasons. The most common was that there was no danger in extension. If the people could safely select lawmakers, they could safely select other officers. Expansionists assured their colleagues that extending popular influence into other branches would not bring new corruption into government. Although on occasion these speakers hinted that being able to select governors or judges was an inherent right, embedded in the same tradition that honored personal rights, for the most part the "right" of popular rule did not extend beyond influence over officers directly associated with lawmaking. Again, this suggests that when expansionists explained the value of voting in agreed-upon liberal language, it might have been clever, but it was somewhat honest. It was building upon the high status that their local forefathers had already granted popular control of legislators. The liberal inalienable right included long-established ideals: life, liberty, property, and voting for lawmakers. The last was the only political influence that states had granted since colonial times.

EXPANDING INALIENABLE RIGHTS

At every state and for nearly every electoral reform issue, at least some of the speakers who supported increasing the people's influence in and over government described political voice as if it were no different from any of the personal, inalienable rights due American citizens. Delegates wishing to increase popular influence in and over lawmakers contended that the same sources making life, liberty, property, happiness, and their security above government manipulation and legislative whim also gave similar inalienable status to political power. As they saw it, neither nature nor the original compact, neither state constitutions nor America's other foundational documents, neither great statesmen nor liberal philosophers differentiated between personal and political rights. And neither should delegates. A few expansionists further emphasized the inalienability of political power by comparing its exercise to the exercise of rational free will. In speeches of this kind, expansionists spoke as if political liberty and economic liberty were the same thing. Life without one or the other was equally dehumanizing. When an individual lost control over government, he lost his freedom as an independent being able to make decisions for himself. Decision making both in and out of government was part of what made individuals essentially human; it distinguished American citizens from slaves, animals, and machines.[36] An individual's political power determined whether he was free to act as a human being.

Despite this equation of political and private rights, it appears that delegates distinguished among the kinds of power that the good state—by definition and inherent high-order principle—had to grant its citizens. In each state examined, delegates created a hierarchy among different types of popular political influence: first a widely inclusive white franchise, then a color-blind franchise, then equal representation in the legislature, then popular election of executive and judicial officials. In other words, some influence over one's lawmakers was an inalienable right of nature. This was the case first and foremost for white men, the individuals who constituted the members of that pregovernment society on the new continent. How much voice these individuals should have in overall government operations was a question of law or possibly of expediency. The more closely connected the influence was to the legislative branch and lawmaking, the more inalienable the right to power was thought to be.

This was the case at *every* state convention examined. The further removed the proposed reform was from expanding the people's legislative influence, the less frequently delegates referred to that influence as an inalienable right. Voting for officers directly involved in lawmaking was always considered a question of rights, but once everyone had some voice, the power question was seen as less pressing.

Embedded in this general pattern are others. Whereas opponents of reform consistently relied on America's legal and historical tradition of selective empowerment to justify restrictions on the people's political influence, reformers did not always look to these documents as the authoritative source of the necessary character of the good state. In the 1820s, questions of legislative control were often phrased as questions of inalienable rights, especially natural rights. Over time, however, the rhetoric of nature subsided and the historical and legal tradition took on its own democratic nature. Delegates felt more comfortable attributing their democratic preferences to their own history. Why?

Perhaps constitutions were beginning to take on a revered status all their own. In most of the cases examined, these documents already applauded popular sovereignty; it was now only a question of implementing what an ideal state had already endorsed in principle. Perhaps the state-of-nature theory had simply lost legitimacy.[37] Perhaps later debates increasingly addressed the status of rights for Americans of African descent brought to this nation as slaves, not freemen. In this particular case, to recall nature was to insist on an equality that the American reality blatantly averted. It was to suppose a pregovernmental state of freedom and equality that did not mesh with the history of African Americans.

In any case, the rhetoric of rights remained alive through the first half of the nineteenth century, but the origin of the immutability of rights had begun to undergo a transformation. In this aspect, the antireformers' traditionalist approach was winning ground. Abstract philosophical rationality was becoming a less attractive and less forceful means of establishing the legitimacy of ideals.

By describing the value of political influence as originating from high-order immutable principle and by giving it high profile among their constitutionally revered ideals, reformers developed a liberal language that not only justified popular sovereignty in the good state for its protective potential but made it an inalienable goal in its own right. Although no one self-consciously quoted Locke to make his case, nonetheless, many of the speeches favoring reform—especially those favoring expansion of white suffrage—appeared to follow the principles and methodology laid out in Locke's *Second Treatise*. Expansionists used reasoned arguments to discover the bases of human freedom, looking outside existing political conditions to circumstances that transcended present power arrangement. They then aimed to ensure procedural designs that enhanced and protected those original, extragovernmental bases. Many of them invoked a simple chain of arguments: having a say in and over one's government was an end in itself; it was one of those rights enjoyed in nature that rational men compacted to keep after the formation of the state; it was one of those rights that just governments included as inalienable and therefore made immutable. Most interpreters of the *Second Treatise* deny any direct democratic aspect in it and would therefore find such early nineteenth-century American interpretations "unLockean." However, Ashcraft recognizes that this democratic reading is plausible, given the views of Locke and some of his contemporaries.[38]

Whether expansionists thought they had the authority of Locke or not, many used his paradigmatic conception regarding the origin and limits of just government in order to redefine the foundations of the good state. They did not regard self-government as an immutable good because it built a better, more virtuous citizenry. They did not endorse its expansion merely for better protection of civil rights. Instead they contended that self-government was an essential right of man. Active popular consent was conceived of as an inherent part of the good state for the same reasons that Locke and America's national designers endorsed personal rights and private property. For nineteenth-century expansionists, self-government was not the expendable instrument that some of their forefathers and adversaries claimed it was.[39] Instead, active popular influence was one of the inalienable rights due each and every citizen by nature and by tradition. Regardless of whether one accepts the Lockean parallels, advocates of increased popular influence based their arguments on the very liberal language that determined rights immutable. Their expansion of the meaning of America's commitment to rights constitutes one of the fractures in American liberalism. It constitutes an important democratic—and yet ignored—feature of liberalism.

Antireformers avidly fought this theoretical explanation of America's commitment to rights. For them, people joined together to protect private rights, which they called "civil" or "personal" rights. By leaving nature, individuals had given up any legislative, executive, or judicial authority they may have once had. The people lost their political control at the signing of the compact. People formed societies for protection, not empowerment. To the extent that they refused to conflate private rights and political voice, they may be seen as the spokesmen of that "traditional" liberalism that scholars of the founding period describe and democratic theorists critique.[40] Although their reading of the nation's commitment to rights is more traditional than how their adversaries depicted it, many reform opponents also redefined the meaning and importance of America's allegiance to rights, stressing the value of material and landed possessions over that of life and liberty.

Antireformers and Property

*N*o one who opposed electoral reform during the first half of the nineteenth century denied that political influence in and over government was an important component of well-designed constitutions. Instead, they adamantly and consistently refuted their adversaries' broad interpretation of that influence as an inalienable right, free from government supervision and restriction. For opponents of electoral reform, political voice and private rights were concerns of different magnitudes; governments were designed only to protect the latter. Self-government was the best-known means to protect personal rights. The ongoing active consent of part of the population ensured that life, liberty, and property were well protected and that the nation's commitment to popular sovereignty was adequately realized. To a large extent, such arguments followed *Publius*'s depiction of the purposes of good government and what might be termed a "traditional" Lockean view of rights. However, not all arguments against electoral reform were quite so conventional. There is a sense to which restrictionists clearly and intentionally deviated from this traditional perspective and instead narrowed the meaning of America's allegiance to rights.

Opponents of reform wanted to reserve political power to those possessing material goods. In defense of this view, many lauded the merits of land and possessions over all other state concerns. Most denied that their praises were aimed at narrowing the list of inalienable rights to include property alone, and instead insisted that their special praises of property did not detract from their simultaneous allegiance to life and liberty. However, by emphasizing these material goods, many restrictionists appear to be applauding a government whose sole aim was to protect property rights; and in some sense they were. Regardless of whether they admitted the consequences of their arguments, many antireform praises of property constituted a reinterpretation of America's commitment to rights and created an explicit hierarchy among inalienable concerns. Their adversaries certainly recognized the implications of these arguments and adamantly rejected them as narrow and a wrongheaded interpretation of America's allegiance to rights.

Given Locke's own ambiguities regarding the value of land and material possessions, the debate between reformers and antireformers on the importance of property does not detract from the general influence of his ideas on their views. Just as Locke claimed to give equal weight to life, liberty, and property, some of his arguments suggest a more narrow and bourgeois interpretation of property.[1] The views of antireformers on the subject of property (narrowly understood as material possessions) demonstrate parallels with the bourgeois Locke. Again, the similarities do not imply that these nineteenth-century delegates read and intentionally quoted him but, rather, demonstrate the kind of liberal bias that was embedded in the antireform position.[2] Although not necessarily their intention, many opponents of reform ultimately endorsed a particular interpretation of the good state, a bourgeois liberal perspective that narrowed the field of inalienable rights. These antireform arguments reflected yet another fracture in American liberalism.

Among scholars who believe Americans have long aimed to ensure that government granted and protected private rights, there remains the question of how important property and economic liberty were, among these aims. Some might argue that the Revolution was fought for America's economic independence, rather than for the right of representation as much of the rhetoric implied. After all even Paine, the supposed great American democrat, found it important to explain that the British were using the colonists for their economic advantage and that America would prosper with independence.[3] Some contend that economic concerns greatly influenced the writing and the passage of the national constitution. Few deny that one of its chief architects, Hamilton, had capitalist designs for the future of the nation; and there is evidence that Madison was concerned primarily with property rights.[4]

Certainly in the American tradition, economic prosperity has always been considered closely related to economic liberty and secure property rights. This was especially so in the nineteenth century, when capital development skyrocketed.[5] Given this historical importance, one would expect that concerns with free exchange and protecting ownership would play a definitive role in delegate understandings of the good state. Since at early nineteenth-century conventions there were so many declarations of property's importance (alongside life and liberty), there should be little doubt that constitutional drafters of the time acknowledged its definitive place in the good state.

The architects of nineteenth-century state constitutions did not agree on how important land and material possessions actually were. For reformers property was just one of the many concerns of the good state, no more special than life, liberty, or self-government, whereas for many of those against reform it was the great and fundamental aim of the good state, worthy of special consideration in any question of government design. It was the great emphasis that so many antireformers placed on property that sometimes made them sound as if they too deviated from the traditional understanding of America's rights commitment as an allegiance to unfettered life, liberty, and property. Their great emphasis made them sound as if they instilled a hierarchy among rights, placing material goods over and above the rights of personhood.

Except in the case of black enfranchisement and the selection of nonlegislative officers, every antireform policy entailed the continuation of some political privilege to owners of land and material possessions. Given that restrictionists were attempting to maintain or even enhance the power of those with material and landholdings, it is not surprising that so many advocates of the status quo would applaud the merits of the goods these individuals held. Although perhaps not astounding, the restrictionists' emphasis is notable for two reasons.

First, reformers rarely placed any right above others. Even though expansionists had to convince skeptical peers to embrace popular political voice unconditionally and even though they had to change the way people thought about personal rights and political privileges, they hardly ever attempted to raise the status of political voice above and beyond the other concerns of government. No advocate of any electoral reform willingly decried the great inalienable importance of America's commitment to property. Unlike their adversaries, who countered claims about voting rights with outright denial, expansionists never denied property's high standing. They merely emphasized property's equal standing among all other inalienable rights; they spoke of its place *alongside* life, liberty, and self-government.

Second, even when restrictionists were not self-conscious of or explicit about theoretical consequences of their constant praises and added protections for property, their adversaries were. Expansionists noted the logical outcome of the antireform argument and sought to refute it. When restrictionists were confronted with these counterattacks, they did not wholly deny the legitimacy of their opponent's critique. Instead, they noted that for practical reasons, protecting property ought to be the primary concern of constitutional writers. According to this argument, life and liberty were important but they could mostly take care of themselves. Everyone valued his life and liberty; few coveted the life and liberty of another. Thus neither was really threatened by popular jealousies. The same could not be said of property, and without full protection, battles would frequently ensue until such disputes destroyed the state. Good constitutional designers recognized this and gave property foremost consideration.

This kind of response suggests that while, as individuals, delegates respected and wished to protect life, liberty, and property, as state builders and government men they concerned themselves primarily with the last. While the reason for this emphasis on property may have been largely practical (that is, because individual property holdings were uniquely at risk of violation), there were elaborate theoretical reasons offered as well. Antireformers occasionally proclaimed property the primary right of nature, the only right that was vulnerable and in need of protection. These emphatic views constitute another, alternative liberal understanding of the good state.

THE BOURGEOIS PERSPECTIVE OF ANTIREFORMERS

Those against electoral reform frequently placed extraordinary emphasis on the right to acquire and dispose of property. *Whenever* antireform delegates talked about or praised property, they always meant something narrow (unlike Locke, who frequently spoke of property as life, liberty, and material possessions). For the antireformers, property consisted of material wares and commodities only; life and liberty were not part of the definition. Thus, when antireform delegates praised the ultimate importance of protected property rights, they were not simply restating their commitment to the Lockean triumvirate. Instead, they were putting forward a bourgeois understanding of the good state, wherein material possessions took priority over personal rights.

The policy a speaker was advocating often defines the meaning he gives the word *property*. In Massachusetts, for example, restrictionists wished to grant taxpayers majority political power. They argued to secure a taxpaying electorate and maintain a senate whose districts were created by measuring the amount of taxes paid by inhabitants. They supported policies that gave privilege and power to persons with material possessions. This meant that to the extent they described their policies as acknowledging the greatness of property and ensuring its protection, they probably understood property broadly. They sometimes gave special applauds to the landed or wealthy, but generally they did not differentiate between the horse owner and the financier. Accumulated possessions—large or small, landed or portable—brought about benefits to the state. Thus, such possessions deserved unqualified government protection.

In Virginia the policies endorsed by restrictionists always sought to retain the political power of the large plantation owners, with large slaveholdings. They endorsed the current county system of representation, which granted two representatives to every county, regardless of population. Not only did they prefer a landed-property qualification for voting, they wanted it to specify the value, not the size of the holding. Both policies gave disproportionate power to residents in the eastern portion of the state where land was extremely valuable, slaveholders abounded, and counties were sparsely populated. These policies prevented many small cattle-raising farmers who lived on inexpensive plots in densely populated western counties from having the vote or their proportionate number of representatives.

Thus when Virginia's restrictionists claimed their policies gave property its fair credit and protection, they were really praising and protecting slaves and the large plantations that housed them and their masters. For these delegates, noteworthy property was any substantial holding that contributed to Virginia's plantation economy. This represented the state's greatest and most profitable interest. The same was true in North Carolina.

In Louisiana, opponents of reform supported a districting system that gave each small farming county as much legislative influence as the entire city of New Orleans, where almost half the population actually resided. When these speakers praised property and called for its special voice and protection, they were applauding and aiming to preserve agriculture and farmland. They rejected the value of land used solely for commercial interests.

In New York, delegates favored restricting the senatorial franchise to those individuals who held land worth over $250. They did not care for what purpose the land was used, only for the land's value. Farmers, landlords, and manufacturers all shared a kind of economic independence that came from owning land. Thus in New York, when restrictionists discussed the merits of property, they had a broader understanding of it than their colleagues in the South, but a narrower view than their colleagues in the North.

The type of property applauded by antireform delegates varied from state to state, but these men never veered from the narrow view that property entailed only possessions of monetary value.[6] Moreover, they always found property to be of primary importance. It was the most insecure of all the rights the good state should protect. Thus when designing government and electoral laws, good constitution writers had to pay extreme and careful attention to it.

The Special Importance of Protecting Property

The great emphasis that antireformers placed on property is apparent in how they described what they considered the real problem with electoral reform. Restrictionists mostly feared property invasions. Some feared the loss of liberty, predicting that a radical move toward universal suffrage would lead to chaos, and ultimately to tyranny as had occurred in France.[7] Yet at every convention, when antireformers discussed the negative consequences of increasing political power, they emphasized the chance of less secure possessions. One still finds this bias even in cases where reform opponents were arguing in favor of policies that did not privilege a particular property-holding group. Thus, in questions of how to select governors or judges or in questions of whether foreigners should be allowed to seek office, these speakers still stressed the threats to property that reform would bring.

In New York, agrarian reformers seeking to equalize landholdings caused fear.[8] At the 1821 convention New Yorkers against electoral reform referred directly to this fear, especially in discussing how far to extend the franchise. Those against removing property qualifications predicted such a change would end the security of landholdings. When the chief justice of New York's supreme court, Ambrose Spencer, argued to maintain the franchise with large property holders, he did so by conjuring up images of redistribution.

> What is there to protect the landed interests of the State . . . if the wide and broad proposition be adopted admitting the whole mass of the adult population of the state to vote? I would venture to predict that landed interests of the State will be at the mercy of the other combined interests, and thus all public burthens [that is, taxes] thrown on the landed property of the State. (NY 1821, 218)

The chief justice and his colleagues believed that a landed franchise would avoid such tyrannous takeovers of property.

Colleagues in Massachusetts who fought to retain a landed-property requirement emphasized the security that property presently enjoyed, which it would lose with further extension. Yet, even those who accepted a tax qualification—a requirement closely resembling the one many New York reformers preferred, but one made in opposition to universal suffrage—applauded material goods. Warren Dutton wanted to retain the freehold qualification, for it was "a wise provision. . . . Without it, the foundations of the republic would be weakened," for property "lay at the foundation of the social state and was the spring of all action. . . . The qualification . . . was intended for the security of property." To remove it would bring "danger to the state" (MA 1820–1821, 247, 248).

Delegates made the same case when justifying the ongoing practice of creating legislative districts that accounted for the taxes paid by inhabitants. Over half the proponents of this status quo agreed with Federalist William Prescott who predicted that, without a senate to represent taxpayers, there would be "no security for that protection of property which is at the foundation of government" (MA 1820–1821, 281). As Joseph Story, famous writer and chief justice of the U.S. Supreme Court, explained, with a number basis "all property would be [available as] . . . booty, to be divided among plunderers" (288). With the tax basis "the liberties of the state [were] secured" (293). Although Story explicitly denied that he was giving priority to property, the implicit assumption of his argument, as well as of his colleagues, was precisely that. Property, at the very foundation, required the special attention of constitutional designers.

Elsewhere, too, antireform delegates stressed the particular vulnerability of property and the need to take special action to protect it. In Virginia, delegates worried about taxes that would unfairly burden slaveholders. At the 1829–1830 convention, fourteen of the fifteen speaking in favor of a property basis in the senate stressed the importance of empowering property in order to avoid this devastating outcome. Many of them specifically aligned themselves with the views of the very first speaker on the subject, Abel Upshur, a prominent state judge, who believed:

> *protection* flows from the possession of power. . . . It is necessary to the well being and even to the very existence of society, that property should be protected; it cannot . . . hope for protection except in the power of protecting itself; and no adequate substitute for that power has been or can be offered in any other form [than the mixed basis]. (VA 1829–1830, 76, 78)

Nearly every speaker who shared Upshur's policy preference referred to this speech, noting that their respective words were merely less eloquent repetitions of Upshur's.[9] Although these men may have found their words less eloquent, their message remained the same: by basing districts on property, one would ensure that government protected the right upon which the well-being of society depended.

At the 1850–1851 Virginia convention, debates regarding the basis of representation looked similar. Six of the seven restrictionists who spoke agreed with the House of Delegates representative Robert Scott's depiction of why property needed special voice in at least one house of the legislature. As Scott put it: "property was entitled to protection and protection [was] to be secured by representation" of large landholdings, in the senate. As Scott noted, those who denied this simple lemma—and would have both houses represent population only—would undermine present constitutional securities:

Those paying less than one-third of the taxes of this commonwealth are eternally clamoring for the possession of the purse strings. . . . If in the adjustment of representation . . . we adopt a ratio of mere numbers—white numbers—we shall organize the government upon a principle that instead of affording protection to property, will lay it open to be plundered at the discretion of a mere majority not paying one-third of the public burdens. (VA 1850–1851, 284)

This same concern arose in other convention debates over representation. In Louisiana, antireform delegates feared that city dwellers would destroy all subsidies to farming areas and instead use the money to build up the commercial industries. These delegates defended the existing system of keeping farmers in control of both house and senate as necessary to protect "property"—in this case, land used for farming. Delegate Wadsworth, for instance, claimed:

all our exertions are to secure property. . . . You have universal suffrage the basis of the house of representatives—for the sake of justice, then, let the senate stand by to prevent the state from being flooded with ruin by the prodigal waste of the treasury funds. . . . What protection have we, then if we have it not in the senate? . . . If the property qualification is abandoned, men will be elected who have nothing to lose, but all to gain. (LA 1845, 503)

In each case, delegates who favored representation systems that secured majority power to the holders of land or material possessions did so because they found property especially vulnerable but still of great importance to the state.

Even where the aim was not to empower property, in some cases restrictionists still emphasized its importance. In Louisiana, for example, speakers against allowing foreigners to run for office justified their policy preference by conjuring up images of foreigners stealing the land of natives. Once in office these foreigners would take away the hard-earned property of other citizens. John Grymes, a New Orleans Democrat, did not want to extend the privilege of officeholding to foreigners, because it afforded them "the privilege of controlling . . . our property." This would ultimately result in "divid[ing] our possessions with them" (LA 1845, 80).

At the same convention, several delegates supporting an appointed judiciary noted that the primary job of a judge was to protect property. They feared that elected judges would become the pawns of the people instead of defenders of the law and would thereby disregard property rights. Few predicted that a loss of life or liberty would follow the popular election of such officials. Instead, they worried about intrusions of property and defended the present system precisely because it protected against such infractions.

In no case did these opponents of electoral reform suppose that property would be the sole right accorded security and unfettered enjoyment. Delegates quoted above are many of the same speakers quoted as praising life and liberty as well. Practically speaking, the good state served to protect all three rights to which individuals had originally agreed to grant immutable status in constitutional government. The particular concern with property was not inconsistent with this understanding, but indicative of what they saw as the purpose of political power, which had positive value when it was distributed properly, and negative consequences when it was overextended. Life, liberty, and property were the aims of the good state, but who governed had far less effect on the first two. Securing property was the people's most difficult task. The value of government was therefore measured first and foremost in its ability to give possessions stability. As constitution writers, then, delegates had first and foremost to concern themselves with securing property. Such rhetoric inevitably established a hierarchy of rights. At least in government, property protection was the first consideration; all else could follow suit behind it.

Property as the Common Good

It was not just its vulnerability that made restrictionists constantly preoccupied with property, and their public language overly bourgeois. For some property was at the very foundation of the good state, which is evident in the way restrictionists subtly and indirectly renamed this valued right. On a number of occasions, restrictionists described property as the common good or as the permanent state interest. Life, liberty, and property were important, inalienable aims, but the last had the attribute of bringing benefit not just to the holder but to the general society. This stands in stark contrast to the arguments of expansionists, who never used any special language to describe property—or for that matter to emphasize the importance of any other right. Yet restrictionists in every state in this study, with the exception of Ohio and Iowa, talked about property, the common good, or the state's great interest all in one breath.

Some opponents of reform equated landed property and its cultivation with the primary interest of the state. In his defense for continuing a propertied franchise, Chancellor James Kent of New York, a Federalist supreme court judge, writer of various political tracts, and great defender of property rights, explained that "The great leading . . . interest of this state is, at present, the agricultural interest" (NY 1821, 220). When justifying Louisiana's senate districting system, William Brent, a retired member of the U.S. Congress, reminded his colleagues that "the interests of agriculture [are in] the permanent interests of the country." Since farmers produced goods that benefited the state and the nation, they deserved an individual powerful voice in at least one branch of the legislature (LA 1845, 435–36). In support of Virginia's similarly based system, Democrat Abel Upshur, a lawyer and Virginia court judge stressed the state's great and special allegiance to property. He explained that a property representation "is right because *our* property, so far as slaves are concerned, is *peculiar*; because it is of imposing magnitude; because it affords almost a full half of the productive labor of the State; . . . and because it is the interest of the whole Commonwealth, that power should not be taken away" (VA 1829–1830, 75). In all cases, speakers wanted property to have adequate voice because, without this primary influence, property, the *great* interest—perhaps the greatest good—would be at the hands of the reckless masses and thus lost.

There are a number of examples of more indirect equations between property and the public good, such as when delegates praised property holders as the only people who had an actual physical stake in the state's main concerns and interests. In his explanation as to why Virginia was better off limiting the franchise only to property holders, Philip Nicholas, who had once served the state as attorney general but who now was in private enterprise as head of the state's Farmers Bank, explained that "evidence of common, permanent interest is only to be found in the lasting ownership of the soil." Giving the vote to those without property meant placing "power in the hands of those who have none or a very trivial stake in the community" (VA 1829–1830, 364, 367). Here property's connection to the public good was put forward in an indirect fashion. If one had property, one respected the common interest of the state. For Nicholas and the many who made statements of this nature, this was the case because property was the public good. Individuals with property simply "owned" a piece of that good; this was why they shared the common interest.[10] This type of argument and that found in the previous paragraph are the two most common ways that restrictionists merged property with the common good.[11] Either they declared government's special duty to preserve property because it was in the great community interest or they declared property holders special because they had a stake in the common good.

Restrictionists intimated that property was intricately tied to the common good also by applauding the great benefits that society gained from those with property. Sometimes the argument was a rather simple one, like the one put forward by Philip P. Barbour, Speaker of the House of Representatives and president of the 1829–1830 Virginia convention, when he explained why property should be the basis for creating legislative districts. He contended that the propertied paid "an enormous disproportion of the tax." Thus they contributed most to the state, for it was with taxes that so many state improvements had been made (VA 1829–1830, 98).

Sometimes the delegate offered a more extensive explanation of the common benefits accruing from property. Justice Story of Massachusetts explained why the franchise should be granted only to taxpayers:

> When I look around and consider the blessings which property bestows, I cannot persuade myself that gentlemen are serious in their views, that it does not deserve our utmost protection. I do not speak of your opulent and munificent citizens, whose wealth has spread itself into a thousand channels of charity and public benevolence. I speak not of those who rear temples. . . . I speak not of those who build your hospitals. . . . I speak not of these, not because they are not worthy of all praise; but because I would dwell rather on those general blessings, which prosperity diffuses through the whole mass of the community. . . . [P]roperty [i]s the source of all comforts over every kind and dispenses its blessings in every form. . . . it conduces to the public good by promoting private happiness; and every man . . . possessing property . . . contributes his portion to the general mass of comfort. The man without any property may desire to do the same; but is necessarily shut out from this most interesting charity. It is in this view that I consider property as the source of all the comforts and advantages we enjoy. (MA 1820–1821, 285–86)

Here Justice Story applauded the general benefits society gained from those with moderate holdings as well as the specific benefits gained from the rich. Both types of taxpayers brought good to the whole community. For both these speakers and for those who made similar cases, property contributed to the public good instrumentally. Those who had land and money paid more taxes, which in turn paid for more services, including public works. Property holders were the major contributors to those institutions, which in turn benefited the greater public.[12]

Restrictionists might have disagreed over the kind of possessions that represented the public good and secured the general interest of the state, but when most talked about property, they agreed on one basic point: a society committed to the good of the whole community was nothing more than a society committed to the protection of property rights against citizen and leadership abuse. This association between the common good and property rights probably arose from the broader American perspective that both economic liberty and property were essential to national prosperity. Nineteenth-century Americans recognized that economic growth relied on the nation's maintaining property as its base.[13] Thus, these delegates specifically connected the rights that supported growth and prosperity with a notion of the common good.

Although reformers shared a respect for property, economic liberty, and economic prosperity, it is curious that they hardly ever discussed these as being in the community interest or representing the common good. Expansionists shied away from using words like these, preferring to talk about varied interests and multiple state concerns. Thus the antireform connection between property and the common good was indicative of their uniquely bourgeois understanding of the good state as economically prosperous. It illustrates the restrictionists' subtle endorsement of private property as an essential—if not the essential—component of the good state. This view was never explicitly rejected by reformers, but it clearly lacked their enthusiastic endorsement. It is likely that the repeated endorsement of such a narrow understanding of the good state was motivated by political aims as well as principled ones.

The Special Importance of Property

Delegates against reform usually did not try and ground the innate superiority of property with subtle references to Locke, nature, or consent. They supported its elevated status by referring to the importance of material prosperity to the welfare of the state. In this sense, justifications for their bourgeois affinities were weak. Yet, in a number of instances, antireformers offered explicit praises of the greatness of property and government's unique role in ensuring its protection, with some remarks being more emphatic and more theoretically grounded than others.

Scattered throughout the debates were various explicit declarations of the special importance of property. In various speeches at the 1829–1830 Virginia convention restrictionists endorsed a property basis for representation. Chapman.Johnson, then a lawyer but soon to be an active state politician, argued that "The indispensable object of every good Government is the security of property . . . . [N]o government which does not afford that security can be a safe depository of the liberty and life of the citizen" (VA 1829–1830, 266). Judge Abel Upshur explained that "it was a fair and just principle that property is entitled to protection . . . because it is an important constituent element in society; without it, society could not exist for a moment" (72). House speaker Philip Barbour contended that if Virginia's representation scheme did not include property as well as persons, it would lead to "bloodshed, civil war, anarchy, and finally the bitter and disastrous downfall of liberty, and the establishment of Despotic Government" (98). Democratic lawyer Benjamin Leigh agreed. He argued that, if property was not given a special voice in government, either "property will purchase power, or power will take property. Either way, there must be an end of Free Government. . . . [E]ssential is property to the very being of civilized society" (156). In all these cases, speakers acknowledged that "good," "free" government was a representative republic that protected life, liberty, and property.

Yet all explained that this government would be dissolved if property was not given adequate protection through its own voice. In each case, no speaker directly argued that there was a hierarchy among rights, with property at the top of the list, or that property ownership rights preceded the institution of government. Nonetheless, property's senior status was implied. Without property protected, there could be no liberty or free government. Surely that kind of acknowledged "power" demonstrated that property deserved elevated stature and a specially secured place in well-constructed governments.

Similar arguments were presented at most other conventions, especially where the power of property holders was at stake. In New York lawyer-trained Elisha Williams, Federalist politician and reputed adversary of Martin Van Buren, favored a property basis for the franchise on the grounds that property "nourishes the whole community." Without "love of property . . . civilized and social life could not be enjoyed" (NY 1821, 253, 249). Lawyer Warren Dutton of Boston agreed. In defense of retaining the freehold qualification in Massachusetts he noted that "without it, the foundation of the republic would be weakened." No men without property "should act . . . upon the property of others," for land "lay at the foundation of the social state; it was the spring of all action" (MA 1820–1821, 247).

Property's greatness was touted especially by delegates as they explained why representation districts were best devised to give disproportionate power to landholders and taxpayers. Leverett Saltonstall, a Federalist from Massachusetts, referred to property as "the greatest object of civil society; . . . it is a living principle which keeps the great machine of society in motion. It is the universal stimulus" (MA 1820–1821, 275–76). On behalf of the same policy his colleague, Justice Joseph Story, asked "What . . . is life worth, if a man cannot eat in security the bread earned by his own industry? If he is not permitted to transmit to his children the little inheritance which his affection has destined for their use?" (286). His implied answer was obvious. Life and liberty were of little consequence without protected property. Delegate Wadsworth from Louisiana made this case explicitly. First, he tried to justify the state's existing county system, a system that perpetuated the legislative influence of agricultural regions, by using a simple example: "as long as a man had a dollar in his pocket, . . . his property was more valuable to him than liberty without it. . . . All our exertions are to secure property" (LA 1845, 503). Later, speaking on the same subject, Wadsworth proclaimed the fundamental importance of property more emphatically: "Life and liberty are perfectly worthless without property"

(548). This same hierarchy was implicit in Virginia delegate Beale's remarks. He defended a property basis for senatorial districts on the grounds that "property is the greatest tie of social life" (VA 1850–1851, 316).

In all these examples, delegates seemingly placed property and its protection a cut above other inalienable rights. For some, property was at the very foundation of government; it was the civilizing tie of social life. For others, all other rights depended on property. With its security, life and liberty would retain respect and free government would survive unharmed. Without its security, government was unsafe. On this last point, the delegates may have had reputable support, for it is said to be part of Madison's constitutional defense.[14]

On some occasions, restrictionists implied that property itself was the only true right of nature; the only real reason people left nature was to protect their material goods. In Virginia, for example, when restrictionists referred back to the story of Robinson Crusoe, they contended that by examining his "savage" life, one also recognized that property was really the only "right" that men cared about before joining government. This kind of argument is elsewhere, for example in the speech of John Adams, one of Massachusetts's greatest statesmen, who not only served in high office as president and vice president but who as a great treatise writer had served at the state's first constitutional convention. When explaining why a senatorial district should be sized according to the taxes paid by its residents, Mr. Adams intimated that there was no truly civilized society without protected property: "Property is the foundation upon which civilization rests. . . . In the state of nature the Indian has no defense for his little hut . . . or anything he acquires. . . . Society furnishes the strength . . . for the protection of the property of each individual" (MA 1820–1821, 278). Another of the state's formidable statesmen, Adams's colleague Daniel Webster, tersely made a similar point: the "nature of institutions [was] founded on property" (312). In cases like these, restrictionists suggested that societies were formed specifically to protect property. Therefore, its ongoing protection must be the first priority of delegates as they rewrite the very document that embodied the principles of the first compact.

These last speakers, it seems, like a number quoted above took the stance that, if government did not afford property complete protection, individuals remained in a kind of state of nature, for all other rights would remain insecure. There would be continual warfare over each other's possessions and continued battles over how to distribute the goods. These arguments rested on a view similar to Calhoun's depiction of government. Calhoun saw government's main role as executing "expensive" services, which meant that governments would always have to collect monies. All political battles were wars of distribution: from whom to take, to whom to give. Unjust outcomes were those that destroyed certain economic interests; regimes that produced such unjust outcomes were despotisms.[15]

The protection of material goods—as both the rationale for creating government and the source of lasting peace—also resembled Hobbes's view of nature and the basis of government. In Hobbes's state of nature there is a continual competition for more power and for more material holdings, which enhance one's power. Man's never-ceasing acquisitive nature brings continual war. Although men join in government to avoid death, it is because they have and want substantial material possessions that they face even possible extinction.[16] Finally, some of their views resemble Locke's who highly valued prosperity and connected it to the public good. To the extent his political allegiance was tied to the landed, the parallels are even clearer.[17]

Whether restrictionists either read Hobbes or Locke or were familiar with Madison's nuanced emphasis on property or Calhoun's more blatant case in his theory of government is not the main issue here. Most noteworthy is that their views, though lacking in elaborate theoretical descriptions, are consistent. Their views partially resemble these other, more detailed explanations of why land and material possessions have such great importance in human affairs and why well-designed governments must take special care to secure them. They had both American contemporaries and liberal philosophers upon whom to build their vision of the good state. Like Madison, Calhoun, Locke, and Hobbes these restrictionists never aimed to deny the importance that individuals placed on their lives and liberties. Instead, they merely wished to convince their adversaries that property protection came first; without it, governments were useless.

Most restrictionists who applauded property rights did not necessarily mean that property replaced life and liberty. Very few declared this their intention. Instead, they adamantly proclaimed their wish to protect "property and persons," to protect "life, liberty and property." Most should not be considered crafty reconstructors of the liberal agreement on rights. They simply stressed a different priority among inalienable constitutional aims. Unlike reformers who used elaborate language to include self-government in the state-of-nature and compact theory, restrictionists rarely raised the status of property through elaborate reinterpretations of either source. Theirs was simply a liberal depiction of the state, albeit with additional stress on the value of owning material possessions. Perhaps antireform arguments like those noted above should be seen as another fracture in American liberalism, for they represent an alternative interpretation of its commitment to rights. After all, restrictionists were thought by their adversaries to be contracting the list of inalienable rights down to one, and antireformers who stressed the great value of property often relied on America's agreed-upon commitment to personal rights to establish that special preeminence.

REFORMERS' RESPONSES

No delegate who favored expanding power beyond the landed and taxed denied that property was an important right, meriting protection from abuse. Not one of these speakers called property the most important right or the pillar or foundation of the American regime. Instead, they usually rejected special status for any right, and they explicitly rejected such a status for property.[18] Reformers responded to their adversaries' depictions of property in various ways. Such claims can be found for each reform issue and at every convention, except in the West where delegates across the aisle also did not tout the virtues of property.

Reformers recognized the theoretical consequences of the great praise and special voice that their adversaries wanted to grant property; so whenever they could they tried to discredit the antireform position. Although no one denied that property was an important societal concern, requiring diligent protection, the reformers did contest the extremity of their opponents' case.

Some denied that property was the most important right, the foundation of the American regime, or requiring special accommodation. Debates in Louisiana over new, high residency requirements for suffrage sometimes centered on whether newcomers or aliens could be entrusted to protect property rights. Solomon Downs, a Whig against these new measures, reminded his colleagues that even despotic governments could protect material possessions. Thus it was heresy to suggest that property "be considered paramount and supersede the protection due to personal rights" (LA 1845, 115). In New York Democratic party leader Daniel Tomkins felt obliged to explain that "property, . . . when compared with our other essential rights, is insignificant and trifling. 'Life, liberty and *the pursuit of happiness*'—not of property are . . . the cardinal objects" of good government (NY 1821, 235).

Other delegates claimed special attention was actually contrary to the spirit of American government. They hinted that the special voice their adversaries wanted to retain for property was actually antirepublican. In Virginia Charles Morgan of Monongalia compared freehold suffrage and its security to "the cold calm of perfect aristocracy or despotism" (VA 1829–1830, 382). In New York Jacob Radcliff declared that giving freeholders the sole right of suffrage was giving them an "odious distinction," a term used also by many of his colleagues. He contended that "property will always carry with it an influence sufficient for its own protection. . . . [To] give it an artificial aid . . . may be dangerous to the other rights of the community" (NY 1821, 225).

Most frequently, reformers simply rejected any special position for property and reminded their colleagues that Americans expected security for a whole gamut of rights. When defending a voter population basis, Eugenius Wilson put forward the following simple lemma:

> The object of all good Government is to protect the citizen in the enjoyment, not only of his property, but also of his life, his personal liberty, his limbs, his character, the freedom of speech and action, and the pursuit of happiness, and that these are all objects of equal and some of them, of higher importance than property. (VA 1829–1830, 352)

Twenty years later, defenders of this basis still refuted property's special role, as Mr. Sheffey states:

> [Man's] first apprehensions must have arisen from dangers to life and liberty; . . . separate property was not essential to the support of life. . . . The common property of all furnished the sustenance of life. . . . Associate . . . was formed to guard rights. . . . The right of property, the right of one man to claim as his own . . . any species of property must have had its origin in the consent of society. . . . Prior to society, the world and its fruits were the domain of the race; . . . such a separate claim or title could only become a right of common consent. . . . [Therefore, property is of] secondary value; it belongs to a class of mere personal rights. (VA 1850–1851, 299)

The implicit assumption of the Sheffey and Wilson speeches was that rights other than property might actually be more immutable and more basic to human beings. Neither speaker was willing to end the guaranteed right of acquiring and disposing of property as one saw fit. In fact, only once did any speaker even hint that America's devotion to property was unnecessary. While perhaps of less relative importance, property remained a fundamental characteristic of the good state. Reformers wanted to reject only the special status ascribed to property, not its overall importance. In his speech to expand the franchise to taxpayers, firemen, and highway workers, lawyer-trained David Buel clarified this point:

> The declared object of the people of this state in associating was, to establish such a government as they deemed best calculated to secure the rights and liberties of the good people of the state, and most conducive to their happiness and safety: Property, it is admitted, is one of the rights to be protected and secured. (NY 1821, 243)

Such statements suggest that, even though few restrictionists claimed explicitly that property deserved to be considered above all other rights, reformers certainly thought this the implicit intention, or at least the logical consequence, of antireform arguments. As a result, expansionists occasionally reminded restrictionists that the stress on the value and importance of property rights ignored the true origins of government and the breadth of its inalienable commitments.

AMERICA'S VARIANT ACCOUNTS OF INALIENABLE RIGHTS

Both sides of the reform debate shared a belief in the importance of protecting private rights. What distinguished restrictionists from expansionists was their tendency to portray property as the most important, and therefore worthy of special and perhaps sole consideration in structuring government designs. For restrictionists, property was the foundation of society, the moral means, the paramount right. Without its protection there would be no secured life or liberty; there could be no free government. In this sense, restrictionists appear to be advocating a bourgeois state, endorsing the empowerment of private property, and overly sympathetic to material prosperity (as Hobbes and Locke are sometimes described also).[19] Antireformers reconstructed America's embrace of liberal government, for they narrowed the list of inalienable rights to one, namely, property.

This reformulation was more subtle and perhaps more blatantly political than the one put forward by advocates of electoral expansion. Reformers supported their arguments favoring greater popular empowerment by openly co-opting language from state-of-nature theorists such as Locke. They simply added self-government to an existing list of agreed-upon inalienable rights. They may have self-consciously extended the notion of private rights to include public activity, but they offered strong theoretical rationales supporting this extension.

The same cannot be said of the antireform arguments aimed at emphasizing the special importance of property. First, this tendency took place mostly in the East, where property owners had previously enjoyed power. Western states had no entrenched power holders to protect and therefore never stressed the states' preeminent commitment to protect material and landed possessions. Second, there was little elaborate theory to support the positions taken by restrictionists. Only a few offered elaborate descriptions of a state of nature wherein property was the only reason for exit. Only a few offered descriptions of the founding compact as an agreement to protect property and property alone. Instead, most stressed the great merits and economic benefits of property, saying nothing about the importance of life or liberty. They stressed the unique need for protecting property, even sometimes making other rights dependent upon its security. For these reasons, while not all restriction arguments resemble a "traditional" understanding of liberalism, their bourgeois leanings toward property rights and economic freedom are difficult to see at first blush. Their arguments are consistent with Macpherson's reading of Locke and are in that sense an alternative liberal interpretation of the characteristic features of constitutional government. However, to the extent that opponents of reform ultimately reformulated and narrowed America's commitment to rights, they usually did so depending on political circumstance and without a self-conscious recourse to the iconoclastic feature of Locke's *Second Treatise*, namely, his state-of-nature or compact theory. In other words, their views were not grounded on firm, abstract theory.

Nineteenth-century public language entailed at least three different liberal understandings of rights, limited government, and the good state. First, for a majority of speakers favoring electoral reform, America's commitment to rights carried with it an inalienable allegiance to life, liberty, property, and self-government. In this case American liberalism is uniquely and intrinsically democratic. Second, for most speakers against reform as well as for a few speaking in its favor, America's founding principles demanded a primary commitment to private rights alone. Self-government had value to the extent that it protected three of these, namely, life, liberty, and property. This is what many would call a traditional conception of liberalism, a vision of the good state ultimately indifferent toward the kinds of procedures preserving it. Third, to a number of those speaking in favor of continued restrictions, America's rights commitment implied paying special attention to property. In this case liberalism is definitely bourgeois, again indifferent to the procedures by which governing officers are selected or controlled. Self-government is prized for its ability to secure property holdings.

Each of these three interpretations of the good state were Lockean in some sense, stressing different aspects of the author's teachings in his *Second Treatise*.[20] Americans did not see themselves as parroting or manipulating the words of Locke. They were far more interested in demonstrating how and why their positions were consistent with America's legal and historical tradition. In many ways, Locke sounds as if he was at the origin of their views, but it is best just to say that his teachings were in the air at the time and were deemed most appropriate to justify America's allegiance to a priori principles. Nature, compact, and constitutional law—not Locke—were the authorities that primarily mattered to the nineteenth-century legal designers. Nonetheless, these authorities led them to Lockean conclusions, namely, to a limited and nonarbitrary government, established to protect those natural inalienable rights left insecure without enforceable rules of law.

Whatever the influence of Locke, the three alternative views represent three different interpretations of what it means to be committed to a state that reveres rights and places them above the manipulation of constitution writers, ordinary legislators, and citizens. Each view can and should be termed liberal. Their differences arose because convention delegates could agree neither on which rights were inalienable nor from what basis well-informed state builders should make that determination. Each view was nonetheless liberal since each rested in the belief that the good state was committed to certain inalienable rights, which had legitimacy before government was instituted and which were now above ordinary legislation. The existence of these three alternative views strongly suggests that it is misleading to speak of nineteenth-century American liberalism in monolithic terms. Rather, embedded in rather general agreements lay important nuanced characterizations of the meaning and origin of America's commitment to rights.

The character of these alternative views make it difficult to determine definitively whether Madison or Jefferson had the more appropriate understanding of the logical consequence of frequent constitutional reform. In one sense, nineteenth-century debates over which rights were inalienable and why suggest that Madison was correct to fear frequent reevaluation of foundational documents and their aims. Originally established rights were up for grabs. However, in another sense, these debates vindicate Jefferson's beliefs and should allay Madisonian fears. Writers of nineteenth-century constitutions never denied that good government protected inalienable private rights and popular sovereignty. Theirs was a debate over emphasis, not fundamentality. Their discussions may have helped solidify differences, but they also reinforced everyone's widespread, unfaltering allegiance to the rights of life, liberty, property, and self-government.

Part Two

Liberalism entails not only an undaunted, higher-order allegiance to rights but also an understanding about how those rights should be protected. Liberal ideology holds that the best laws are those that allow human beings to follow their natural inclinations in ways that avoid capricious and arbitrary infringements on those rights. Behind this belief is a recognition that all individuals share the same basic nature, one that defies alteration through state engineering. Shared tendencies are rarely, if ever, described as righteous or virtuous; in fact the expectation is usually that individuals will selfishly follow their own economic interests or desire for power. That natural, self-interested behavior is to be accepted as inevitable and that it can be channeled safely to protect rights are foundational assumptions of the liberalism of Hobbes and Locke, as well as of modern economic liberalism.

These assumptions inform America's constitutional design as well. Although no advocate of the national document would dare claim that citizen and leadership virtue was unnecessary for Republican success, there were no provisions in the document to encourage morality, selflessness, or country-motivated behavior. God's glory is never advocated; nor are the duties of citizenship ever outlined. Instead, certain procedures, including competitive elections across large areas and a state-appointed senate, are introduced to replace the nation's dependence on popular virtue and vigilance. Clearly, national designers used competitive elections and appointive offices because they saw great merit in leadership virtue. Nonetheless, other features suggest that they were also skeptical about the nation's ability to rely on the good character of those in power. To prevent government tyranny, mechanistic designs channeled hunger for power and allowed ambition to counteract ambition. In theory, then, well-designed procedures and clever institutional checks and balances could keep government limited and nonarbitrary, even when neither citizens nor their leaders were committed to the protection of rights and freedoms.[1]

An examination of early state constitutions suggests that designers of these documents approached rights protection in a way that appeared more reliant on virtue and less tolerant of selfishness than was the national constitution. Only half the state constitutions written in the mid-1770s contained some institutional check on the legislature's power, and in most cases the check was weak. The most popular means for moderating legislative control was either by granting the governor a term longer than that of the lawmakers who appointed him or by letting the people elect him directly. The executor had little actual power. Only two states initially gave him veto power; nearly every one made his powers subject to council approval or review. Many of these councils were selected by the legislature, thus facilitating legislative influence over the executive. Furthermore, throughout the late eighteenth century no state meaningfully empowered the judicial branch. Some states, like Pennsylvania, did not even have one. All told, initial constitutions gave the legislative branch great power and control in matters of political importance. No other branch had sufficient independence or influence to check the legislature.[2]

This legislative sovereignty did not reflect a carte blanche of unlimited power or a foolish trust in government. Original state constitutions reflected a liberal concern with nonarbitrary, rights-preserving government.[3] The difference between these early documents and the U.S. Constitution that followed them was how each provided protection against abuse. At the state level, this guardian role was left mainly with the people, through procedural provisions. The assumption was that frequent elections would ensure that legislators remained good servants, because the people could and would guard against extravagant legislative behavior.

This reliance on the people reflected a naive belief that the people would never hurt themselves, that is, that there could be no popular tyranny. It reflected a fairly widespread faith in the people's general virtue, at least the virtue of its male, property-holding population.[4] What they meant by virtue remains an open question. Miscellaneous pamphlets suggest that revolutionaries offered different interpretations. Some praised the classical virtues of patriotism and independence, others praised the Christian virtues of piety and humility, still others admired the private commercial virtues of moderation, frugality, and industry.[5] Thus, knowing that state builders hoped for virtue insufficiently captures the relative influence of liberalism on their thinking.

More helpful is knowing whether these first constitution writers found virtue natural, or whether they thought it required careful human sacrifice or manipulative state intervention. Most early state constitutions contained provisions that could be interpreted as attempting to instill moral virtue among citizens, suggesting that early designers thought the state should encourage good, selfless behavior. Although every initial constitution granted individuals the right of free conscience, most documents were actually quite restrictive on the religious freedoms individuals could enjoy. Often there existed legal and social prohibitions against atheism, as well as specific legal disincentives for practicing Catholicism, Judaism, Hinduism, and Islam (at conventions held during the first half of the nineteenth century these religions were specifically mentioned as the ones that should be discouraged).

As of 1790 six constitutions specifically required all officeholders to swear allegiance to God or the Trinity prior to taking office. Many constitutions explicitly forbade forced support to any particular church, yet three permitted mandatory support of some church, and some taxed citizens in order to fund their preferred church. As of 1780 only three states had absolutely no restriction on the freedom of individuals to practice the faith of their choice, in any manner they deemed appropriate.[6] Such designs were part of a larger theory of constitutionalism and good government that included a range of intellectual influences, including a Protestant demand for spiritual virtue and free conscience, and a Republican desire for popular virtue and popular participation.[7]

State constitutions created after the national founding and during America's first experiment with Jeffersonian constitutionalism were markedly different from their predecessors and far more similar to their national counterpart. Stipulations regarding the formation of moral character declined significantly. By the late 1830s no state gave money to a specific church, and nearly every constitution contained a specific declaration prohibiting state preference to a particular religious sect. By 1850 over half the states unconditionally asserted religious freedom, restricting religious freedom only when it disturbed the peace. There remained few legal provisions and prohibitions specifically aimed at encouraging citizens to be good Christians in particular, and moral in general.[8] Local statesmen were beginning to realize that the state could not transform individuals into moral citizens. This was a private, internal affair.

As virtue-instilling provisions disappeared, institutional checks and balances emerged. Starting in the 1790s state legislative dominance waned as states introduced additional institutional checks, expanding the independence of both governors and judges. By the 1850s governors had full independence from the legislative branch, since all were elected by the people. Although six constitutions, including Ohio and Iowa, denied the governor veto power, most had dissolved their early executive councils.[9] Judges had also gained independence. No longer did they depend solely on the legislature for appointment; many were popularly elected while others were selected by the governor and granted terms longer than their appointee. State judges began to exercise constitutional review.[10] By midcentury, state constitutions contained many of the same procedures and institutional designs found in the national document. Given that national designers introduced those features in order to limit the abusive capabilities of the legislature, one might conclude that state constitution writers introduced these features for the same reasons.

The question remains whether this assumption is true. The changes in institutional designs likely reflect a shift in constitutional thinking about human nature and how to best provide for rights safety. Politicians and citizens relied less on virtue and state manufacture of morality and more on natural selfish behavior and the institutional channeling of interests. These changes occurred as other new provisions were added that would increase the people's direct influence in political affairs and thus sidestep the ability of certain appointed officers to moderate the people's behavior and channel any inappropriate popular demands made upon them. Were state builders finally accepting human nature as self-interested? Or were there a series of complicated, perhaps contradictory sentiments at work?

As designers of electoral laws were deciding who should vote, for which representatives, and why, they asked themselves about human nature and the constitutional designs best suited to harness and control that nature. What, if any, is the role of virtue and good citizenship in protecting rights? Is it human nature to be a good citizen? How, if at all, can procedural features and arrangements channel nature so as to utilize virtue when possible, and yet render interests and power lusts harmless when necessary?

In all cases, regardless of their position on electoral reform, delegates answered these questions using language filled with liberal assumptions. Institutional checks and balances were necessary and useful for protecting rights. So was virtue, understood as a desire and willingness to protect rights. Yet, savvy government designers knew they could not manufacture virtue or change human nature. They would have to design electoral procedures so that citizens and leaders could build on their own nature and yet protect rights and limit government as they should. At the same time, as was the case with discussions on the meaning and origin of America's rights commitment, the views of constitution writers did not constitute a coherent, monolithic set of liberal ideas. Behind agreements lay important differences, which followed policy preferences, revealing more fractures inherent in American liberalism.

he electoral reforms enacted throughout the first half of the nineteenth century indirectly affected how government branches could check and balance one another. Suffrage reforms would change the leadership selection process, expanding the sphere that leaders would actually represent. Districting reforms would alter bicameralism, by making the two houses more similar to each other than they had been previously. Reforms seeking to make various nonlegislative officers popularly elected would make branches more independent and possibly more powerful, given that they would now have the force of popular mandate behind them. Although not their main aim, these electoral reforms encouraged a reevaluation of the relationship between popular character and government designs. They also encouraged new theoretical interpretations of how well-designed constitutions balanced the two and thereby protected against arbitrary government and potential rights abuses. The question, then, is how closely did their views of the subject resemble those attributed to their forefathers who recognized the instrumental value of virtue but nonetheless prepared for its takeover by citizens who were selfish and money hungry and leaders who were ambitious and power lusting?

Each electoral reform issue might well have encouraged delegates to consult the *Federalist Papers*. Take questions of suffrage expansion, for example. Delegates—especially those favoring reform—could have used various arguments from essay 10 to support their case. In response to fears regarding the vices of the masses, supporters of mass enfranchisement might have argued that the selection process itself would not be altered. They might have argued that competitive elections naturally produced leaders of a character superior to their electors, that new voters would not discourage excellent men from running for office, and that, after all, the caliber of officers not electors was most important for securing against government abuse. Alternatively, supporters of an expanded suffrage could have described reform as "extending the sphere." They might have argued that, by increasing the number of voters, delegates would include additional constituent interests and thereby decrease the chance that any given representative would be elected by a singularly factious majority.[1]

Debates surrounding the basis of representation could have engendered discussions informed by arguments found in such essays as 62 and 63. A change in a state's districting system could undermine—or at least fundamentally alter—the basic structure supporting bicameralism. If voter population became the basis of both legislative houses, states would look less like the national model, where each branch was supposed to represent a different constituency, and where the second house was supposed to speak for a broader group and to be composed of individuals who would exercise great reason when deliberating and making laws. Opponents of reform might have construed such a change as upsetting the ability of one house to check power abuses of the other. With both houses being elected by the same constituency, there would not exist a house of more trustworthy members.

Advocates of a population basis might have stressed ongoing differences between branches such as the age of the representative or the length of his term to explain why changing the basis would not really alter the benefits offered by a bicameral system. These adversaries might have claimed that the size of the senatorial district, usually larger, incorporated more diverse interests and therefore was even more likely to encourage men of caliber to run for office as well as to prevent elected members from representing a particular majority faction. In each instance constitution writers would have been stressing how legislators could be virtuous even when those who elected them were selfish and politically disinterested.

Debates over how executive and judicial officials should be selected might also have reflected and incorporated the views of their nation-building forefathers. By becoming free from legislative appointment, governors would gain legislative independence, of the kind enjoyed by the U.S. president. By becoming free of legislative and executive selection, judges could safely curtail the excesses of these other branches without fear of losing their jobs, the ultimate reason that U.S. Supreme Court justices were granted life tenure.

In various essays in the *Federalist Papers* Madison and Hamilton discussed the importance of independence in facilitating internal checks on government abuse. The hope was to select governors and judges so that both could guard the U.S. Constitution against legislative abuses, according to their consciences, without worrying that the very lawmakers they scrutinized would retaliate by reducing their salaries or taking away their jobs. *Publius* (the pen name for the authors of these pages) had faith this system would work because it cleverly went beyond virtue and relied on interests as well. Independent members shared responsibilities across branches and therefore had a personal interest in guarding constitutional guarantees. Although the design was meant to harness both interests and virtues, as *Federalist* essay 51 makes clear, the most reliable security was the former. The best designs allowed ambition to counteract ambition.

State delegates could have relied on some of these very arguments as they discussed whether governors and judges should be directly elected by the people. Reformers might have contended that the popular election of nonlegislative officers would both create institutional independence and supplement the operation of other institutional checks and balances; they might have argued that the new selection process would have little policy impact so long as powers were realigned such that ambition could successfully counteract ambition. Opponents of these reforms might have countered with descriptions of how these changes would actually upset existing arrangements, for with them every branch would mirror the same interest—namely, the people's—and there would be no branch with interests of its own.

All the above possibilities reflect a particular liberal interpretation of how constitutions and their writers understood the relationship between mechanisms and good men. All assume a reduced faith in the virtue of the general population, and a belief that arrangements could adequately substitute for its absence. Some of the scenarios entail the argument that people need procedural assistance to help them select good leaders and to evict bad ones. Some go further and say that clever procedures select and maintain high-quality candidates and officeholders at least as well as—if not better than—a virtuous, vigilant public.

Underlying other possibilities is the argument that even good procedures will sometimes fail to bring elevated statesmen and that therefore other institutional checks are needed for when corrupt leaders make their way into office. In these cases clever procedures and institutions are claimed to check against abuse better than a vigilant public; it is thought better to let power-hungry leaders check one another than expect self-interested citizens to guard their guardians. These are some of the liberal arguments nineteenth-century constitution writers could have made. Were any of these their position on why electoral reform was worth supporting or undermining?

SHARED VIEWS ABOUT INSTITUTIONAL DESIGNS

Debates over the extension of popular influence—whether in questions of suffrage, representation, or leadership selection—suggest that nineteenth-century state builders were familiar with and embraced certain features of *Publius's* theory regarding the independent value of procedural and institutional design. In various contexts, speakers for and against electoral reform commented on the great merits of competitive elections and representation. Debates over the basis of representation testify that delegates found bicameralism necessary to avoid legislative abuses. Debates over the popular selection of executive and judicial officials indicate a desire to maintain the integrity of the individual branches, precisely to assist in the prevention of overall government corruption. However, in no case were these unambiguous endorsements that government could manage without virtue and vigilance among citizens and leaders. In fact, a more careful look at their views shows precisely the opposite.

On Elections, Representation, and the Extended Republic

State-level politicians of the nineteenth century undoubtedly considered frequent, regular elections essential for the successful continuance of republican government. Theirs was a debate over who should participate in this practice and how direct the participants' voice should be. Even when the politicians said their aim was to sustain a democracy, they really were supporting the representative republic that Madison described as different from and preferable to democracy. It is no surprise, then, that throughout the first half of the century there remained unanimous support to continue competitive elections for the selection of lawmakers, not just in the sense that no one suggested a dictatorship or an aristocracy should replace the state's present representative republic, but also in the sense that there remained numerous unsolicited declarations on both sides about the great importance of this procedural government.

At every convention delegates extolled the benefits of a popularly elected legislature—regardless of whether they wanted an expanded or restricted franchise or a voter-, tax-, or property-based districting system. The following excerpt from a speech by Robert B. Taylor, a delegate from the eastern part of Virginia, is just one example of the many accolades offered in favor of popular government. Mr. Taylor began his speech in favor of an extended franchise by emphasizing the "principles of *Representative Republics*" upon which the Virginia constitution was based, including "(1) that a free Government is best calculated to promote human happiness; . . . (2) that the sovereignty resides, of right, and in fact, in the people; (3) that the best mode of administering Government is by Agents" (VA 1829–1830, 47).

At no convention did any delegate suggest that he or his constituents wished to undermine this set of principles; instead, praises for popular sovereignty and the election of representatives abounded. Those against expanding popular influence less frequently offered long speeches extolling the merits of self-government, but they were no less adamant regarding their allegiance to this fundamental American ideal. Convention delegates may not have agreed on who should elect legislative agents, what qualifications those agents should have before seeking office, or whether other government officers should also be subject to direct popular influence. They were, however, in unanimous agreement that the regular election of lawmakers was the best system for their individual states.

For obvious reasons, state-level politicians had less to say than their national forefathers about the benefits of an extended republic. States were geographic entities smaller and less diverse than the nation. Many of the particular states examined suffered from sectional and bipolar interests. There was little discussion among delegates regarding how the electoral process and the system of representation benefited from constituent diversity and district size. Nonetheless, in certain contexts, scattered remarks suggest that some state builders agreed there were some circumstances outside popular virtue that could assist in electing to office men of integrity, who were unwilling to harm the rights of their constituents. Although Ohio politicians and citizens were committed to the popular election of high-level judges, for example, they disagreed over whether these individuals should be selected from statewide districts or from smaller areas such as counties and boroughs.[2]

In this state nearly everyone who spoke in favor of at-large judicial elections did so at least partially on the ground that such a system would encourage highly reputable statesmen to run for office, thereby offering the people the chance to select among truly judicial individuals. Joseph McCormick, a lawyer who represented the Democratic district of Adams, argued for statewide elections on the grounds that the selection process should be designed to choose "the *best* individuals the state had to offer." For him, extending the sphere facilitated this process (OH 1850–1851, 585). Other supporters, such as delegate Robertson, contended that if elected by local districts judges would represent sectional interests, but if elected from across the state the process would avert particularistic views rising to power (585). These delegates might be seen as suggesting that procedures could supplement for missing popular virtue, or that the people's good intentions were insufficient to elect good judges. However, in both cases, speakers were clearly expressing their belief that leadership integrity was of great value. They hoped to ensure that the very best men would run and be selected for office.

On rare occasions delegates noted that diversity within the general popula-tion helped prevent majority tyranny. This was especially the case in debates over the basis of representation. Some delegates at Virginia's 1829–1830 con-vention who favored a districting system based strictly on voter population claimed that their state had multiple interests, all needing adequate voice. Two of these advocates of reform intimated that such diversity brought independent benefit by helping prevent any group from trampling the rights of another. In Louisiana the issue of diversity and its benefits also occasionally emerged. This time its merits were put forward by advocates of a land-based senate, who fa-vored a moderately revised county system, which gave majority voice to outlying agricultural areas. Three individuals noted that the state contained various inter-ests and that each needed to be empowered to avoid granting one interest (the city) majority power to destroy the rest. For example, Beatty praised the county system because it gave voice not just to the commercial interests of the city, but also to others such as "the sugar interest, the cotton interest, [and] the grazing interest" (LA 1845, 367). In both Virginia and Louisiana the implication was that diversity would prevent a majority of legislators reflecting the same narrow factious interests, but in neither instance was the case made explicit.

In Ohio debates over the basis of representation brought yet another point of view connecting size and diversity to security. Advocates argued that a popula-tion basis would increase the overall number of representatives in each legislative chamber. By enlarging the number of lawmakers one could reduce the chance of corrupt policies being passed by that powerful branch, for a larger number of representatives reduced the likelihood that lawmakers would join together mali-ciously. Here too the sense was that enough diversity would negate the power of malicious leaders. Diversity—not virtue—was being advanced as a means to con-trol the adverse effects of a vicious populace or of power-hungry leaders.

These are all isolated examples, however, and the argument was not robustly made. Even to these speakers, size and diversity were neither the sole nor the major reason citizens retained rights protection. That such arguments were put forward at all suggests that nineteenth-century delegates understood and per-haps endorsed the idea, laid out in *Federalist* essay 10, that government could survive powerful passions without relying strictly on virtue. Delegates may not have used it more broadly because they found it inapplicable at the state level.

On Bicameralism

In addition to their devoted commitment to elections and representation at the legislative level, delegates never questioned the benefits of a two-house law-making branch. Bicameralism had long been a feature of every state constitution. Although the initial constitutions of two states—Georgia and Pennsylvania—had only one legislative house, both had added a second before the turn of the century. Thus, by 1800 bicameralism was a widely accepted institution. With the exception of one or two speeches among the hundreds examined, no delegate proposed the abolition of this system.[3]

Any single state's debate on the basis of representation illustrates both the widespread acceptance of bicameralism and the general belief that a second chamber helped avoid the easy passage of passionate legislation (which a single-house system facilitated). Delegates who supported different representation bases in each house repeatedly described this system as a good means to assure that one branch checked abuses by the other. The overwhelming majority of Massachusetts's representatives wanted to maintain the present system for apportioning senators, whereby district size took account of the taxes paid by the inhabitants. Nearly every speaker in favor of this basis reiterated the view put forward by Isaac Parker, the first to speak on the subject. Parker claimed that "a system of checks and balances in the different departments of the government and between the branches of the Legislature, was essential to the preservation of liberty. . . . The principle required that there should be two bodies organized in such a manner that each might have an effectual check upon the other." As he saw it, the measure in question "would subvert this fundamental principle" (MA 1820–1821, 262, 264). His words would have been greatly respected; not only was he the president of the convention but he was chief justice of the state's supreme court and a professor of law at Harvard. Delegates in other states who supported existing or new bases giving disproportional power to owners of property (land- and slaveholdings) frequently intimated that devising senate and house districts according to different standards was an important mechanism for checking legislative abuse.

Opponents of reform repeatedly described their task as preserving the safeguard offered by bicameralism. They supported alternative district bases for each legislative house for some of the reasons Madison laid out in *Federalist* essays 62 and 63. Most of the convention delegates who opposed any radical reform of the basis of representation recognized that to gain from a second legislative house one must ensure that members of one house were more virtuous, deliberative, and reflective than members of the other. The arguments were not that virtuous behavior was a mere pleasant aside. Senator integrity was deemed essential. However, the argument indirectly implied a distrust in the people's integrity, a belief that some were not capable of electing good men and vigilantly guarding their actions thereafter. The question remained whether a senator's good character would be assured without a substantially virtuous populace, whether there were any innate features of bicameralism that would make senators trustworthy even when their selectors were as factious as the electors of the lower house.[4]

On Maintaining Separate Branches of Government

The most famous aspect of America's checks and balances is its institutional design of shared powers among separate independent branches. Almost all initial state constitutions provided for three separate branches of government, each with distinct functions; but the executive and the judicial branches gained independence and power mostly in the following generations (during the period under study). Even though many electoral reforms were discussed before questions of how much new power should be granted to governors and judges, the general belief seems to have been that uniting the powers of the three branches was the very definition of tyranny and that the best selection procedures ensured each branch was independent of the others.

Delegates often referred to the importance of institutional independence when debating the selection of nonlegislative officers. On several occasions they specifically declared allegiance to the principle that separated branches facilitated checks and balances. Read of Louisiana, one of two delegates to speak in favor of directly electing supreme court justices, gave various reasons for the superiority of this selection process. He began his speech by describing the important, specific role that judges played in the overall framework of government. The judges' job was to "decide controversies between individuals . . . [and] interpret and construe the constitution and the laws" (LA 1845, 743). He later explained that judicial independence was imperative to ensure that judges did their job well (747). Although he was speaking in favor of a popularly elected judiciary, and he certainly believed this selection process would assure the needed independence (747–48), Read included in his speech remarks about how separate divided powers helped protect rights and avoid despotism: "Safety consisted in keeping each of [government's] departments separate from and independent of others. In a pure despotism, all power centers in the monarch. . . . [I]n proportion as you divide and separate . . . powers [of the legislator, judge, and executive], you advance from monarchy to republicanism" (749).

Even opponents of the popular selection alluded to the importance of independence and separation, and to how both features helped maintain checks and balances. Soon after Read's speech, delegates voted to make supreme court justices appointed by the governor. The debate then moved on to how to select district-level judges. Delegate Porter, who favored joint ballot by the General Assembly, argued for this arrangement as a check on the governor's power, which would be too great if he was able to select all high-level judges (LA 1845, 771). Porter's suggestion failed to garner majority approval, and delegates began discussing a plan to permit the governor to offer three candidates and then let the senate decide among them. Democrat Pierre Soule, a jurist, diplomat, and criminal lawyer who entered politics after the convention and ultimately succeeded Calhoun as the leader of states rights in the South, offered the first speech in favor of this proposal. He supported the plan as an alternative means to restrain the potential corruption in the governor's office (785). In each case, speakers intimated that a well-designed government never allowed one branch to control the actions of another. Temptation for corruption and tyranny was too great. Although no one made the explicit case that each branch would check the others, they nonetheless endorsed officer independence as an important means to avoid government tyranny and an essential feature of well-designed government.

This argument surfaced in every state where the election of judges was at issue. When newspaper editor James Taylor explained why Ohio should popularly elect its judges, he described it as the best means "to guard against the tendency to[ward] centralization," a tendency he described as "great and dangerous" (OH 1850–1851, 355). These were the words of a judicious man, who worked with both Democratic and Republican administrations and who was therefore noted for being above party politics and without a specific partisan agenda. When New Yorkers in 1821 explained why justices of the peace should be elected, they alluded to the intrigue and patronage that appointment by the governor permitted. Popular election helped separate these justices from administrative control; it gave them an opportunity to pursue policies different from executive officials.

This kind of argument regarding the value of maintaining the integrity of separate branches also occurred in states where questions of governor selection arose. Advocates of popular election touted the procedure's ability to assure separation and independence. For example, when U.S. House representative and noted orator Philip Doddridge spoke in favor of popularly electing the governor, he began his speech by reminding his fellow delegates, "If we agreed on any one principle which has been discussed amongst us, it is that the Executive, Legislative and Judicial Departments of the Government, should be separated and that the duties of neither should be exercised by another department." Yet from his perspective, the governor is currently "nothing more or less than an emanation of the Legislative power. He is appointed every year" by that branch and is therefore "responsible to the Legislature alone." Doddridge reminded his colleagues that, when the legislature controls all three branches, "it is a precise definition of despotic power." To ensure separation, branches must be independent from one another, and for Doddridge popular election brought the executive his needed independence (VA 1829–1830, 466).

Even advocates of a governor being selected by the legislature declared the fundamental importance of independence along with separated powers. Former president James Monroe agreed with Doddridge on the importance of separation, but not on the necessity of popular election to obtain it. In his speech in favor of Virginia's current system, Monroe acknowledged that a well-designed constitution ensured "all three branches of Government be separated," with each branch's "power[s] clearly defined." He agreed that placing all "three powers of Government in one body . . . gives it [government] the character of despotism" (VA 1829–1830, 481). Because Monroe saw the present system of selecting a governor as consistent with this institutional independence, he thought any change unnecessary.

Here, as in all debates over how to select nonlegislative officers, arguments included allusions to the problems of government collusion and to the benefits of separated and independent branches. Speakers appeared to have embraced many of the same arguments one finds in *Federalist* essays 47–51. However, nowhere did delegates demand that overlapping shared powers supplement independence. Nowhere is it implied that independence, with or without this supplement, led any particular officer to check the abuses of another branch. Most relevant here was that no checks were promised in the absence of leadership virtue, nor predicted to work with widespread ambition.

Remaining Questions

The above illustrates that state constitutional designers of the early nineteenth century saw some of the same advantages with representation, bicameralism, and institutional independence that *Publius* outlined. However, two important components of the national vision were absent: first, regarding how much narrow self-interest the system could manage, and second, how designs would respond to such narrow behavior. Did delegates suppose that the electoral process refined and enlarged the public views so well that government easily survived bouts of popular corruption? Did they think a bicameral legislature or independent governors and judges would be able to check against government abuse even if the majority of them were primarily concerned with maintaining their own power and authority? Did they think ambition would counteract ambition? The question remains whether state delegates generally believed that procedural and institutional designs could impede the power of popular factions and power-hungry leaders, without the simultaneous existence of virtue somewhere in the system.

As it turns out, state constitution writers never suggested that their system was designed to work when both citizens and leaders were uninterested in the good of the state. Instead, they proclaimed repeatedly that popular virtue and leadership integrity had important instrumental value in the good state. If the people did not act as good citizens, if they did not think about the good of the state as they selected rulers and evaluated policy, then every officer elected would also be of unacceptable character and ultimately act in harmful ways. If leaders were too self-interested or too power-hungry, representative government would not survive. Institutional branches checked each other only when leaders within them cared about the public good. Although constitutional writers during the first half of the nineteenth century expected that there would be bouts of corruption both in and outside government, they also recognized that only the virtue of people and their leaders would effectively battle it. Thus, they had a view different from their national forefathers regarding the extent to which a republican government relied on virtue and how successfully it could manage behavior not directed toward the public good.

ON THE IMPORTANCE OF VIRTUE

National designers certainly hoped for citizens and leaders of integrity. The very best governments empowered such people, for they promised security. Drafters of state constitutions agreed on the instrumental importance of virtue in constitutional government. In the conventions examined, nearly three-quarters of the recorded speeches mentioned how or why the nature of the people and their leaders directly affected their state's ability to limit government power and preserve the rights and freedoms of its citizens. At each convention one finds plaudits for virtue, morality, patriotism, moderation, rationality, independence, and intelligence. Speakers did not always use the same words or elaborately describe the characteristics they desired, but they usually found it necessary to remind their peers that without good citizens and leaders there was little chance of protected rights, limited government, or economic prosperity.[5]

Constitutional designers' attention to the character of citizens took various forms. During the 1820s delegates often commented on the fundamental place of intelligence, morality, and virtue in republican government. At the 1821 New York convention, three-quarters of those wanting to extend the franchise to taxpayers, military men, and highway workers made statements like lawyer David Buel's. He declared that "Virtue and intelligence are the true basis on which every republican government must rest. When these are lost, freedom will no longer exist" (NY 1821, 239).

Opponents also invoked the fundamental role of character in republican government. John Duer, a Federalist politician who later became chief justice of the state's superior court, argued on behalf of a landed franchise by noting that "excellence in a republican form of government . . . depended on its adaptation to the habits and manners of the people. Where the people were sunk in vice, it was perhaps the worst government. . . . But where the people were intelligent and moral—where there existed habits of attachment to liberty and law, a republican government was, of all others, the most excellent" (NY 1821, 271). In questions about the franchise the two sides differed on who had the necessary character, not on the fundamental nature of its importance.

One finds such general statements about character in debates over other issues as well. When Democratic-Republican Henry Childs of Massachusetts spoke in favor of a voter population basis for the state senate, he explained that the United States was an "experiment, made to test the power of the people to govern themselves." The experiment was successful precisely because "government was founded on [the] intelligence and morality" of its people (MA 1820–1821, 295). His adversaries chimed in agreement. A third of those preferring the existing taxed-based districting system agreed with Federalist Supreme Court Justice Joseph Story, who noted that good government "depends on the habits, manners, character and institutions of the people, who are to be represented." Without appropriate inclinations, "there cannot be public security and happiness" (288). His equally prestigious colleague the Whig leader Daniel Webster was even more forceful on this point, when he reminded his fellow delegates that "We do not . . . expect all men to be philosophers, or statesmen; but we confidently trust, and our expectation of the duration of our system of government rests on that trust, that by the diffusion of general knowledge, and good and virtuous sentiments, the political fabric may be secure, as well against open violence and overthrow, as against the slow but sure undermining of licentiousness" (315).

Speakers at the earlier conventions particularly praised those parts of the community they wanted to have political influence. Advocates of suffrage expansion praised the heroic acts of the Revolutionary soldiers they wanted to enfranchise. They commented that blacks and whites and men both with and without property had proven their virtue by fighting for American freedom. Because of their good character, they could and should be included in the participating body politic. Opponents of reform likewise praised those they hoped would retain majority influence in political affairs and defamed those whose voice they wished to restrain. In debates over the franchise and the appropriate basis for representation, advocates of the status quo depicted property owners and taxpayers as extraordinary individuals. These people had displayed great generosity over the generations by helping to fund the construction of churches, schools, and roads. Their contributions, as well as their productive use of land, added to America's greatness. These praises were accompanied by detailed descriptions of the wretched dependence of renters, military personnel, highway workers, and the like. According to opponents of reform, should the latter gain an influential voice in the political process, then anarchy, violence, and general destruction would follow.[6]

By the 1840s and 1850s, there were fewer general declarations concerning the independent importance of citizen character. Speakers at later conventions seldom used terms such as *virtue* and *morality*. Nonetheless, they intimated that the people's disposition ultimately determined republican success. Those in favor of expanding popular power found it necessary to offer testaments regarding the good character of those they wished to empower. Whig farmer Benjamin Bruce argued that because blacks had proved themselves worthy defenders of the country, they deserved the vote (NY 1846, 776). Neeson, a member of Virginia's western delegation, extolled the merits of his constituents, who remained underrepresented in the present districting system. Inhabitants of western Virginia were "honest and capable of administering the government wisely and faithfully with due regard to all interests." They would not, as his adversaries claimed, heavily tax their slaveholding brethren to the east and thereby undermine the state's economy (VA 1850–1851, 476). In these later debates, the word *virtue* was often conspicuously absent. Nonetheless, constitutional writers stressed the admirable traits of those who had little or no political voice and thereby implied their ongoing concern with the electorate's character.

Later opponents of reform were equally indirect regarding the importance of good citizenship. They honed in on the specific attributes that made various groups in American society either worthy or unworthy of the governing privilege. The words of Virginia's Robert Scott, a lawyer then serving in the state's house of delegates, exemplify the kind of character arguments found at these later conventions. Scott rejected a population basis for senate electoral districts precisely because it would lay eastern Virginia "open to be plundered" by greedy westerners "clamoring for the possession of the purse strings" and advocating policies undermining the "protection of property" (VA 1850–1851, 284). Scott later noted that only large property owners "will be just and reasonable [and] let equity govern" (341). Here and elsewhere, restricting the expansion of popular influence was justified by doubts about the integrity of those who would be newly empowered.

Speakers sometimes accompanied this kind of argument with reminders concerning the need for responsible leadership. Henry Childs not only stressed the value of a virtuous citizenry, he also reminded his colleagues of the merit of empowering good leaders. He praised the overall constitutional design of his home state, in large measure because it empowered "men . . . well-qualified to fill the different offices with dignity." He acknowledged the fundamental importance of good leadership by conceding that he would endorse a property-based districting system if his adversaries could prove it "could and would elect better men" (MA 1820–1821, 296). Childs thought such a proof impossible and made his statement to illustrate why Boston should not be granted the extra voice its wealth currently gave it. Nevertheless, the spirit of his argument shows that underlying his position was a recognition that the quality of leadership mattered. This assumption was embedded in many speeches about the appropriate basis for representation.

The value of ensuring that officials were men of integrity was a theme that received great attention in debates over selection procedures for nonlegislative officials and officeholding requirements for popularly elected representatives. Kenneth Rayner, a Whig planter and state legislator of North Carolina, argued that requiring a religious oath for elected officials denied the fundamental principle that civic virtue was necessary and sufficient for serving in office. He objected to incorporating "into our fundamental law the doctrine that 'honesty, capability, and faithfulness to the constitution,' are not sufficient for office." Religious affiliation was not the only test of a good statesman (NC 1835, 264). Although he was rejecting a particular measure of good leadership ("moral virtue"), his words indicate he was by no means rejecting the need for high quality and integrity among officers. Throughout his speech in favor of allowing foreigners to run for governor, Louisiana delegate Brent alluded to the great importance of being governed by men devoted to national good. He then explained that foreigners too "love their country . . . and [are committed] to liberty and equality" (LA 1845, 247). Brent justified his choice of policy by trying to assure adversaries that it would empower men of the appropriate character. As his colleague Marigny said so well, "the talents and character of a man should be passports to office" (259). In these and other debates over who should be eligible for elected office, speakers illustrated their belief in the importance of good leadership by trying to show how or why their preferred policy would enhance or maintain the present quality of governing officers.

Throughout the first half of the century, constitutional designers found it necessary to declare that the good state depended on the disposition of those with power to influence government. By the late 1840s explanations of what made specific individuals worthy, or not, replaced shorthand words such as *virtue* and *morality*. The basic argument remained the same: the people's disposition influenced whether republican government would be successful and whether leaders would abuse individual rights. Also important for good governing was the character of leaders.

These views are certainly consistent with the views of their forefathers and with the liberal tradition in general, for they assume that the character of the people—their virtue, morality, intelligence, and independence—mattered for instrumental reasons only. In no case was that valued disposition claimed important as a higher-order good, worthy of cultivation because of its innate ability to elevate the human soul. Their national forefathers and the strand of liberalism they represented embraced virtue as a beneficial aside, knowing that government design could serve in its absence. Some nineteenth-century designers seemed to agree. However, prevailing views on how procedural features and institutional designs were thought to operate in the absence of any interest in either the public good or generally protected rights show that these later constitution writers never supposed mechanisms could survive, even temporarily, without good men somewhere in the system.

Nineteenth-century delegates applauded good character because it prompted citizens and leaders to act for the benefit of the republic. By looking closely at the arguments for and against electoral reform, and then reading between the lines, one finds that good citizenship and leadership may not have been sufficient, but both were deemed necessary to support a popularly based government and secure it against potential abuses. Whereas both sides endorsed aspects of the Federalist perspective regarding the electoral process, bicameralism, and the separation of branches, neither side thought those procedures and institutional mechanisms protected against oppressive government if those with political influence were narrowly interested or hungry for power. The majority of speakers for and against electoral reform supposed that, when and if people and their representatives were predisposed against the public good and did not hold the general enjoyment and protection of rights as their primary concern, state governments were in trouble. Certain electoral procedures might help enlarge the public view, but this did not mean leaders would be elevated from their factious constituents or that popular opinions would be sufficiently diverse to exorcise the explicit need for a public-minded citizenry. Neither members of an upper house nor independent governors and judges would impede government abuse if their constituents made passionate demands upon them or if they themselves were motivated by ambition and hunger for power. Politicians at state conventions never mentioned the possibility that self-serving ambition could be channeled positively to motivate members of one branch to check members in another. Instead speakers for and against electoral reform offered repeated reminders that no branch of government prevented government abuses by another unless it was directed by good citizens or housed leaders of integrity.

Underlying the argument of both sides of the debate was the basic premise that designs could not effectively filter out or positively channel self-serving sentiments once they gained power in the system. The only counterbalance was virtue itself, broadly understood to include any behavior that consciously or unconsciously supported the public good and protected the fundamental rights of all citizens.[7] Thus, the point of checks and balances was to empower virtue, not channel self-interest and render it harmless.

Behind this shared vision lay a bone of contention. Whereas delegates agreed that the integrity of leaders mattered and that no government could protect rights without good men in office, they disputed which part of the citizenry—the general populace or selected voters—were ultimately responsible for ensuring the reign of appropriately minded leaders. Constitution writers agreed that, overall, the system intended to select officers of integrity but they disagreed as to whether procedures could do anything to counteract malicious undercurrents, that is, whether electoral stipulations could silence factions when they existed.

The Voices of Restriction

Why restrict voting? Those against reform believed that voters directly determined who came to power. Leaders reflected the interests and attachments of those who selected them. If voters lacked any commitment to protecting the inalienable constitutional rights and instead cared only about their narrow interests, then leaders and the policies they passed would reflect these same sentiments, including any problematic features embedded in them.

Why endorse representation by property? The rationale was similar. As suffrage requirements waned, supporters of a property basis saw the legislative branch as increasingly vulnerable to factious voter demands. By creating districts weighed by property holdings, delegates could limit the general population's governing influence in the second chamber. Here a majority of districts would consist of upstanding citizens—that is, those who could be trusted to elect fine statesmen—and therefore the majority of legislators would have good character. With majority control in the hands of the trustworthy, this branch would approve only policies that reflected the general good. They would veto any destructive policies proposed by the lower house, by the house whose members mirrored the more general population.

Why appoint certain officials? Appointments avoided direct contact between leaders and the corrupted segments of the population. They kept certain officials above petty electioneering and away from factious party dogma. The expectation was that appointers would choose individuals that were virtuous and qualified for the job, whereas the people would not.

In each case, the whole point of restrictions was to ensure voters and leaders had good character. The same underlying assumption prevailed: if a majority of government branches lapsed from the hands of the competent and into the hands of those selected by the less virtuous masses, the state could not survive, fancy checks notwithstanding. Competition for office was insufficient insurance for acquiring good candidates. The electoral process produced leaders who mirrored their constituents. Only virtuous, moral, independent voters could select sound leaders. Only these kinds of voters would be able to recognize demagoguery and bad policy making; only they would deny office to individuals thereby inclined. One government branch would not check the other, unless the members of at least one were of good character. Ambition alone insufficiently countered ambition. In all cases the implication was that a well-designed government ensured its voting citizens and government officers were interested in pursuing the common good and protecting everyone's life, liberty, and property. Security came only when these mechanisms were designed so that one or more branches of government empowered the virtuous. It came when those with unsatisfactory dispositions were denied majority control in or over government.

This philosophy can be unmasked in various arguments supporting ongoing or new restrictions on the people's political influence. Take, for example, arguments favoring a limited franchise. To advocates of ongoing restrictions, whole sections of the population lacked the necessary commitment to the state and its fundamental principles and therefore were best kept silent. Those supporting a white-only franchise considered blacks degraded, immoral, and lacking in the necessary rational capacities. Those aiming to preserve property requirements saw the landless as dependent and easily tempted by malicious interests to steal the property of others. Those against a more universal suffrage saw military personnel as too deferential to authority and renters too dependent on their landlords.

In each case the contention was that such individuals must be kept from exercising the vote, because these individuals would either seek policies that were destructive to the public interest or ignore politics completely and defer to corrupt leaders and party hacks. As a direct result of a poorly designed franchise, officials intent on equalizing property to benefit their constituents would rise to power. Or the ambitious would increase their power and destroy the people's rights while military personnel, blacks, and other apolitical groups deferentially stood by and accepted such ruinous behavior.

Advocates of ongoing suffrage restrictions believed disaster would follow the extension of suffrage to the unworthy. Joseph Crudup opposed black suffrage on the grounds that "Some intelligence and moral character were necessary to qualify a man to exercise this privilege [of the franchise]." Those who lacked that character would permit tyranny (NC 1835, 74). In his view, voter vigilance was essential, and some individuals would never pay attention to politics. Federalist lawyer Elisha Williams, who was then serving in New York's state assembly, argued that a freehold franchise was one of "those checks and balances, which the experience of nearly half a century has sanctified, . . . and without which a well organized government cannot exist [or] . . . be perpetuated" (NY 1821, 255). He believed one should confer the franchise only "on those who may exercise it discreetly." Advocates of reform wanted to enfranchise the "ring streaked and speckled population of our large towns and cities," but Williams saw the cities as "great sores" and worried that the general populations within them would seek sustenance by plundering. Thus from his view without a propertied franchise "a stable and free government . . . will [not] be transmitted . . . to the latest posterity."[8] Philip Nicholas, a Virginia delegate who had once served as the state's attorney general and who now headed the Farmers Bank, agreed. He rejected calls for extending the franchise beyond property holders, for if you place "power in the hands of those who have none, or a very trivial stake in the community, ... [y]ou immediately open the floodgates of corruption, . . . undermine the public and private virtue of your people," and cause the "gradual decline, and final extinction" of the state's republican government (VA 1829–1830, 367). According to Nicholas, freeholders would never elect officers who could be bought or convinced to harm rights. As he saw it, "Our institutions are free, no man is oppressed, and every man is secure. . . . [because] power is in the hands of the great body of the yeomanry" (368).

Implicit in the majority of arguments against suffrage reform was the denial of any "elevated separation" between electors and the men they selected. Speakers repeatedly spoke as if there existed no meaningful distinction between leaders and electors, as if the character of voters determined the kinds of policies that were ultimately passed. These arguments imply a shared understanding of constitutionalism: the competitive electoral process neither raised representatives above the ordinary nor weeded out the ill effects of improper voter sentiments. It was not a mechanism that worked independently of the character of voters. Elections filtered out the negative effects of individuals who ignored the public good only by silencing them. Lawmakers mirrored their electorate. These representatives acted however their selectors demanded. Thus the integrity and intentions of electors mattered greatly. In this sense, the voters' virtue and morality explained why representative government secured rights. Without such sentiments among citizens with influence, the process would never bring elevated statesmen to the helm.

Only one restriction speech (from all the conventions examined) appeared to echo the view of James Madison that the electoral process itself both naturally elevated to office men of a caliber higher than those who selected them and served as a check by itself against government corruption. The speaker was James Monroe, one of America's first presidents, someone active during the creation of the national government and known for his ongoing allegiance to the nation's first principles. Monroe wanted to keep Virginia's existing system of governor selection, whereby the governor was chosen by the general assembly. He explained that "if they [the people] are confined to the election of their Representatives, they will sustain their dignity, and their judgment will be enlightened by the competition of the candidates, whose mutual rivalry will expose their errors to the public view" (VA 1829–1830, 482). In his view the electoral competition would encourage good candidates and help voters choose an enlightened statesman. But Monroe appears alone on this issue. Although in numerous other instances Virginia's delegates deferred to Monroe, using his opinion to bolster their own, they never repeated this particular argument. Even Madison himself, who was present at Virginia's 1829–1830 convention, did not chime in agreement.

Despite Monroe's faith in leadership competition, it appears he also thought that popular virtue was necessary to ensure that the process worked well. Earlier in this same speech he explicitly noted, "The people have a complete check upon them [the legislature] *if* they are only true to themselves, intelligent and virtuous" (481; emphasis added). By such a remark, he left open the question of what would happen if the people were not so true and virtuous. Could legislators still be checked? Would laws still be appropriately restrictive? How he would have answered such questions is ambiguous.

Arguments made in favor of a property or tax basis for (at least) one legislative house also demonstrate how little faith delegates placed in the workability of procedural and institutional mechanisms if electors ignored the good of the state. Advocates of district bases that favored the propertied saw these systems as offering a security similar to one ensured by a property or tax-based franchise. Drawing districts according to the resident property holdings would ensure that a majority of lawmakers represented property holders, that they were selected by and therefore spoke for men of good character.

Underlying this argument was one of the same assumptions. Those favoring an unequal basis assumed that officers mirrored the character of those who elected them. No elevation took place from the electoral process per se. Leaders elected from districts housing apolitical, wrongly interested voters were equally problematic. Leaders elected from districts where the virtuous presided would act in the interests of the state. These speakers also indirectly referred to the inability of ambition to counteract ambition. The assumption was that the success of a two-chamber legislature depended on at least one branch's housing men of integrity. Simple bicameralism would not quiet the potentially harmful interests that might find their way into the house. Neither branch could be trusted to avoid factious legislation or to restrain itself in power, unless a majority of its members had the interests of the state and its inhabitants in mind. Again, this would occur only if representatives were elected and continually watched over by the virtuous segments of the population.

Those who opposed forming districts solely on the basis of voter population argued that the quality of the electorate—not the existence of a second chamber—was primarily responsible for the sound, rights-protecting legislation states currently enjoyed. Nowhere was this position made more explicit than in Massachusetts where eight of the ten delegates arguing for tax-based senate districts described this system as absolutely essential if one branch was to check the other. Daniel Webster began his speech by acknowledging, "We have already decided that the legislative power shall exist . . . in two separate and distinct branches, . . . that these branches shall . . . possess a negative on each other, . . . [and] that members . . . be chosen annually. The immediate question . . . is, *in what manner* . . . shall the senators be elected?" (MA 1820–1821, 304). To him, the question warranted special attention because its answer determined whether the senate would check abuses by the house. Related to this was another query: "shall the legislative department be constructed with any other *check*, than such as arises simply from dividing the members of this department into two houses" (305)? For Webster, merely separating the legislature into two houses had no independent value. "Legislative bodies . . . consider themselves as the immediate representatives of the people. They depend on public opinion to sustain their measures" (306). "The senate is not to be a check on the *people*" (307). It could not be, for legislators reflect the views of their electors. This kind of position implied a particular theory of legislative behavior: that lawmakers blindly endorsed the policies of their constituents. The position also entails the underlying assumption that the electoral process did little to elevate leaders above their constituents. To bring in men of high integrity, something more had to be done.

After outlining this view, Webster explained how he thought it best to ensure that the senate checked the house. He suggested manipulating districts so there would be "some difference of origin, or character, or interest, or feeling, or sentiment" (MA 1820–1821, 307). This was done well in the state's present system of districting, which enabled senators to echo the voices of "small proprietors, acting with intelligence, and that enthusiasm which a common cause inspires" (311). For him, "property should have its due weight and consideration in political arrangements" for this helped avoid "confiscation and plunder" (312). "Party and passion" would have no practical effect so long as one house spoke on behalf of property holders. This arrangement would ensure that at least one chamber reflected the views of "intelligent, . . . common-cause minded" individuals (312). It was exactly this system that had so far provided the inhabitants of the state with "general security for public and private rights." This system ensured "no violent measures, affecting property, ha[d ever] been attempted" (317).

Embedded in Webster's argument was the idea put forward explicitly by his colleague Justice Joseph Story, that power given to mere numbers would cause the legislature to fall prey to the "wretched inhabitants," and then "all property [w]ould be booty . . . divided among plunderers" (MA 1820–1821, 288). The senate could not prevent this dreadful occurrence if all its members were elected by the same potential rabble who selected assemblymen. Again, the arguments of antireformers made sense only if one assumed they believed that electors ruled and that representatives were mere agents of their will, enacting only those policies that their constituents demanded. Since legislators would mirror the interests of those who selected them, constitutions had to be designed so that the majority of legislators in at least one house had the kind of character that would recognize when policies went against the interest of the state and its inhabitants in order to then veto them. The aim was to grant good citizens disproportionate influence so that good leadership would dominate in at least one legislative branch. The assumption was that right-minded lawmakers would prevent rights-abusing policies. The mere existence of a second house was useless, unless its members were of good character.

This position was echoed in other debates over representation. Those who opposed a voter population basis argued that, unless respected men of property elected the majority of representatives in at least one branch of government, then inappropriate intrusive legislation would inevitably occur and no one would have any inclination to stop it. Leaders elected by the general population would surely endorse policies that harmed the rights of some, simply to satisfy their constituencies. As Mr. Wadsworth put it: "let the senate stand by to prevent the state from being flooded with ruin by a prodigal waste of the treasury funds. . . . if the property qualification is abandoned, Men will be elected who have nothing to lose, but all to gain" (LA 1845, 503). In the words of Mr. Meredith, the mixed basis of representation provided a "check on our rulers, a check without which . . . every government degenerates into tyranny" (VA 1850–1851, 458).

Again, the implicit assumption was that the senate would check against the invasion of rights only when members were elected by—and therefore represented—appropriately minded citizens. Only then would representatives be of a disposition willing to protect fundamental rights, especially property rights.

Those who were against systems that further empowered the general population rejected outright the argument that lengthy staggered office terms could filter out the negative demands of a wrongly motivated populace. Proponents of the status quo or similar bases were afraid of letting less trustworthy masses elect members in both houses, for then both branches would be the same, with neither branch housing men of integrity who were willing to keep rights protected from factious demands or government tyranny.

Some speakers opposing a voter population basis (including Webster and Meredith) noted explicitly that their position was consistent with the national case for bicameralism, and in important respects it was. The national constitution created two houses representing different constituencies, precisely so that one branch might check the abuses of the other. Madison expected that members of the senate—elected from a broader constituency and for longer terms— would be more stately and thoughtful as well as better experienced than their peers in the house. He, like the state constitution writers who followed him, recognized the value of having senators of high caliber.

Local designers differed from their national forefathers mainly in that these later constitution writers emphasized the necessary role that voter character played in producing such men. Many of these subsequent writers implied that bicameralism prevented the invasion of rights only when appropriately minded citizens (that is, the propertied, taxpayers, or slaveholders) elected a majority of the members in at least one chamber, for only then would representatives in that branch be virtuous, well guided, and willing to secure the rights of all citizens— especially the property rights these designers found so important and so much in need of special protection. Their argument rejected staggered terms as well as the belief that electoral process could serve mechanistically as its own filter.

Debates over the selection of judicial and executive officials illustrate the same general pattern. Opponents of electoral reform believed that the character of the selectors directly affected the character of the selected. They saw their task as devising a government that ensured the virtue of as many government officers as possible. Also apparent is the belief that the way to check legislative abuse was not to empower separate and independent officials, grant them overlapping power, and then not pay attention to their character. Well-designed constitutions entailed selection procedures aimed at choosing leaders that were disinterested in power and concerned with protecting rights and preserving government limits. These arguments for restricting popular control over nonlegislative officers reflected sentiments similar to the ones already outlined in this section in that they too stressed the inherent importance of empowering leaders of integrity. The differing aspect here is that delegates sought to keep some officers completely out of the people's hands and therefore had less to say about the value of a quality electorate. In this case, delegates called to separate leaders from the masses so as to silence the problematic influences and give voice to high-minded leaders, above the factious fray of party politics.[9]

Arguments favoring the continued appointment of various nonlegislative officials illustrate this point. Delegates against the popular election of judges argued that only appointment guaranteed a virtuous judiciary, capable of protecting rights. Independence from the virtue-lacking masses—not from the legislature or executive—inspired men in robes to do good. Federalist politician Elisha Williams contended that justices of the peace controlled "the reputation, liberty and property of their very neighbors." These individuals should be appointed by the governor, for if the people elected them, these justices would become a "corps of pettifoggers." This he strongly wished to avoid (NY 1821, 308). He feared that officers would directly mirror the sentiments of the electorate, which delegates had already extended to include taxpayers, military men, and roadworkers. New York Democrats also supported the continued appointment of these petty officers. Martin Van Buren, then still a U.S. senator, argued that by permitting the election of justices of the peace, you "render their judgment subservient to their desire for a continuance in office." This would lower their quality, which was dangerous since "their duties were so important" (321). His position emphasized the importance of high-minded officers. Van Buren did not believe that other officers—whether men of integrity or not—would counterbalance corrupt justices of the peace. In judicial matters the electoral process would attract individuals who devoted all their attention to retaining office. Such politically ambitious officers were problematic.[10]

Delegates wanted even sheriffs to have a certain amount of virtue. Charles Conrad of Louisiana, longtime politician who started as a Democrat in the U.S. Senate and later became a Whig serving in the Fillmore administration, was against the popular election of sheriffs, precisely because he expected this procedure would lower their character. He feared that, if popularly elected, sheriffs would "harass the poor, and uninfluential men [and] w[ould] hesitate to do anything that w[ould] include the displeasure of the rich and powerful." The end result of election would be "to produce corruption" among these officials (LA 1845, 818). The underlying assumption was again that appointment ensured virtue, whereas elections would allow vices to surface. There was never any indication that officers without the general common interest in mind could offer unexpected benefits to the system. Neither would they be controlled by the zealous watch of other officers. Ambition was not expected to counteract ambition. Put simply, if leaders lacked virtue then security was unlikely.

Delegates endorsed special qualifications for officeholders by stressing the importance of their job, the independent merit of empowering good men, and the inability of the election process to select good leadership. In his explanation as to why foreigners should not be given the privilege of running for office, conservative Whig Judah Benjamin discussed the role of the representative. To him a lawmaker was "here to guard the interests of his constituents. . . . How very important it is to have men in our legislature that are imbued with our feelings and sentiments, and are identified with our interests and institutions." Foreigners might well place the concern for their homeland over concern for the state, and the electorate might overlook this (LA 1845, 89). Thus, from Benjamin's perspective, better to prevent foreigners from running for office than to allow voters the opportunity to empower such undesirables. The underlying rationale was twofold. Individuals in power who did not identify their interests with the state's were dangerous to security. The electoral process could not be expected to filter out such individuals.

One can see traces of the same position in debates over whether to maintain a religious oath for officeholding. Jesse Cooper contended that "the Roman Catholic is the very offspring of a despot." Such a person must be denied office (NC 1835, 242). Cooper claimed that if a Catholic were among "permissible" candidates, the people could not be trusted to ignore his candidacy. Should they elect such a despot, then the other branches would be unable to quiet the Catholic's potential evils. Americans would become papal servants. Although it was seemingly an implausible position, both Cooper and Benjamin took the stand that the legislature could not withstand even one corrupt or wrongly motivated representative. Underlying this particularly implausible case—as well as the many other arguments in favor of restricting who could run for office—was the idea that, in order to survive, republics required leaders of good character in some, if not all, government branches. Restricting some from the privilege of leadership on account of their inability to pursue America's public good helped ensure that responsible individuals gained office. Neither voters nor the election process itself could be expected to do so in all cases.

Across conventions and reform issues, advocates of restriction never even hinted that the good state could or would survive if apathetic or self-interested citizens, coupled with power-hungry ambitious leaders, controlled all areas of government. Clearly the restrictionists recognized that negative influences would creep into politics now and again. But every policy they advocated was an attempt to restrain the influence of the self-interested, ambitious, and corrupt by counteracting it with virtue. They held that institutional arrangements had thus far avoided tyranny, not because competitive elections naturally brought elevated leaders to the fore, or because ambition countered ambition, but because at least some branches had given men of appropriate character decisive influence in government.

The case for ongoing restrictions entailed the belief that some (if not all) branches of government needed leaders who were virtuous enough to check vice wherever it reared its ugly head. A *propertied* electorate, a *nonelected* judiciary, *God-fearing* officials, and a senate *based on taxation* could all be trusted, precisely because these officers would be concerned with the needs of the good state—that is, with the protection of everyone's life, liberty, and possessions. Advocates of restriction contended that as long as these "rights-minded" men had louder and more powerful voices in some (or all) branches of government, states could forever avoid government oppression.

The Voices of Expansion

When responding to these theories, reformers never once countered by claiming that procedures and institutional mechanisms would help ensure that the newly empowered did not harm the rights and freedoms of their neighbors. They too found institutional designs unable to cover for the negative consequences that would occur when self-interested individuals, who ignored the common good, had significant political sway. State-level republics could not function when narrow interests and leadership ambition were the forces behind political action. Their quarrel was largely one of degree. Those favoring the expansion of popular influence thought that successful republics required widespread virtue. They denied emphatically that any institutional check or popular restriction would work, if parts of the population were as corrupt and misdirected as the restrictionists implied. Not only did the electoral process and the separation of powers fail when corrupted subsets of the population had political voice, but these designs failed *whenever* such subsets existed, even when the corrupt lacked direct influence in government. Thus, the expansionist case for the independent security that might be offered by institutional designs was even weaker than the antireform perspective.

The minimal independent role of institutions was forcefully made in several instances. At the 1821 New York convention a majority of the advocates of an expanded franchise adamantly declared that restrictions would not effectively curtail the effects of factions. Should portions of the people be as corrupt as the restrictionists claimed, denying them the right to vote would not hold back their destructive power. David Buel's rhetorical question put the matter simply: "It may be that mobs will occasionally be collected and commit depredation in a great city; but, . . . if such a state of things were possible, would a senate, elected by freeholders afford any security?" (NY 1821, 242). Democratic party leader Martin Van Buren made the case even more clearly:

> When the people of this state shall have so far degenerated; when the principles of order or of good government which now characterize our people, and afford security to our institutions, shall have so far given way to those of anarchy and violence, as to lead an attack on private property, or on agrarian law; . . . or by an attempt to throw all the public burthens on any particular class of man; then all constitutional provisions will be idle and unavailing, because they will have lost all their force and influence. (259)

This argument also underlay various expansion arguments elsewhere. One might look to the speech of Democrat John Branch, a wealthy planter and a formidable politician (who already had served as state senator, governor, U.S. senator, Navy secretary, and U.S. representative, and later would become governor of the Florida Territory). In his justification for the enfranchisement of freed blacks with property, he explained why Americans remained free to this date: "our social compact is held together . . . [by] the mutual interest which binds us to each other." The binding, shared commitment he spoke of was among Americans—black and white, not just voters (NC 1835, 70). For him and his peers in other states, the general population had virtuous intentions. The proof was that no tumultuous upheavals had yet destroyed the people's rights and liberties. In a free republic, if those segments of the population who lacked formal influence wished to abuse the rights and freedoms of their fellow citizens, they could. With or without a powerful voice, those people could and would rise up and use force to destroy the good state. Neither the electoral process nor a restricted electorate would keep them quiet.[11] The people's virtue and commitment to just laws—not the electoral process or representation system—elevated the character of lawmakers and their policies.

Advocates of the voter population basis offered similar arguments, denying that securities now enjoyed resulted from the current practice of silencing certain groups. These delegates agreed with their adversaries that electors and leaders were men of good character, but they disagreed about how much of the success and security currently enjoyed should be credited to these individuals alone. The virtue of the broader American constituency was ultimately responsible for present rights security. At both the 1829–1830 and the 1850–1851 Virginia conventions, advocates of a voter population basis refused outright to accept that a legislature controlled by the eastern part of the state could avoid looting by inhabitants of the western part. Alfred Powell, an ardent reformist who fought not only for a population-based legislature but also for the extension of suffrage, made this case explicitly when he asked his colleagues how they might design government so it avoided legislative abuses and overall corruption:

> [By] parchment stipulations in the compact of Government? By giving to property . . . political power? By declaring the minority . . . shall govern the majority because of their wealth? By placing wealth in a hostile attitude to physical strength? Certainly not! The only effectual guarantee against the abuse of power in a republic is to be found and to be found only in the *virtue and intelligence of the people* in whom all power rests. While virtuous and intelligent, they will do no act of injustice or rapine. And when they become vicious, and fit for violence and spoil, it is in vain to attempt to restrain them. . . . [I]f those fears are well founded [and westerners are plunderers], . . . no security is to be found in any paper stipulation . . . or by the adoption of the [property basis] amendment, because these fears suppose that the people are vicious, corrupt and dishonest and if such be the fact, no possible security can be formed, recognizing the right of self government in the people. (VA 1829–1830, 107)

Powell believed that "a Representative Republic . . . is the best and happiest system for obtaining the end of all Government . . . , when the people have the essential qualities to suit them to such a form." Without the appropriate qualities, there could be no representative system (104).

Many other speakers there and at the later convention agreed: giving property special voice in one area of government would never, on its own, protect rights. Neither would the system of bicameralism alone. Staggering the terms of office might prove useful, but the real reason the present system worked, the real reason a more egalitarian system of representation would work in the future, was that the people as a whole had the appropriate character for governing themselves. These reform advocates spoke as if the people really ruled, as if members of a bicameral legislature would respond to the views and demands of the greater population, not just of those individuals who specifically elected them. This meant that government avoided the negative consequences of factious demands only when the public were sufficiently concerned with protecting the rights of all inhabitants.

Delegates in favor of increasing the number of elected officials made a similar case when belittling the restrictionists' rationale for ongoing appointments. Here, reformers noted that powerful officers needed independence to prevent legislative abuse and that only with elections would governors and judges be free from other branches. However, their arguments built on the assumption that independence, while essential, was insufficient. The individual officer must be a man of virtue. Furthermore, the disposition of the general populace influenced the kind of people who held office as well as the policies they enacted. For the reformers, appointing a few select officials would not ensure that officers were removed from popular factions and misconduct. If the people lacked the character to elect judges or governors, they were likewise incapable of electing legislators who would appoint other officials, which meant that the people were incapable of maintaining a republican form of government, a claim reformers knew no one was willing to make. Once again, advocates of reform saw far less means to silence mischievous sentiments.

The speech of Louisiana delegate Brent serves as a good example, for it contains many of these assumptions. Brent began his defense of popularly elected supreme court justices by referring to the foundational importance of relying on the good character of the people: "Any government . . . must have its foundations laid deep in the respect and affections of the people . . . [and must be] sustained by the stout hearts . . . of the people. . . . Laws may be framed . . . but cannot be executed and enforced, if passed in defiance of the public will." In a well-designed government, "there is no power . . . antagonistical to that of the people" (LA 1845, 744, 747). Here, Brent was suggesting that the people—not their high-minded leaders—lay at the foundation of government success. The rest of Brent's argument stressed the dual import of independence and good leadership, how one was useless without the other, and how good leadership arose as a result of the electorate's character. He agreed with his opponents that the judiciary was an important branch of government, requiring independence. Its job was "not only to decide disputes among citizens, but to keep other departments from shooting madly from the spheres allotted to them" (748). He explained why judges selected by the legislature or the executive would be dependent, corrupt, and of low caliber and why popular election would avoid these pitfalls. The people will select "a good judge," of "high and striking qualities" (751). Since "the great object is to obtain capable and honest judges," that is, "the best men upon the bench," election should be the preferable selection process (752). The character of judges influenced whether an independent bench could check abuses. For Brent, obtaining such men in office should be a constitution writer's primary aim. Since in his view the people had worthy character, elections were the best means.[12]

This argument surfaced in every state where delegates debated how to select nonlegislative officers. In many cases, advocates of popular election added another twist: if the people could elect legislatures, they could elect governors and judges. If they could not select good executive or judicial officers, how could they demonstrate any better judgment in the legislative department?

When explaining his support of the popular election of governors Porter explained, "The governor and the judges are but servants of the people, and the people are as capable of appointing their other servants as they are of appointing the governor" (LA 1845, 822). Stephen Hemstead, a Democratic lawyer from Iowa, explained why high-level state judges should be popularly elected. When a legislator, senator, or governor appoints officers, he acts as a proxy for the people. "If the people were capable of electing these proxies, they were capable of electing the officers themselves" (IA 1844, 103). For Federalist Judge William Van Ness, the argument against popularly elected justices of the peace "is founded on the supposition of the total corruption of the whole body of the people. . . . If that be the case, it is a matter of no moment who appoints or who are public officers" (NY 1821, 337–38). His case made good sense since restrictionists were proposing that legislators appoint these officers, the very legislators who were currently selected by that populace deemed too corrupt or incompetent to elect justices.

Like the opponents of increasing the number of elected officers, these delegates spoke as if no rights-protecting government could manage if leaders selected were power-hungry or exactly mirrored a corrupt public. As in other arguments in favor of electoral reform, these delegates went beyond the restrictionists. To reformers, describing the general public as incapable of guiding leaders in one branch was the same as proclaiming that the whole foundation of republican government was unstable. These delegates endorsed an important mechanistic feature of constitutional design: institutional independence. However, they explicitly outlined its conditional use: countering ambitious leaders in one branch required more than independence. It required that vigilant, virtuous individuals had power somewhere in the system.

By denying the people their right to select nonlegislative officials, one implied that these people were too stupid or too corrupt to choose lawmakers as well. To admit incompetence in one area was to admit the whole foundation of republican government unstable, for an unfit populace would select bad legislative officers, and these officers would appoint misguided officials in other branches. Underlying their arguments was the same assumption their adversaries had implied: the people's character determined who got elected. No rights-protecting government could long withstand the power-hungry leaders that a corrupted public might support or ignore. Such leaders spelled trouble; their ambitions would not be countered by their peers.

No matter what electoral reform issue was being debated, those favoring the expansion of popular influence might have made an alternative case. They might have argued that extension was safe precisely because state governments were designed with sufficient checks and balances to ameliorate the occasional negative influences brought by mass participation. Instead, expansionists usually rejected this proposition and attributed the successes of America's institutional provisions to the virtue of the people and the people alone. Why had state governments remained free from oppression? Advocates of greater popular empowerment contended that the character of ordinary citizens—both those with and those without formal government power—explained why Americans still enjoyed free government. The people's general respect and willingness to fight for the state, their ability to know good laws and follow them, their ability to recognize and choose high-quality officials whenever the opportunity arose, together explained the success of America's state republics. In this sense expansionists saw institutional provisions as even more conditionally useful than restrictionists did. Not only did expansionists deny that checks and balances could diminish the ill effects of self-interest and channel the excesses of ambition, they denied that these devices could filter out the negative features of certain wrongly motivated individuals by keeping them out of power. No procedural or institutional design brought success by empowering a selective part. Restricting the franchise or keeping certain officers appointive could never stop mischievous individuals from exercising their will and promoting destructive policies.

STATES VERSUS THE NATION: A LIBERAL FRACTURE

Despite all the talk about the instrumental necessity of virtue to protect rights, state constitution writers never directly asserted that procedure or institutional designs had no function in preserving free government. Almost no one wanted to dissolve the senate; only a few isolated delegates wondered about the additional security that came from this branch or attempted to disband it. Surprisingly few worried that abolishing executive councils would make governors dangerously independent (there was a short debate in Massachusetts whether to keep the executive council). Executive councils were abolished and senates remained. Most moves from an appointed to an elected governorship happened without a disruptive incident (only in Virginia was the proposal debated somewhat and even rejected at the last minute; it was not until 1851 that governors became popularly elected).

With each new constitution, the executive and judiciary both obtained more power and more independence than they previously had. Absolutely no one argued in favor of merging the responsibilities of the individual branches. The constitutions written and defended during the early nineteenth century and antebellum period explicitly declared "that the legislative, executive and judicial powers should be separate and distinct."[13] In these senses, delegates on both sides of the debate clearly recognized that institutional provisions such as frequent elections, representation, bicameralism, and separated branches had an important role to play in assuring the continuance of protected rights and free, limited government. Their position was not that these features were unnecessary, only that they were insufficient on their own.

Both sides found institutional arrangements conditionally useful only to the extent that "rights-minded" citizens supported them. The electoral process and separation of powers helped avoid government oppression if, and only if, leaders were dedicated to protecting rights and a trustworthy, well-intentioned citizenry stood behind them. Together leaders and citizens were responsible for the lack of factious uprising and bad policies. Good citizenship and responsible leadership—not the institutional channeling of ambition—countered the dangers of despotic quests for power and control. Institutional designs were a means to empower the virtuous. They were only successful in avoiding government tyranny to the extent they helped ensure that the unvirtuous masses lacked a powerful voice in government. Institutions had their place, but so did virtue. Institutions had no means to protect rights independently; it required the presence of virtue.

The question remains whether these views reflect affinities with the liberal tradition, whether the ideas underlying how constitutions should protect against rights abuse have meaningful roots in liberal ideology. On one hand they clearly do. No speaker claimed virtue had anything but instrumental value. Both sides recognized that the primary point of institutional designs was to help empower the virtuous and thereby maintain rights security and limited government. Representation and the regular popular election of lawmakers were necessary components of successful republican government. Bicameralism allowed one house to check the potential abuses of the other. Institutional independence further facilitated cross-departmental checks. To this extent, their views signal a basic liberal agreement among themselves and with their national forefathers.[14]

They did not, however, share *Publius*'s theory of how checks and balances managed problems of narrow interests and factious demands. Nineteenth-century designers rarely described institutional arrangements as powerful enough to overcome the potential negative effects of self-interested citizens. They rarely described these arrangements as clever means to have ambition counter ambition. Instead, their comments reinforced their position that good citizenship and virtuous leadership (by which they meant individual behavior that aimed toward the vigilant protection of rights) were not only instrumentally useful but absolutely necessary to the success of republican government. From this perspective their views represent a fracture in American liberalism, not a fracture among themselves but between them and the writers contributing to *Publius*, the best-remembered voice of their national forefathers.[15]

Human Nature and Good Citizenship

oth sides of the reform debate talked about the importance of a virtuous, intelligent, independent, rational, competent populace to guide the arm of government. They often used these words simultaneously and interchangeably to describe the qualities of good citizenship. The purpose of these applauded characteristics was to ensure the selection of good officers, who would then secure legislation that protected the lives, liberties, and possessions of all inhabitants. The instrumental role of good character is certainly consistent with a liberal framework but does not necessarily reflect an undisputed link. In addition to a strict instrumental value, a liberal conception of virtue differs from the virtues of, say, classical antiquity, civic republicanism, or Christianity in another way also.

Liberal virtues are thought to require less self-discipline, sacrifice, or inner struggle than other virtues do. Liberals anticipate that individuals will be private-minded and self-interested both in and out of government affairs, for this self-absorption supposedly constitutes natural behavior. Spokesmen from other traditions chastise such behavior as dangerous and hope that with conscious effort it can be overcome or at least carefully contained by moral legisation. Liberals accept this behavior and chastise government attempts to change it.[1] The question, then, is how did nineteenth-century delegates understand the relationship between natural behavior and the character that representative government required for its survival?

The dispute among nineteenth-century convention delegates went beyond the question of who could be trusted to defend the public good and the private rights of all and instead included profound questions about human nature and how it manifested itself in the political realm. Although not every speaker offered a detailed theory addressing these topics, nearly everyone who discussed them believed that government must take individuals as they are. In nearly all cases where good character was depicted, good citizens were described as just naturally behaving that way. Almost never did good character entail great personal sacrifice or sublimation of instincts. In many cases, convention speakers specifically noted that to try and transform people or to pretend that individuals would ignore their natural inclinations in questions of politics was a foolish mistake. In this sense, liberal values and beliefs clearly influenced the delegates' perspective on human nature and state building. At the same time, convention speakers differed among themselves regarding what was natural human behavior and what constituted sufficient citizen virtue upon which to build a government. Again, their differences generally followed political preferences.

On one hand, those who supported ongoing restrictions to the people's political power tied human nature and the characteristics of good citizenship with actions and motivations completely unpolitical. The good individual was one who quietly pursued economic prosperity through hard work and the accumulation of property. The mark of a good citizen was the successful accumulation of valuable possessions. In this view the public good was thought to spring from each individual's pursuit of private interests. In a general sense the restrictionist view resembled Adam Smith's metaphorical invisible hand, for in all cases opponents of reform spoke as if individuals, who pursued their narrow economic concerns within the limits of the law, could and would bring about the desired social outcome of protected rights. In many cases, however, arguments against electoral reform actually resembled Locke's, since many applauded property accumulation precisely because it led to economic prosperity and virtues associated with the work ethic and because it de facto convinced citizens that work—not government largess—brought success and independence.[2] In both instances, the resemblances do not necessarily show direct inspirational influence. They only illustrate the particular nature of their liberal affinities.

On the other hand, those supporting the extension of popular power usually dismissed any inexorable link between good citizenship and private interests and activities. Accumulated possessions were noteworthy, but they were neither a mark of distinction nor an indication of how an individual behaved in political affairs. Good citizens were still those individuals who were able to make political decisions by considering what was good for the state and its inhabitants, but, as reformers saw it, the rich and poor might equally rise to this standard. Both did, in fact, for the kind of social sentiment necessary for good citizenship was natural and characteristic of ordinary behavior.

This view resembles Scottish Enlightenment views about the natural origin of moral and social sentiments and about individuals as "naturally sympathetic." Adam Smith contended that "reason, principle, [and] conscience" inhabited "the breast, the man within, the great judge and arbiter of . . . conduct" (Smith 1982, 137). Social sentiments resulted from people's natural desire to dignify their own characters. For reformers as well, private interests might contribute to one's political inclinations, but those interests were driven by a public-mindedness, for example, a personal love of country. This reliance on natural sentiments also makes the reformers' views consistent with liberalism, albeit of a brand that differs from the restrictionists'. Thus, once again, amid general liberal agreements about certain characteristic features of the good state stood differing conceptions that constituted a decisive fracture in nineteenth-century American liberalism.

ON HUMAN NATURE, VIRTUE, AND GOOD CITIZENSHIP

Some delegates were quite explicit about what constituted human nature and to what extent citizens relied on their natural inclinations when making political decisions. Others merely alluded to images constructed by their colleagues. Many remained silent. Restrictionists largely described good citizenship in terms of how individuals behaved in their private, economic life. They were clear that well-designed government took men as they were, not as it hoped they would be. Expansionists largely described good citizenship politically, in terms of how individuals behaved toward their country. They were less explicit about the origin of this character.

Despite this difference, there remained an important and fundamental agreement. Neither side expected that any of the traits they applauded required a population of high-minded seekers of the noble life. Both sides sought to discover the minimum standard that both characterized human nature and nonetheless sufficiently avoided government oppression. Almost no one concluded that individuals would rise above nature and go beyond their natural inclinations. Instead, most delegates concluded that representative government could and should rely on the people's ordinary innate dispositions. In this sense, convention delegates on both sides of the electoral reform debate offered liberal theories of human nature and its relationship to the public sphere.

On the Private Nature of Citizen Behavior: Restrictionists' Views

In every state, if and when an antireformer detailed why an individual or group should or should not have additional influence in and over government, he referred back to that individual's or group's behavior in private life. The argument contained a set of recurrent themes: a person's behavior in economic matters indicated how he would act in political affairs. Everyone had the same personal interest: to enhance his economic prosperity. Everyone would seek to gain wealth by whatever means chance afforded him. This constituted human nature. Good citizens were those individuals who had shown themselves successful in accumulating personal and landed property in peaceful nonthreatening ways, by law and tradition. The rest could not be trusted with power, for they would seek prosperity through the ballot box. They would steal from the well-off through unfair taxation rather than prosper legitimately through the existing opportunities that America's foundational principles and practices afforded them.

Restrictionists most commonly explained that only those who had a personal stake in the common good could be expected to behave "appropriately" when deciding public issues. Only these individuals would do what was in the best interest of the state and therefore act virtuously. A number of assumptions underlay this position. First, proponents of this view usually admitted that the security of the land brought great benefits to the nation; it was the state's first and primary interest (see Chapter 3). To be virtuous, one must not only respect life and liberty, but also property. Second, proponents of this view usually suggested that it was human nature to be *narrowly* self-interested. This natural interest was less connected to desires for power and more connected to desires for property. A man with property had the great and narrow desire to forever protect his holdings. A man without property was mostly interested in acquiring some material possessions for himself, by the least costly means available, including stealing it from others when possible. (This closely resembles Hobbes's view of human nature.[3]) Third, proponents of this view contended that individuals could never be trusted to go beyond their narrow self-interests. Since the state nonetheless required virtue at its foundation, framers needed to figure out how to empower citizens who would work to preserve the common good.

The restrictionists' solution was rather straightforward: one finds good citizens wherever and whenever one finds a coincidental equation of personal and state interests. The state cannot create goodwill among its citizens. Therefore it seeks to empower those whose private wants and concerns are the same as the state's public wants and concerns. Those with a personal stake in the common good (namely, property holders) make good citizens. Man's self-interested nature could never be transformed. It was conducive to good citizenship only in select instances.[4]

At other times restrictionists tied good citizenship to a set of "private" virtues.[5] Certain kinds of activities, most especially the acquisition of property, required industry, frugality, hard work, and honesty. These acquired characteristics were the model characteristics of the good private man. How did these virtues lead individuals to be better voters and leaders? Sometimes restriction-ists did not say how, except to note that it benefited the state to encourage these virtues. Perhaps the implicit assumption was that "private" virtue was an inherent good.[6] Other times restrictionists did explain how and why the "pri-vate" virtues inadvertently led to protection of the state and the rights it aimed to protect. For these speakers, industrious, modest, frugal individuals were not ambitious or power-hungry. They could be trusted to use their political influ-ence wisely, since—rather than abuse government to gain power and wealth—they would use it to protect the features of government that had helped them procure the advantages they currently enjoyed. They would willingly protect rights, especially property rights.[7]

In some ways the two restrictionist arguments are tied closely to one an-other. In both cases it was a person's narrow economic interest to acquire prop-erty that motivated behavior. The results from the pursuit of this interest were outcomes in the state's interest. In both cases the good citizen needed neither public nor social awareness of his fellow citizens. He did not need to sacrifice his personal wants or desires in order to serve the public good. The two argu-ments differ in one fundamental respect: in one case self-interest was the neces-sary virtue; in the other case self-interest was the means to acquire the neces-sary moderating virtues.

At each of the conventions held in the 1820s, delegates in favor of restricting the people's power offered detailed accounts of their conceptions of how it was that certain individuals made good citizens and others did not. The 1821 New York convention serves as a good example. All ten delegates speaking to keep property as the basis of the franchise discussed the importance of character among the electorate. In all cases these men agreed that the appropriate char-acter was acquired indirectly, by simply living a private life and by not paying any particular attention to political affairs. Eight of the ten delegates described why they considered property owners the best guardians over government. They discussed both those "private" virtues, which owners obtained from working hard on the land, and the appropriately directed private interests, which all owners had precisely because they had a personal stake in the public good. Restrictionists contrasted this latter trait with the narrow interests of those without accumulated possessions. The poor had no stake in the existing system of rights and liberties; it was in their interest to ignore existing constitu-tional restrictions and plunder the rich.

The tone was set by Chancellor James Kent, one of the state's most notable judges and the first to speak against an extended franchise. He explained, "The great body of the people are now the owners and cultivators of the soil." In this group one finds "moderation, frugality, order, honesty and a due sense of independence, liberty and justice. . . . They are the safest guardians of property and the laws." Those without property "do not have the same inducement to care." In fact, "there is a tendency in the poor to covet and to share the plunder of the rich" (NY 1821, 221). Most of the others who supported Kent's policy preference echoed many of his very arguments. One of the many Federalist lawyers at the convention, Jacob Van Rensselaer explained, "The farmers and mechanics, who own portions of property procured by the practice of all the moral virtues, are uniformly and constantly bound to afford support and protection, in peace and in war, to your government" (360–61). Possessors of property "are moral in their habit, moderate in their desires, free from personal ambition, and a desire of political elevation" (363). In addition to their "private" virtues, property holders had a unique character. They had a stake in protecting a very important concern:

> Man has been and probably always will be subject to the same passions and feelings. It is . . . the providence of prudence and of wisdom . . . to exclude those from a participation in the political power of this government, who have nothing to lose by the enactment of bad laws, and who may feel . . . a desire to violate private rights for the gratification of their cupidity. (363)

As in these cases, the majority of delegates endorsing a white-only propertied franchise believed that the best citizens were property holders, both because they had acquired those "private" virtues that moderated ambition and because they had a personal interest in protecting property, the great common good of the state.

At this convention, delegates also discussed briefly whether to elect justices of the peace by popular election. The entire debate dealt indirectly with the question of popular competence, with those against expanding the number of popularly elected officials mostly fretting about party politics. They worried that these instruments of faction would control the elections and put into power narrow-minded, ambitious officials. In this context, Chancellor Kent explained:

> All unchecked democracies are better calculated for man as he ought to be, than for man as he is, and as he has always appeared to be in the faithful pages of history and as he is declared to be in the volume of divine inspiration. . . . I believe . . . that unless we remove the means of concentrating at the seat of government . . . the elements of faction and the struggles for office . . . our future career will be exceedingly tempestuous and corrupt. (319–20)

These points, together with the chancellor's other comments on the franchise, show that he obviously believed "man as he is" was narrowly self-interested in acquiring wealth and power and passionately willing to join with others to get what he wanted, by any means and without necessarily exercising reason. The chancellor wanted to restrain the political power of those with wrongly directed self-interests. By this point in the convention the extension of suffrage seemed assured; an appointed judiciary was simply another means to prevent such individuals from gaining dominant control.

The same general pattern existed at both the other conventions held in the 1820s. In Massachusetts six of the seven delegates speaking against universal male suffrage discussed the importance of empowering only those who could ensure the protection of rights against abuse. Five delegates explained what this character entailed, and in each case the speaker connected it to private interest, as their colleagues in New York had done. Three delegates took the position of Warren Dutton, a Boston lawyer, who applauded the present taxation requirement for voters because it encouraged people to work hard, acquire property, and thereby attain "private" virtue. The requirement made the vote "a distinction to be sought for; it was the reward of good conduct. It encouraged industry, economy and prudence" (MA 1820–1821, 247). Dutton intimated that individuals naturally sought a kind of public glory, namely, the distinction to vote, and that this (along with expected economic benefits) would motivate individuals to accumulate property and virtue. In recognizing that ambition could lead an individual to serve the public good, Dutton appears to be echoing a practical perspective associated with republican ideology. However, he hoped that the applauded ambition would lead to "private" virtue; the admirable human actions were those that aimed at personal gain, and only indirectly enhanced the public good. Good citizenship did not flow from a sacrificing love of one's country nor from an ambition to better the state as a means to better oneself.

A couple of Massachusetts delegates agreed with the case put forward by Federalist Josiah Quincy, a lawyer, politician, and scholar.[8] He made the case that present voting requirements gave political power to "men who would have a greater interest in promoting the general good. . . . To convene the right of voting to persons who are directly interested in the protection of rights of property as well as of life and liberty was the most probable mode of securing the enactment of just, equal and useful laws" (MA 1820–1821, 254). Here the implication was that only the propertied could be trusted, for only they had a personal interest in procuring the public good. Whether protection by the propertied resulted from their virtue or interest, the character applauded was a private character, motivated by a desire to accumulate wealth. This private character was thought to bring indirect public benefit. None here purported that constitution writers or structural government designs could transform individuals into publicly minded citizens. Security resulted from the ordinary, natural behavior of economically successful individuals.

At this Massachusetts convention delegates spent more time discussing the basis of representation than the franchise. Those arguing in favor of a tax basis explained that if property were to be secure it must be guarded by its owners, the taxed. Most simply contended that, if individuals without significant holdings gained majority power in both houses, they would heavily tax those who did. They would then use these tax dollars strictly to benefit themselves. Their arguments contained no direct analysis of what constituted good citizenship; yet speakers indirectly equated self-interest with natural behavior in the public realm. When making public decisions, the propertyless were expected to tax and spend in recklessly self-serving ways; that is, they were expected to plunder owners and to fund unnecessary and expensive projects. Of the many speeches put forward against reform, the speech of John Adams, one of the architects of the state's first constitution, captured many of the main points repeatedly mentioned by others. Adams explained that it was always important to ask

> how the property-holding part of the community may be sustained against the inroads of poverty and vice. Poverty leads to temptation and temptation often leads to vice, and vice to military despotism. . . . The hardy yeoman . . . in the preservation of property and virtue . . . has the deepest and most permanent interest. (MA 1820–1821, 286)

Adams also made the case that property came from "toil and diligence of a long life of enterprise and industry" (286). In other words, constitution writers had another reason to trust property holders; their accumulations had come from previously cultivated "private" virtues. As Adams himself noted, giving majority power to taxpayers did not permanently disenfranchise anyone. Instead it served to encourage everyone to obtain property and therefore exercise virtue.[9]

In all cases restrictionists spoke about personal interests and "private" virtues as the bases of good citizenship. Their views were more sketchy than those of New Yorkers, but here too, no restrictionist supposed that ordinary individuals would address political issues with a disinterested public outlook. By nature, people were concerned with their own economic gain. The propertied classes could be trusted because their personal gains benefited everyone and because they had a great interest in maintaining secured rights and liberties. On the other hand, those with no material possessions could not be trusted; they would plunder the goods of honest, hard-working citizens.

At the 1829–1830 Virginia convention, supporters of a freehold suffrage and a property-based representation system put forward the same arguments found in New York and Massachusetts. Here, because the state's declaration of rights specifically stated that all who demonstrated attachment to and permanent common interest with the community may vote, attachment became the synonym for good citizenship. Debates here centered on questions of who had that attachment and why. Six of the seven delegates wanting to keep the franchise with landholders connected the behavior of good citizens to actions in the private realm. No delegate favoring a property basis elaborated on the "private" virtues of property holders, but every single speaker elaborated on the innate relationships between self-interest, human nature, and rights security.

The only difference between debates in this state and debates in the other two was that many of Virginia's delegates who opposed a voter population basis for legislative districting explicitly denied that the interest foundation for security they endorsed had anything to do with virtue. Constitutional makers must rely on appropriately directed private interest. Richard Morris explained that people of the east are told "we must rely on the morality, on the integrity and the virtue of the majority as a sufficient guarantee." While he believed "the people west of the Ridge are [as] . . . moral [as] . . . those to the east of it," he was adamant that

> the principle on which all free Governments rest is not confidence but jealousy and watchfulness. . . . Men vote taxes with much less caution and care when they do not expect themselves to pay any part of the tax than when they are personally interested in its effects and responsibility to those who must pay. (VA 1829–1830, 113)

Here again we find the same underlying assumption: personal interest naturally motivated human behavior in private and public matters. People could not be made to love the common good for its own sake; they would act in its behalf only when it coincidentally concurred with their interest. From the perspective of this speaker, as well as from that of most other Virginia restrictionists who endorsed property's ongoing disproportionate influence in the legislature, interest was not virtue. Virtue entailed selfless attachment to the good of the country; it was neither a natural nor a reliable sentiment.

Although most restrictionists who conceded that all Virginians might be honest and virtuous used thoughtful phrases like Morris's, there was something condescending and contradictory in their concession. Inhabitants of the western part of Virginia were virtuous, but they could not be trusted to protect rights. Why? One possibility was that virtue itself was not the ability to pursue the common good, for if it were, then clearly virtuous West Virginians would pursue the good of the state. Another possibility was that interest would always trump virtue, meaning that the West Virginians were really not so virtuous after all, for they were deemed incapable of rising above interests in pursuit of a greater good.[10] In both cases civic virtue in the traditional sense was a meaningless concept for understanding how a popularly elected government protected rights. The only dependable sentiment was interest, and interest was not virtue, period.

Another characteristic of good citizenship—mentioned at each of these three conventions, but not again—was independence. With this argument restrictionists did not exactly equate private behavior with good citizenship. Perhaps independence deserves its own "category," for embedded in calls for independence was the assumption that good citizenship came from freedom of thought, not from a principled or interested love of rights and freedoms. Chancellor Kent of New York argued, "Every man should be excluded who has not the *capacity* to give an impartial and independent suffrage, or who was habitually and necessarily influenced by other men" (NY 1821, 273). His argument seemed to have nothing to do with narrow private activities and interests, but in fact it did.

Chancellor Kent, and every restrictionist who talked about the importance of independence, tied freedom of thought to *economic* self-reliance. Independence could not be gained from enlightenment. An individual always had an interest in following the views of those he depended on for his livelihood. One's private economic life determined how independently one behaved in questions of politics. Almost every delegate who discussed the importance of independence also considered interests or "private" virtue as defining attributes of good citizenship. In Virginia, for example, everyone who mentioned the importance of financial independence did so to supplement a more general connection between good citizenship and success in one's private life. In Massachusetts only Josiah Quincy of Boston insisted on the importance of economic independence, but he also discussed virtue in terms of a personal interest in the public good (MA 1820–1821, 251–52).[11]

At later conventions delegates against reform justified their positions by complimenting the good nature of the empowered and admonishing the vices of those who were currently deprived of influential political voice in the selection of various leaders. However (except in Virginia), there was far less "evidence" of what restrictionists meant by good citizenship. The only obvious factor was that the character they expected was not the result of selfless denial of one's interests. The character anticipated was consistent with the person's innate nature.

At the 1850–1851 Ohio convention two speakers against black enfranchisement briefly noted that these individuals lacked the appropriate character to vote and that empowering Americans of African descent would bring "harm" to the state. Neither explained the great faults of this group; both speakers mentioned competence in passing, almost as an afterthought. At other conventions where the issue of black enfranchisement was discussed, delegates raised the question of competence, but (as in Ohio) their discussions lacked the detailed explanations present at earlier debates. At the 1835 North Carolina convention one finds similarly general complaints among two-thirds of the restrictionists. Delegates there explained that Americans of African descent were, in the words of Mr. Bryan, a "miserable and worthless population" (NC 1835, 68), or in the words of Louis Wilson, they "had not the requisite intelligence or integrity" (80).

For these restrictionists, the issue remained competence, that is, the perceived inability of Americans of African descent to make judicious electoral decisions. But what these men thought constituted the basis of good citizenship or the origin of black incompetence was left unclear. At the 1846 New York convention, half the delegates against black enfranchisement alluded to the faulty character of African Americans. Yet none gave more detail than lawyer John Russell who charged, "The Almighty had created blacks inferior to whites" and that only whites were "capable of self government" (NY 1846, 777).

In all cases the probable underlying issue was restrictionists' disbelief in racial equality. For most advocates of restriction, blacks were different: they had second-class-citizenship status and were innately inferior to whites. Although it was not always explicit, restrictionists probably endorsed these differences because they considered blacks to be naturally lacking in the capacity to rise above temptation and exercise reason. Contextual evidence in the debates themselves cannot verify this interpretation definitively, but discussions over other issues strongly suggest it. Some clergy made this case to support the lowly fate of blacks. In other contexts, state-level spokesmen emphasized their irrationality. Debates over why the nation should not liberate slaves included arguments such as Fitzhugh's that blacks were like dependent irrational children. Although many of these arguments use liberal assumptions about the importance of rationality for political inclusion, the views underlying them—that is, a priori denials that certain races are rational—are probably best understood as illiberal and therefore a signal that other intellectual traditions beside liberalism influenced nineteenth-century state builders.[12] Nonetheless, these views are consistent with the view that human nature, whatever it may be, is immutable, and government must accept it as is.

At these later conventions, delegates debating whether to subject nonlegislative officials to popular election rarely offered detailed descriptions of what constituted necessary good citizenship. This was partly because of the position they took. Delegates were explaining why people should *not* be politically active; they were not explaining what characteristics would be necessary for people to participate. Some delegates against the popular election of governors and judges did offer views about human nature and the origin of good character, but they generally expressed their views indirectly, voicing worries about party passions predominating over individual rationality and about officers becoming like monarchs.

Although these delegates were rarely as explicit and detailed as Chancellor Kent in his speech against the popular election of justices of the peace, his position is worth quoting at length. He began his discussion on party by noting that "The *spirit of party* in popular government is . . . truly the [people's] worst enemy." He then explained the mischiefs and negative effects of party rule. When parties controlled public affairs, the people experienced

> The alternate dominion of *one faction* over another, sharpened by the spirit of revenge, natural to party dissention, which . . . is itself a frightful despotism. . . . The disorders which result . . . incline the minds of men to seek security and repose in the absolute power of an individual; and sooner or later, the chief of some prevailing faction . . . turns this disposition to the purposes of his own elevation on the ruins of public liberty. . . . [These are] the common and continual mischiefs of the *spirit of party* [which] are sufficient to make it the interest and duty of a wise people to discourage and restrain it. (NY 1821, 320)

This negative characterization of party governance had been with American state builders since independence. In early debates over the constitutionality of the U.S. Bank, three of America's greatest leaders worried about parties and monarchy, tying the two issues together. Jefferson accused Hamilton of being a friend of monarchy; Madison decried the Federalist party as allies of hereditary rule; Hamilton described Jefferson and Madison as heads of a faction, hostile to and subversive of the principles of good government.[13] Chancellor Kent claimed his views were taken directly from Hamilton.

By the mid–nineteenth century, party politics was well established in America, yet convention rhetoric suggests that Americans still saw political parties as organized factions, as the new and powerful instrument of passionate, narrow, potentially rights-violating legislation, as able to facilitate the rise of a charismatic dictator. Parties enabled the people to join together, en masse. With parties people ignored rational considerations and merely supported their party's candidate and policies. Party representatives were seen as supporters of the party's interests, not the state's. Party candidates, in pursuit of reelection, would forever remain party puppets.[14] Such depictions implicitly questioned the people's character. The depictions implicitly supposed that individuals naturally formed factious groups and then misdirected officers. They assumed that with little encouragement people would forfeit reasoning and remain part of the

fray. Many delegates argued against the direct selection of nonlegislative officers on the grounds that it would promote blind party voting and therefore bad
government; it seems likely they shared many of these prevalent views.

At the 1850–1851 Virginia convention, a few restrictionists discussing issues
related to popular influence over government made references to the capricious
nature of a government relying on abstract selfless love of the common good. A
third of those speaking against the indefinite reelection of governors depicted
the expansionists as implying that the people were infallible, a view they found
absurd. Robert Scott, a lawyer then serving in the house of delegates, contended that unrestricted reeligibility would be possible only

> if we were to regard men as perfect and exempt from those frailties which neces-
> sarily connect themselves to human nature. But looking at this as he is, it is neces-
> sary that some restraints should be imposed . . . for the purpose of checking the
> passions . . . [and] regulating and controlling [a person's] otherwise uncontrollable
> actions. . . . If men were angels and perfect in character, then I would be willing to
> say "give them all power". . . . But so long as we are to regard men as men, the
> creature of passion, avarice and ambition . . . it is necessary that such checks
> should be placed on his action to prevent . . . in all that abuse of power. (VA
> 1850–1851, 177)

As in most speeches on the issue of electing governors and judges, Scott did not
discuss directly what interests would serve the state. He made it clear, however,
that there were no public selfless sentiments driving citizen behavior. People
naturally, passionately, pursued their personal ambitions.

The only time after 1830 that antireform delegates both discussed the importance of competence and carefully explained the qualities necessary for good
governing was in Virginia's debates over the basis of representation. There,
every restrictionist who insisted that government must retain majority power in
the eastern part of the state explained that this design empowered people of the
appropriate character. They explained human nature and good citizenship in
narrow terms of interest. Robert Scott explained:

> Reason, justice and equity never had weight enough . . . to govern the councils of
> men. It is interest alone which does it, and it is interest alone which can be
> trusted. . . . In public and private affairs we secure, if possible, the services of
> agents whose interests incline them to be faithful. . . . Interest is the mainspring of
> action. . . . It is a great moral law. . . . if, in the organization of government, we
> discard all consideration of this great influence, we lose sight of the very principle
> itself out of which the system springs. (VA 1850–1851, 342)

Again, it was human nature to follow one's personal interests. Good constitutional designers recognized this and therefore empowered only appropriately directed interests.

For nearly every electoral issue discussed, the question of competency remained at the core of the restrictionists' position. Opponents of reform maintained that the good state first and foremost protected personal rights. Self-government was the means of protection. In order to ensure that the means achieved its end, designers necessarily had to take competence into account. Whenever they explained the origin of this competence and what this implied for constitutional design, antireformers had the same explanations: savvy planners examined man as he was, not as they hoped he might be. They set up government not to change the natural character of man but to utilize his best features. At early conventions restrictionists were explicit: the people's sovereignty would have to be limited according to known theories of human nature, that is, with the knowledge that all men were narrowly self-interested and would rely on personal interests alone when making political decisions. Even though at later conventions restrictionists did not usually explain what constituted human nature and the kind of individuals that made good citizens, there is no evidence that a different perspective informed these antebellum state builders. Even later, restrictionists never contended that ordinary citizens could be trusted to rise above their natural sentiments. Moreover, on the rare occasions that they described natural sentiments or expected citizen behavior, they most commonly spoke of each in terms of a narrow self-interested pursuit, a disinterest in politics, and an obsession with economic prosperity.

Restriction advocates argued that all individual actions were driven by the same instincts: people naturally followed their own personal desires and economic interests, with the most forceful drive being avarice. To ensure good government, those with political influence needed personal interests that led them to behave in de facto virtuous ways. This meant that wise delegates sponsored laws and a social order that accepted human nature as it was and merely granted participatory privileges on a selected basis. These views share little with the principles of classical or renaissance republicanism. Moreover, with the exception of their views on black enfranchisement, restrictionist arguments did not depend on the innate superiority of property holders and taxpayers. The distinctions emphasized were ones that could be acquired by the individual himself, without ever veering from his personal concerns. The idea that wise statesmen should accept naturally avaricious tendencies as inevitable and potentially beneficial, that statesmen should nourish and empower these sentiments, is a distinctly liberal assumption; it is at the foundation of Hobbes's and Locke's liberalism as well as of modern economic liberalism. Furthermore, the idea that the character developed by hard work and industry is an important component to good citizenship—a kind of virtue—is yet another defining aspect of early modern liberalism. Although this view shares Protestant roots, it is also an integral part of Locke's theory of property and good government.[15] In short, much of the exclusionary language of nineteenth-century America shares affinities with the language of early liberalism.

Private Character and Public Consciousness: Expansionists' Views

Calls for expansion, on the other hand, did not have the issue of competence at their core. Advocates of greater popular empowerment emphasized the people's good character in order to explain why expansion would be safe, not in order to explain why more popular influence was necessary. Expansionists first and foremost argued to increase popular control because it was an inherent right and freedom, which every individual (man) deserved. Republican government required popular sovereignty, and widespread equal power was the only and best practical application of this ideal. Nonetheless, most reform delegates made passing references to the competence of the people they wished to empower. They responded to the detailed theories that the restrictionists laid before them. One therefore finds various theories of human nature and good citizenship among arguments favoring expansion.

Expansionists usually sought to disconnect citizenship from private activities and pursuits. They did this in one of two ways. Sometimes they emphasized the importance of loving one's country and of being willing to fight to defend its principles. In this case advocates of reform usually noted that patriotism was a natural sentiment, born with the individual or readily acquired from living in our free nation. It was thus in an individual's nature to love the land he inhabited, especially a land that had given him freedom and economic opportunity.

At other times, expansionists conceded that good citizenship did require an interest in the community. But they adamantly disconnected this interest sentiment from a notion of self-interest, narrowly understood. In their view almost everyone could differentiate between what was good for the country and what was good for himself. Americans recognized that actions of the former kind were in their interest, broadly understood. Citizens recognized that unearned economic gains—that is, material good taken from others through heavy taxation and the like—was really not in their best interest. Here, the implication was that it was natural for individuals to consider their interests, but an interest in the country's well-being was as strong a drive as personal material gain. Furthermore, in questions dealing with politics, the two interest motivations were not in conflict, for then the country primarily mattered. In both cases, expansionists proclaimed that people would protect all rights and freedoms, including those that did not personally bring them direct, monetary gain. Behaving appropriately in the public sphere was considered a natural inclination.

In Virginia where the constitution explicitly mentioned the importance of common interests and attachments, expansionists agreed that the necessary qualification for good citizenship was an interest in protecting the essential rights and freedoms that all Americans ought freely and securely to enjoy. However, they disagreed with the restrictionists' interpretation that an interest in this general concern could arise only when the citizen had a narrow personal interest in the public good. Interest in the state did not necessarily translate into a personal stake in property.

At the 1829–1830 Virginia convention nine of the delegates in favor of extending the franchise talked about the need for virtue or for an interest in the common good. Those who discussed "interests" as the motivator for citizen activity specifically separated this notion from narrowly construed selfish desires, contending that patriotic sentiments held individuals to the interest of their country. Eugenius Wilson, for example, thought that equating property with good citizenship required assuming "that a man cannot love a country or take an interest in its good government unless he owns a portion of its soil" (VA 1829–1830, 351). Wilson strongly disagreed with this assumption. He countered by noting that in Virginia all the people were "intelligent, virtuous and patriotic"; that is why we have a "free representative Republic, wherein the administrators of public affairs are the agents of the people, and chosen by those people who have . . . a free will, a matured intellect and an interest and attachment to the community" (351). He found every citizen virtuous, intelligent, and patriotic. Every citizen could be trusted to protect against government corruption—in part because everyone cared about the great ends of government, that is, life, liberty, property, and security. Individuals cared for these things even when it was not in their direct self-interest to do so:

> The object of all good Government is to protect the citizen in the enjoyment not only of his property, but also of his life, his personal liberty, his limbs, his character, the freedom of speech and action and the pursuit of happiness. . . . In all these, the rich and poor stand on a level—they are equally valuable to both. . . . The rich and poor have equal virtue. . . . the poor man must, and does take as great an interest in the good government of the country as the rich man. (352)

Nearly every expansionist who followed Wilson also disentangled narrow personal interests from human nature, especially from one's natural behavior in questions of politics. Lucas Thompson was explicit in denouncing the restrictionist conception of good character: "In the opinion of some Gentlemen, Government has no principles. The idea of patriotism and virtue even are exploded and self-love and self-interest are the only springs of human action. . . . Against this, I solemnly protest" (VA 1829–1830, 411). Thompson characterized his adversaries as saying "that inherent love of distinction in man, that overwhelming self-love, and that . . . spirit which induces a frail man to plume himself on the infirmities of his fellow-man" controls how citizens behave in political matters. Again, he strongly disagreed (411). He believed that patriotism was the true test of interest. And since "no man contends that the land is a test of patriotism," land should not be the test for voting. Instead, "Every man is more or less a patriot if patriotism means love of country. . . . The love of country is formed in the heart of man in childhood, in youth, and does not grow out of self-love and self-interest of mature years." Therefore, all taxpayers deserved the vote (415).[16] In short, many who wanted to extend suffrage denied the connection between good citizenship and self-interest, at least self-interest narrowly understood as a personal interest in one's own economic prosperity.

Discussions among advocates of a voter population basis for representation also contained these same general arguments. Expansionists here once again tied citizenship to public patriotic sentiments and general interests in the nation as a whole. They denied that voters would seek to further their narrow private interests and act to further their prosperity in any possible way, including through the ballot box. Of the thirteen Virginia delegates speaking in favor of using population as the basis of representation, four simply mentioned that the republic required "virtue and intelligence" and would falter if the people were "vicious and corrupt." But seven others who spoke about the importance of good character attempted to detail the difference between narrow interests and the virtues necessary for exercising political power appropriately. A good example of this kind of argument can be seen in the vision of human nature put forward by Democrat John Rogers Cooke, one of the leaders of the western reform movement:

> Man, though sometimes driven by stormy passions to the commission of atrocious crimes, is by nature and habit neither a wolf nor a tiger. . . . He is an *affectionate*, a *social*, a *patriotic*, a *conscientious*, and a *religious* creature. . . . [Man has] *love of country or patriotism*, designing that he should obtain to happiness through the practice of virtue. (VA 1829–1830, 59–60)

Mr. Cooke mocked the claim of his adversaries, because they asked delegates to forget this true human nature. Restrictionists contended that men did not care about future rewards and punishment and that "love of property is the great engrossing passion which swallows up all other passions, and feelings, and principles . . . in all men." Cooke found this "a doctrine monstrous, hateful and incredible!" (60).[17] Private individuals were not so acquisitive or robberlike as the restrictionists contended. Although everyone might be governed by something called interest, it was in each individual's interest to be a "Virginian," not merely an individual owning or wanting property.

In Massachusetts delegates favoring universal suffrage and a population-based representation system mostly avoided the issue of popular competence. Four of the eight speaking in favor of an extended franchise made at least a passing reference to its importance; two of these offered an assessment of human behavior in politics that corresponded to that of their contemporaries in other states, connecting good character with regard for country, not property. Avid abolitionist and Republican lawyer James Austin, for example, argued that "Regard for country . . . did not depend on property, but upon institutions, laws, habits and association" (MA 1820–1821, 252). For him, ownership of real and landed property served as no good indicator of how well individuals would behave politically. A minimum patriotic sentiment was all that was necessary among voters. Everyone living in a well-ordered society had this sentiment. The implication here might be that government design might affect character and improve a person's behavior as citizen. In this sense, perhaps his views suggest republican influence.

Of the three Massachusetts delegates who spoke in favor of a voter population basis for representation in both houses, only one delegate gave any indication of what he considered the appropriate character for those with power. This was Democratic-Republican Henry Childs, who began his speech by explaining: "government was founded on intelligence and morality" (MA 1820–1821, 295) and ended it by noting that the propertied did not have a monopoly on virtue (296). His few words suggest that he too did not think individuals acted only as their narrow, economic interests dictated.

Expansionists at the 1821 New York convention offered a distinct vision of what constituted human nature and good citizenship. Whereas all opposition to an expanded suffrage connected good character with narrow private pursuits, no expansion delegate made a parallel claim. None contended that taxpayers, military men, and highway workers should be given the right to vote because they had a personal stake in the rights and liberties that were protected by the state. For them the important qualification for participating in government was a heartfelt, political sentiment—which arose because individuals contributed to the state by their employment and which was rightfully termed a patriotic love of country. All who lived on American soil could be trusted with political voice, because in political matters citizens did not consult their private situation; they naturally looked to the country as a whole. Six of the expansionist speeches on record resembled merchant Jacob Radcliff's, who merely mentioned that, because "the people of this country, above all others, were intelligent and virtuous," there was little to fear from expanding the voter population (NY 1821, 281).

He (and five others) explained neither why the people were virtuous nor what that character entailed, but the other five delegates who discussed the matter outright rejected the interest connection and declared the people's patriotic sentiment as the one important factor in good citizenship. When General Erastus Root, a Democratic-Republican state senator who later became a member of the Whig party, first spoke in favor of electoral expansion, he devoted his entire speech to severing the connections restrictionists wanted to make between money, interests, and political behavior. Root refuted the idea that a "manufacturer [will] . . . control the votes of the hundred men he employs." Employees do not necessarily vote as their employer counsels. He also denied that "the landed classes have any more interest or occasion to protect rights," including property rights (NY 1821, 223). Root also applauded the character of some of the disenfranchised. He depicted men in the military as "young men whose patriotic bosoms burn[ed] with a love of country. . . . They will vote for the good of their country." They are "friends of order and of law" (360). Here again, good citizenship was tied to qualities of the heart, not to economic prosperity. A personal stake in the economic well-being of the country was not the deciding factor whether people would serve the state well. An abstract, general love for one's country and its laws was the force behind people's political decisions.

At most of the later conventions, speeches favoring expansion did not contain as many elaborate descriptions of what constituted good citizenship. Delegates still insisted that popular character mattered, and that institutional checks on governmental abuse would not work in its absence, but these speakers no longer carefully explained what kind of political behavior was to be expected among a sovereign people. In debates in Ohio over the basis of representation, only one speaker, Simeon Nash, who preferred a representation system based on the general population, offered the beginning of a definition of citizenship. He explained that, although most regard "self interest . . . as the interest which . . . govern[s]," in fact this was the basis of corruption. "It is the duty of every man who has any regard for the obligations of conscience to discharge his duty so that he may not lead his neighbors into temptation" (OH 1850–1851, 135). Nash obviously denied that good citizenship would spring from purely self-interested motivations and behavior, but unlike most of his cohorts elsewhere, he apparently believed that the good citizen had to rise to meet his political duties.[18]

In later debates over the political status of freemen of African descent the question was never whether to grant them unconditional suffrage but, rather, whether to enfranchise those holding property or to outlaw the privilege completely. Unlike restrictionists who merely declared blacks "incompetent," expansionists wanted to enfranchise some of these individuals and therefore occasionally offered explanations as to when and why blacks had the capacity to rule. Since expansionists were arguing to empower blacks with property, they were free to emphasize the connections between "private" virtues and the smooth operation of government. At the 1846 New York convention, physician William Taylor advocated the continuation of the state's policy of enfranchising property-holding blacks because the requirement encouraged blacks to be "industrious and of good morals" (NY 1846, 777). He applauded such encouragement. The same argument was made in North Carolina and Ohio, but it appeared unconvincing since in both these states freemen of color lost the voting privilege.[19]

In 1850–1851, debates in Virginia over the basis of representation resembled debates that had taken place there twenty years earlier. Speakers in favor of expansion relied mostly on principles, but in response to the restrictionists they also offered detailed comments on the nature and importance of popular competence. Waitman Willey, a leading Whig in the western part of the state typified the views there offered. He began his speech by asking a series of questions, which intimated his denial that citizens were strictly and narrowly interested in their personal life and individual economic prosperity.[20] "Does the mere fact that a man possess a great amount of goods . . . necessarily qualify him . . . for a faithful and efficient discharge of the duties of a good citizen? Is property the source of patriotism? Is love of country . . . love of money?" Willey found such pretensions "abhorrent," for they were "downright presumpt[uous], wrong in principle . . . and anti-republican in nature" (VA 1850–1851, 333). Instead, Willey believed that West Virginia could be trusted with power. Why? Because they "are at least as virtuous, patriotic and trustworthy as the people of East Virginia" (334). All Virginians were interested in the welfare of the community. "A person may possess the property of a freehold without the attachment. . . . the landed and the tenant may have, as far as law or reason can determine, the same permanency of interest" (335). Again, his speech—like so many of those preceding—contained the common litany of expansionist responses. Citizenship was a political activity, and when engaged in political activities individuals did not rely on those narrow personal interests that inspired their economic behavior and private activities. Moreover, to the extent that voters consulted their interests when making political decisions, they consulted their *general* interests, interests they shared with others.

Most often, delegates favoring electoral reform simply sought to refute the restrictionists' claim. They detached narrow, personal concerns from the more broad, public job of governing. As Mr. Hoge put it, "[l]ove of country . . . does not . . . grow out of self love" (VA 1850–1851, 174), or as Mr. Campbell put it, "[c]ommon interest with and attachment to the community" does not come from being a freeholder (VA 1829–1830, 385). While good citizenship did not arise from following one's strong drive to benefit oneself, it did not require a sacrifice or struggle either. Most delegates hinted that the necessary level of disinterestedness was implanted on the heart; it glowed in the bosom and was the only guide available. Usually, it was patriotic love of one's country—a simple sentiment, felt by all. Sometimes it was understood in terms of interests, but then always general interests, interests in the welfare of the community of which citizens were a part.

In any case, either explicit or implicit, it seems expansionists believed that, when it came to political decision making, individuals could easily sublimate their personal desires. Citizens could refrain from putting their narrow self-interests into public policy. Americans naturally behaved patriotically, with the state's concerns at heart. Being a good citizen—that is, interested in protecting everyone's rights and liberties and desirous of limiting government power—was an act natural enough that most people rose easily to the occasion.

The ideological influences on advocates of expansion are less obvious than they were for their adversaries. Their primary case for expansion did not rest on demonstrable mass competence. Nonetheless, advocates of extending the people's political power (especially for white males) openly agreed with their adversaries that successful government depended on voters willing and able to protect people's rights from government abuse. Although some advocates of expansion elaborated upon the character or origin of this necessary good citizenship, describing it as a universal sentiment of the heart and easily acquired by anyone, many remained silent or vague on the source of this important social sentiment. The most consistent view offered was reactive and negative, that is, that love of country and allegiance to its principles had no relation to the wealth or material holdings of specific individuals.

Thus, expansionist language regarding the relationship between human nature and the traits of good citizenship has ambiguous roots. Repudiating narrow economic interests and applauding patriotism and civic virtue are features of the language of republicanism.[21] At the same time, reformers contended openly that every American—at least every potential voter—had the innate capacity to be a good patriotic citizen. Everyone naturally cared about the rights and privileges of his fellow citizens. In no case did expansionists discuss the need for individuals to rise above nature and go beyond their natural inclinations. Good citizens need not pursue the high-minded, noble life.

These views did have the stamp of approval among some of the expansionists' predecessors, that is, they resemble those attributed to James Wilson, one of the nation's constitution writers. Although his views did not win out in 1787, it seems they carried policy consequence in the decades that followed. Moreover (at least in a general sense), the case for the expanded power was also liberal at its core. However, to the extent that expansionists' supporting arguments resembled the ideas of prominent liberal theorists, they resembled those associated with the Scottish Enlightenment.[22]

LIBERAL IDEOLOGY AND HUMAN NATURE

Not all delegates described what they believed constituted human nature and good citizenship; but when they did, their responses followed distinct patterns. Those against expanding the suffrage and taking away property's disproportional influence in legislative districts contended that what it took to be a good citizen was acquired in private life. Government received "public" use from one's private concerns and aspirations. Those favoring an expanded suffrage and a representation system approximating one man/one vote mostly contended that good citizens recognized the public nature of their job; therefore good designers need not look to an individual's personal situation when determining whether that individual would be a good protectorate of inalienable rights and freedoms. Although neither side always specifically called good citizenship virtue, and although some (like Virginia restrictionists) denied any equation between the two concepts, both sides understood them similarly. Good citizens, like virtuous individuals, were those who acted in ways that were beneficial to the common good, namely, in ways that protected the state's commitment to life, liberty, and property. True to liberal interpretations of virtue, both sides agreed that good citizenship did not require much sacrifice or self-restraint. They agreed that constitution writers could not design governments which attempted to transform individuals or relied on noble pursuits.

Electoral debate disagreements regarding the characteristics of human nature and the basis of "virtuous" citizenship reflected differences within a liberal perspective; they did not signify the ongoing influence of competing ideological traditions.[23] Those in favor of restriction offered arguments similar to those fleshed out by Locke, in his writings about prosperity and property accumulation. Individuals who *privately* sought their own economic gains would also enhance the public good, because their actions required "private" virtues, because they would seek a government limited to one aim: the protection of rights, especially property rights. These individuals would not look to government as the answer to their problems. In this, the adversaries of reform were putting forward conceptions of virtue that were distinctively liberal and in many ways similar to those of their prominent, national forefathers.

In some ways their views also resemble Adam Smith's notion of the invisible hand. Like Smith, restrictionists contended that individuals, acting in their own economic interest and seeking private material gains, inadvertently benefited the common good. Like Smith, restrictionists contended that these beneficial acts occurred without any personal sacrifice in the name of a higher public good, and without state intervention in or control over human behavior. At the same time, neither of these restrictionist constructions exactly fits Smith's theory of societal equilibrium. In one case individuals contributed to the common good only if their private activities elevated their character and only if their actions cultivated the "private" virtues. In the other case individuals contributed to the common good only if they had a personal stake in it; they were depicted as being so self-interested they looked more like individuals in Hobbes's state of nature than civilized citizens. In any event, both arguments rested on the assumption that some economic pursuits harmed the common, public good. Working in factories, serving in the military, or raising cattle would have been beneficial private pursuits according to Smith, but according to advocates of limited popular influence, none contributed to the common good.

Like their adversaries, expansionists appeared not to expect any high-minded noble character from Americans. In this sense their views about virtue are uniquely liberal as well. However, parallels—especially ones to specific individuals—are less obvious and precise. In some sense, the views of expansionists resemble the late eighteenth-century Scottish Enlightenment perspective that social and moral sentiments are as natural as personal and economic ones. Certainly the reformists believed that people were naturally inclined to overlook their narrow economic interests when decisions of social or political ramification were at stake. For some, these natural inclinations arose from a type of interest, that is, because citizens were members of a country that had benefited them over the years. For others, good citizenship was tied to patriotic sentiments, grounded in a natural desire to protect the land they loved. In both cases, individuals' social nature was driven by inner instincts.

In sum, the two sides of the electoral reform debate looked to different theories of what constitutes natural behavior in politics. For one side it was narrow self-interest; for the other side it was social sentiments. What should one make of their differences? For one, they suggest that in antebellum America there were two conceptions of human nature, one private, one public. Since both sides equated virtue and appropriate political behavior with natural human behavior, this also means there were two conceptions of the good citizen, one private, one public. Some delegates were able to devise a vision of the state wherein individuals were not involved in political activities merely to benefit themselves, their narrow rights and concerns. Instead, the liberal state became a public one, in which individuals had civic responsibilities toward their fellow citizens.

The similarities and differences characterizing nineteenth-century views regarding human nature, virtue, and institutional design also give insights into the consequences of frequent constitutional reform. Despite the repeated reevaluation of foundational law taking place during this period, certain fundamental ideals remained at the core of good state building: constitutions must be carefully designed so as to empower virtue. At the same time, these documents were not meant to transform individuals into noble characters. Instead, good constitution writers were to recognize and respond to the fact that human beings followed their "instincts."

The strength of the writers' commitment to these ideals suggests that frequent reevaluation had yet to dissolve important constitutional components aimed at protecting rights. In other words, Madison's fears were probably premature. At the same time, state builders interpreted those various protective components in different ways: stressing either the public virtue of the entire citizenry or the strength of people's narrow economic concerns. Such differences suggest that frequent reevaluation was not without consequences, for it did solidify alternative interpretations of the underlying features of well-designed constitutional government.

Conclusion
America's Constitutional Traditions

*O*ver the course of America's history as an independent nation, its constitutions have attempted to embody a particular reasoned understanding of the good state, one that balances a commitment to an active popular sovereignty with a commitment to inalienable private rights. In the early years of U.S. development, as today, not all of America's foundational documents endorse the same equilibrium between these two ideals. The national constitution has always tipped the scales in favor of inalienable rights. Original protections to personal and property rights, now expanded to include a vast array of private freedoms, continue to enjoy distinct preferential status. At the same time, self-government remains an instrumental good, cautiously awarded when and where it can safely be exercised.

State constitutions, on the other hand, have always tipped the scales in favor of popular sovereignty. Today, states allow nearly all adults to elect lawmakers, governors, and various low-level executive and judicial officers; many permit the direct election of supreme or district court judges. Half the states also grant citizens the power to initiate new legislation or directly approve referenda. By now, all states require direct popular approval of constitutional revision, with half of them permitting citizens to initiate change themselves. Since neither amendment process requires a prohibitively high super-majority, documents are still regularly revised and rewritten. All this suggests that, even though state constitutions enumerate rights and government prohibitions in far more detail than their national counterpart, they do not grant private rights the same unequivocal priority. Unlike the national document, these local constitutions give citizens substantial political influence, including the power to overturn supposedly sacred, constitutional ideals. In short, there has never been a singular constitutional tradition in the United States. The handiwork of designers in 1787 did not represent America's definitive solution for negotiating its dual commitment to private rights and popular sovereignty. States retained their own solution and thereby took a developmental path different from that taken by the union.

What are the consequences of this alternative approach to balancing constitutional commitments to rights and self-government? In what sense does the granting of broad popular influence affect the substance and spirit of foundational laws and principles? These questions lay at the root of Madison and Jefferson's 1790 debate over the value of constitutional reverence and stability.

Madison thought changes like the ones sanctioned by the states would bring legal chaos. For him a well-designed constitution was the product of careful reasoned discourse. He thought the national convention—which had brought together great minds and produced a document that balanced rights and self-government extraordinarily well—was no easy feat. Individuals were too passionate and self-centered to be trusted to re-create that original well-balanced foundation. Give the people regular opportunities to rewrite the laws designed to bound their behavior, thought Madison, and they will ultimately destroy the very rights that constitutions protect and reasonable men cherish. Such views led Madison to embrace stability and limited popular influence as the best means to retain constitutional integrity and protect rights. Only in this case would fundamental law acquire the reverential character that was necessary to ensure that the public and their leaders never upset its spirit or intent.[1]

Jefferson found this prediction specious. For him, stability was deadening, even dangerous, to the American ideal. Intentionally preventing the people and their elected representatives from regularly reinvestigating constitutional principle would suppress one of America's primary aims, namely, its allegiance to popular rule. Although Jefferson was willing to promote frequent constitutional revision, even if it put everything else at risk, he denied that disorder would ever result. People could and would regenerate new and better constitutional means to pursue the nation's fundamental commitments. In addition to the creation of better documents, Jefferson also expected that frequent recurrence to basic principles would keep the document and its underlying ideals meaningful and alive. Laws that did not reflect the people's contemporary understanding of the good state would ultimately lack the authority and legitimacy necessary to enforce them.[2]

It is no simple task to discover who had the more accurate prognosis. The national document has been the model of Madisonian stability and has remained a revered emblem of fundamental principle. Those affected by its contents—that is, the general population of all fifty states—recognize the power and significance of this document. Many deem it the most important protection of inalienable rights, especially of every individual's freedom to act in private matters without government intervention. Today, as in 1790, the U.S. Constitution contains a relatively concise set of foundational directives, coupled with a series of procedures necessary to support them. Through the help of certain judicial approaches to constitutional interpretation, original integrity remains a credible and important factor in determining the limits to this expansion of power (although the national government has usurped far more power than even its most nationalist supporters ever considered possible).

At the same time, the people's direct influence over ordinary and constitutional lawmaking remains almost as limited as it was in 1790. Everyday policy making is still distributed among officers of varying popular accountability. Although, in theory, the powers of constitutional reform lie with elected lawmakers at the state and national levels, in practice, nine elite justices hold the lion's share of influence in this regard. Although it is unclear whether the people's limited influence is directly responsible for constitutional reverence and long-standing rights protections, the correlation is certainly there—as is the connection between those limits and the ongoing stability of the document's contents.[3]

State constitutions, on the other hand, are modeled on Jeffersonian practice. They are frequently revised and give extensive governing powers to ordinary citizens. As a result, these documents look markedly different from their original Revolutionary models. Whereas New England constitutions remain relatively short and concise, most state documents do not; several actually fill over a hundred pages of text. As a result, local constitutions now contain extensive, far-ranging declarations of rights as well as detailed, particularistic limits on government activity. However, these additions do not necessarily signal better legal protections. Many of the limiting provisions, as well as the dozens of other miscellaneous features contained in the text, are probably best understood as ordinary statutes, for they are particularistic and are constantly amended. Today many constitutional provisions are treated as mutable law, not sacred principle.[4] One turn-of-the-century observer, James Bryce, described a state constitution as "nothing but a law made directly by the people voting at the polls upon a draft submitted to them. . . . It deals with a variety of topics which in Europe would be left to the ordinary action of the legislature or of administrative authorities; and it pursues these topics in a minute detail hardly to be looked for in a fundamental instrument."[5]

Perhaps even more disconcerting than this widespread tendency to incorporate minutely detailed statutory features into supposed high-law documents is that state documents seem to lack stature among those they govern. Close to half the population are not even aware that their state has its own constitution, and this even though at least once in their lifetime, most of these inhabitants will determine the fate of at least one constitutional amendment.[6] Thus, while the national constitution has become much like an arc of covenant, its ever-changing counterparts at the state level have never been treated or conceived of in this manner. At first glance, the comparison suggests that Madison was correct in his fear that frequent constitutional revision would undermine the stature and legitimacy of these important documents. Regular, unimpeded opportunities for revision may well have contributed substantially to the population's current disregard for state constitutions as authoritative documents, delimiting those fundamental principles and ideals that they as good citizens ought to follow.

Similarly, because opportunities for constitutional reformulation necessarily foster regular constitutional change, they probably encourage the incorporation of legislative-like features into those very documents. Constitutions that underwent serious evaluation during the late nineteenth and early twentieth century, for example, now contain detailed regulations on railroads and public utilities. Those that escaped scrutiny during this period regulated these industries with legislative provisions. Such examples suggest that contemporary issues of relevance make their way into constitutions rather than ordinary legislation primarily when convention meetings make the option easy and available.

We must be careful not to misinterpret these phenomena. Although the frequency of revision is a plausible explanation for prevailing disregard for state constitutions, an equally viable candidate for the uninformed and dismissive attitudes of the general public is the by now all-consuming sovereignty that the national government enjoys in resolving matters of constitutional dispute. Judicial interpretations of, say, the fourteenth amendment have reduced the power of states to use their constitutions as authorities for delimiting rights or determining various internal affairs. Such loss of power probably contributed to the demise of those documents' status.

Moreover, though the convenience of constitutional conventions have contributed to the incorporation of statutory policies in foundational documents, this does not verify that frequent opportunities for revision necessarily result in Madison's worst fear—that is, that they pollute the document by transforming it from a representation of society's reasoned understanding of the good state into a collection of laws lacking principle and high standards. Size and superfluous content do not necessarily mean a document empty of principle. They only signal a document cluttered with extraneous features, features that may actually cohabit alongside original fundamental purposes, rather than corrupt them.

In fact, contemporary actions by interested citizens and politicians suggest that these local documents retain substantial legitimacy. Some constitutional amendments, for example, still engender heated debate over what role the documents ought to play in the protection of rights.[7] Constitutional dictates regarding popular influence and leadership accountability are strictly followed by all affected parties. Not only do elections proceed according to document guidelines, but local governing officers use state constitutions to direct and delimit their actions when writing and executing ordinary law.[8] Finally, judges at both levels of government still evaluate state documents and their contents according to how well they secure private rights and maintain active popular sovereignty.[9]

All this suggests that neither popular attitudes nor statutory incorporations portend the demise of state constitutions as sacred foundations seeking to balance the nation's two fundamental commitments. The behavior of interested citizens and politicians verifies only that constitutions remain keepers of the good state. Whether frequent reform altered that guiding vision—for better or worse, or not at all—still remains an open question. To address this question requires looking to the ideas underlying the document and directing the various revisions made to it over the years. It also requires looking to the way constitution writers and ratifiers interpreted the meaning and relative value of the nation's commitment to rights and popular sovereignty and to the assumptions driving their interpretations. This is what I have tried to do in this book— albeit for only one particular feature of constitutional reform, and during only a limited period of U.S. history.

Antebellum state constitution writers as they revised electoral provisions concerning who should vote, for which officers, and under what conditions debated the character of human nature and its expected political consequences. They discussed the meaning of America's commitment to rights, and the place reserved for popular sovereignty. No matter what electoral issue was at stake, they grappled with two important questions. First, was their allegiance to popular sovereignty as important as their commitment to rights? Second, what kind of restrictions on the people's power did human nature and government purpose mandate? Delegates across the aisle saw both matters as essential concerns for constitution writers to resolve before designing good foundational law. Although the intensity of their discussions depended on various factors, their thoughts on these matters always contributed to their particular stand on electoral reform and their general interpretation of constitutional design and purpose.

These factors in the setting up of legal provisions have a long tradition in

American political thought. Colonists crafted their own theories of human nature and the relative importance of private rights versus popular sovereignty as they devised colonial laws and charters. Then, religion and British common law were among the most useful guides for constructing viable theories of government design.[10] Revolutionaries concerned themselves with the same issues as they wrote their first state constitutions. Although religion and common law continued to sway them, by now liberal and republican values also influenced their handiwork.[11] Finally, writers of the national constitution continued to discuss human nature and the relative values of private rights versus popular sovereignty. Their changing views on these matters, particularly their newfound emphasis on liberal parlance, are apparent in the popular document they created.[12]

Antebellum constitution writers were debating the same issues, this time strongly influenced by a liberal tradition, seemingly, albeit a tradition rather more multifaceted than was used by their predecessors. From the time Americans first relied on foundational documents to speak for their reasoned understanding of the good state, and at least through the mid–nineteenth century, constitution writers have consulted theories of human nature and the relative value of rights versus popular sovereignty before designing the documents everyone was expected to live by. In this sense, convention debates should actually give solace to those Madisonian skeptics who worry that frequent constitutional reform will create documents void of reason and principle and lacking in commitment to private rights.

For several decades after the national founding, frequent reevaluation and resultant legal changes altered neither the extent of reasoned debate nor the questions on which it focused. Constitution writers saw the same issues as pertinent for designing constitutional law; that is, the quest for theories of rights and human nature still guided them. This is remarkable, for constitutional conventions theoretically released popularly elected representatives from all constraints. These individuals had full authority to refashion fundamental principles and construct wholly new foundational documents should they choose to do so. They were speaking in the name of the people and their wishes, not in the name of their ancestors or the principles and concerns embossed in previous documents.[13]

There were no limits on their behavior except those that designers felt public opinion imposed upon them. Yet impose limits and principled guidelines these delegates did. When considering the meaning and relative value of their rights commitment, some looked back to nature, a pregovernmental state of principle. Others looked back to U.S. foundational documents, to the ideals that had been part of America's legal tradition for some time. Both were established foundations of the good state; their forefathers had relied on the same ones. Reasoned discourse produced carefully considered theories of human nature, which also built upon existing theories. Delegates described the features of good citizenship, the limits of government manufacture of it, and the purpose of procedures and institutional designs in ways that built upon some of their forefathers' views. In all cases questions regarding the fair distribution of popular sovereignty, one of the primary purposes of American constitutionalism, engendered scrupulous, thoughtful debate and followed the general guidelines that had directed past generations. Although nineteenth-century delegates did not always reach the same conclusions, they remained faithful to the view that good constitutional design required serious consideration of certain fundamental questions and concerns.

There are some features of antebellum constitutional debate that Madisonian skeptics might find problematic, however. For one, over time writers gave fewer (and less detailed) accounts of the theories driving their actions. They still talked about human nature and the importance of rights, but the ideological clarity and principled intensity of their positions dissipated over time. When debating enfranchisement of African Americans during the 1820s, for example, convention delegates regularly considered the content and origin of inalienable rights as well as the relevant factors underlying natural political behavior. Thirty years later, debates on this same issue, were vacuous in comparison. Few individuals cared to explain in theoretical detail why they took the positions they did. This was especially the case in North Carolina and Ohio where blacks were termed incompetent and rights were considered grants of citizenship, where both epithets were claimed without much reliance on reasoned theory or attempt at coherent ideology.[14]

In addition, delegates representing western states seemed to approach constitution making in a pragmatic fashion. Some speakers from Ohio and Iowa considered the theoretical underpinnings of the good state, but the majority did not. These conventions were held later, but it is not at all clear that time alone accounted for this behavior. New York, Virginia, and Louisiana held conventions in between the two western meetings, and yet, in these places, at least some issues encouraged delegates to think seriously about the origin of their rights commitments and the nature of human political behavior.

Finally, in addition to time and regional factors, the kind of stipulation under discussion seemingly affected the seriousness that constitution writers applied to their job. Electoral issues dealing with officer qualifications and the selection of nonlegislative officials engendered little principled debate, even during the early years. Throughout the first half of the nineteenth century, discussions about who should elect judges focused mainly on questions of expedience. Few if any of the delegates debating this issue talked about the content or origin of inalienable rights. It was as if certain electoral provisions—despite their direct effect on the people's political influence—were considered policy concerns, and not important component features of the state's fundamental commitment to popular sovereignty.

By midcentury, most of the electoral issues discussed at constitutional conventions were of this latter type: questions of policy and expediency. Perhaps this character best explains why constitution writers grew more silent on questions of principle. If so, the trend brings problems of its own. Was it not intellectually dangerous to use constitutional conventions—forums for designing fundamental law—as the means for deciding matters considered practical? As more questions of practical policy infiltrated foundational documents, would reminders of underlying theory and principle completely disappear from designer deliberations? Without reminders of the fundamental issues underlying constitutions, would documents and ideals lose credibility and force? If so, the decline noted in this study portends the ultimate demise of constitutions as higher law, the consequence Madison most feared. However, the decline probably resulted from many causes—including the issue discussed, the cultural tradition of the state, and various time-related factors.

Although it is difficult to determine whether, in the long run, Madison was right to fear frequent constitutional reform, in the short run, part of Jefferson's hope came to fruition. Jefferson anticipated that regular reevaluation would allow laws and institutions to progress with the progress of the human mind. He believed that America's reasoned understanding of the good state would evolve over time; if frequent constitutional change was encouraged, revised documents would reflect and incorporate inevitable ideological shifts.

If earlier studies on the Revolutionary and national founding period are correct, then this is certainly what happened. In the late eighteenth century, accolades for private rights and the acceptance of narrow self-interest in politics were the prevailing views of liberal spokesmen in America. Such views meant that self-government was a secondary concern, no more than a potentially good means to protect revered rights. During this period many believed simultaneously that self-government had innate value and that good government required public-spirited inhabitants. The prevalence of these views meant only that liberalism was not the sole legitimate political language of the time; republicanism had ongoing influence. Constitutions written during this period are thought to have relied on a complicated combination of at least two of these ideological traditions. The decrease in popular influence in the national document, together with its increased reliance on institutional checks and balances, are thought to reflect liberalism's increasing dominance.[15]

Debates among antebellum constitution writers illustrate the changing ideologies underlying constitutional design. Virtue and popular sovereignty were important considerations, but designers rarely relied on republican language to support their ongoing value. Liberal language now dominated the scene.

Although liberalism may have begun as a set of ideas justifying the priority of private rights over popular sovereignty and accepting narrow self-interest as the inevitable basis of political behavior, by the early nineteenth century this particular theoretical tradition—associated with stressing natural and contractual rights and recognizing government's need to accept natural behavior—had expanded. For a significant number of Americans, the underlying assumptions of liberal ideology now dictated equal treatment of private and public rights; these assumptions placed social sentiments among the politically natural behaviors that were expected of citizens. Although it is likely these views existed earlier (in the political positions of Thomas Paine and James Wilson, for example), at that time such views were not deemed prevalent or legitimate enough to be successfully co-opted into constitutional designs.[16] Thus, as the usable political language shifted and expanded, constitutional designs moved right along with it. Broader contours of liberalism gained credence in the fifty years following independence and therefore found their way into constitutional electoral policies.[17]

Thus, just as Jefferson hoped, ideological shifts affected the behavior of politicians and citizens as they rebuilt their foundational documents. Participants at constitutional conventions knew their handiwork would be evaluated by their peers who listened to speeches as they delivered them. They knew the broader constituency would soon read their views in newspapers, political pamphlets, and later convention records.[18]

Wise delegates therefore sought to find a rationale that these evaluating audiences would find familiar, acceptable, and ultimately persuasive. This meant speaking a political language they would understand, which meant working with preexisting, agreed-upon concerns, with theories of the good state that they and their listeners could endorse in good conscience. In this sense, prevailing ideas and any new twists to them would necessarily find their way into revised documents. Any shift in ideology would become part of constitutional intention.

The relationship between ideas and constitutional design was probably not unidirectional. Instead, it is likely that writers of state documents contributed to the changing course taken by American ideology. Delegates came to conventions with certain preconceived notions of how they wanted documents to look, that is, having decided whether they would support particular electoral reforms. Although principled values and beliefs certainly influenced their preferences, so did practical concerns, including the long-run consequences that various proposals would have on the distribution of power. Thus, legitimating their electoral law preferences might sometimes require that constitution writers subtly alter the prevailing political language, by stressing, ignoring, or even re-defining previously revered concerns. Participants at these meetings might sometimes find themselves reshaping prevalent ideas to serve their cause. Con-stitutional conventions were not just opportunities to recite existing and incor-porate new shared values; they were also forums to give values useful interpre-tations. These meetings allowed for a dialectical interaction between prevailing ideas and an individual's policy preferences.[19]

Given the kinds of arguments that antebellum constitution writers put for-ward for and against electoral reform, they clearly considered the values and as-sumptions handed down to them—from liberal theorists such as Locke and Adam Smith—the most reasonable to use for constitutional questions regarding popular sovereignty. They found interpretations of those values and assump-tions rich and multifaceted enough to support their disagreements about how or why their state should approach electoral reform. This does not mean the liberal issues raised at the constitutional conventions were the only ones constitution drafters and contemporaries understood. Nor does it mean their views repre-sented American ideology *toute force*. The liberal assumptions these delegates stressed, about rights and human nature, were clearly those they had determined the most persuasive for constitutional questions of popular sovereignty; they were not necessarily the best for every other political question facing America at the time, as other scholars of the period have convincingly shown.

Some scholars contend that nineteenth-century politicians debating certain national policy matters stressed different features of liberal ideology. For in-stance, the nullification controversy supposedly raised questions about whether good government should be an interest provider or an advocate of the common good. Theories of natural behavior and government's best responses to it were not part of the nullification discourse.[20] Others find nineteenth-century political debate laced with views best understood as entirely distinct from liberalism, as when debates over the role of government in promoting manufacturing encour-aged republican concerns about the importance of land and self-sufficiency. De-bates over the meaning of liberty often inspired religious reflections, whereas debates over immigration policy fueled ethnocentric biases to support policies promoting America's white, Anglo-Saxon heritage.[21]

The ongoing presence of other ideological traditions and different liberal concerns suggests that the kind of policies considered affects the evolution of American ideology. The nature of the political question under debate helps de-termine which values and beliefs are brought to the forefront and debated. This then shapes how the selected values and beliefs develop or transform. So, that nineteenth-century designers of electoral laws found the liberal language of na-ture and compact pertinent to questions of representation and suffrage did not preclude them or their contemporaries from using racist and ethnocentric language to justify political decisions regarding African Americans or immigrants, whether these decisions would impact ordinary policy or constitutional law. This kind of intellectual cohabitation demonstrates that there is a deliberative and dialectical process between ideology and practice, that when reasonable people debate, what they think and say are sensitive to the issues being discussed.

That Jefferson's experiment thrived at the state level and actually resulted in some of the outcomes he anticipated ultimately means we must revise our understanding of American constitutionalism. On the one hand, these documents all form part of a single tradition. Each and every foundational document represents a vision of the nation's understanding of the good state, wherein both private rights and popular sovereignty are given just due. At least through the antebellum period, each document had its origin in the reasoned debate and careful consideration of politicians and citizens, struggling to justify why they advocated the particular balance they did. In this sense, all U.S. constitutions share a common origin and a common purpose. On the other hand, these commonalties tell only a partial story. Across America, there are different constitutional traditions regarding how often to return to origins and how to best implement constitutional purpose.

As was the case in the 1800s, today no two documents distribute rights and powers in exactly the same fashion. That the nation and its states take radically different approaches in this matter is just one facet of difference. Different states choose different rights and electoral provisions; each choice represents a different balance. The varying configurations mean there is no single constitutional vision of how best to codify America's allegiance to popular sovereignty. Because states so frequently returned to their origins to reinvestigate foundational principles and constitutional provisions, it is almost impossible to characterize the ideological underpinning of even one document.

As the antebellum debates over electoral reform make clear, behind each document feature lay at least two contending visions of how that provision should have been written and why. Although all individuals shared basic assumptions, the process of debate necessarily brought out and defined subtle and consequential differences. In the end, the final wording of any given electoral law did not definitively resolve the ideological disputes underlying alternative proposals. Instead, the stipulations that were finally approved either ignored the battles behind them or at best represented a compromise. In this case, the ideas guiding electoral reform policies comprised a consistent and limited set—there were only two or three contending theories about the value of rights or the character of human nature. Because policies and ideology are intricately connected, however, it is unlikely that the same ideas influenced other, wholly distinct provisions. This means that not only was each electoral provision the product of varying interpretations about the good state, but each document—the product of hundreds of passages—contained many other contentious and differing readings of the ideal.

These complications do not mean that scholars and judges should abandon the quest to uncover what writers and ratifiers understood to be the meaning and purpose of foundational documents. It is just that a search for some singular, original meaning would be mistaken. Not only are there significant differences between state and national approaches to devising the good state, but each individual document contains multiple intentions. Behind each constitution are numerous provisions, each supported by principles whose meaning and relative value were originally contested and never fully resolved.

This does not mean, either, that there are no important founding principles behind U.S. constitutions. This was Madison's nightmare, neither Jefferson's hope nor America's reality, at least until 1850. Then, and today, foundational principles delimit and guide political debate and constitutional design. Debate and legal practices affect American ideology and thereby the nation's reasoned understanding of the good state. Jefferson's hope for both was not some idle dream. At the state level, his dream quickly came to fruition. The practice of ongoing debate and subsequent revision has helped ensure that the meaning and relative importance of America's initial foundational principles remained neither static nor detached from practical concerns and has contributed to the evolution of liberalism and constitutionalism in the United States.

Notes

PREFACE

1. On the British origins of America's allegiance to popular sovereignty, see Morgan (1988) and Pole (1966) as well as Reid (1989). On America's restructuring of the British system into one advocating active consent, see each of these as well as Bailyn (1967, ch. 5), Lutz (1980, esp. ch. 1) and Wood (1969, ch. 5; 1991, chs. 13, 14).

2. Daniel Elazar, Christian Fritz, and Kermit Hall are notable exceptions. Each has studied various aspects of state constitutional development during the nineteenth century. See Elazar (1994), Fritz (1989, 1994, 1997), and Hall (1983, 1991, 1992).

3. A quick library search under constitutions in the United States will easily show the truth of this claim. There are literally hundreds of books on the national Constitution, the theories of *Publius*, and Supreme Court activity over the years. Only in the last few years has there been any interest in state constitutions, and this has been mainly among legal scholars and historians, not political scientists. For a discussion of this bias, see Fritz (1994).

4. See Barber (1991, 25–27) and Wolin (1989, esp. ch. 8) and also Miller (1988). Wolin does note that America's tradition, as inherited from the colonies and states, is actually more democratic than the national experience.

5. See Appleby (1984) and Pangle (1988, ch. 12) as well as Anderson (1993, ch. 5), Diggins (1984, 61–62, 133–35), Kammen (1988, ch. 1, esp. 29), and Wood (1969, 475–524). Early twentieth-century Progressive historians made an even more forceful case, depicting the national constitution as antidemocratic and concerned only with property rights. See Beard (1986, esp. 324–25) and Croly (1911, esp. 32–43).

6. See Hofstadter (1973, 26–30) and Reimer (1967, esp. conclusion), as well as Ashworth (1983, 10–12, 56–57), Garry (1992, ch. 4), Howe (1979, 81–86, 236), Remini (1981, ch. 2), and Welter (1975, ch. 7).

7. Nine documents contained stipulations similar to the one quoted. Since Revolutionary Americans had rejected the British notion of virtual representation (that leaders could or would represent a people's interest even when the holders of that interest had not directly selected them), declarations like the one found in Delaware were statements applauding the people's direct influence in government formation. On revolutionary conceptions of representation and active consent, see Bailyn (1967, ch. 5), Lutz (1980, 37–46), Morgan (1988, 240–59), Pole (1966), and Wood (1969, pt. 2, esp. ch. 5).

8. For a discussion of these institutional features or the theory underlying them, see Adams (1980, ch. 12), Hall (1991, 396), Kruman (1997, chs. 4–5), Main (1973, 151–200), Nevins (1969, ch. 4), Sturm (1982, 61), and Wood (1969, ch. 5).

9. Pennsylvania and Vermont provided specific procedures for constitutional revision every seven years. Georgia allowed the legislature to call a convention if the people deemed it necessary. Massachusetts required a popular referendum in 1795 to consider constitutional revision. Although then most states let legislative bodies design and approve change, as Kruman (1997, ch. 2) and Fritz (1997, 329–38) have illustrated, the prevailing sentiment was that legislatures were the people's delegates and servants and that the documents produced by them contained only popularly endorsed fundamental laws.

10. There remains widespread agreement that the political philosophy of John Locke and the liberal tradition he inspired have influenced American political thought during the Revolutionary period. For example, see Diggins (1984), Dworetz (1990), Hartz (1955), and Zuckert (1994, 18–25). At the same time, many have discussed the other sources of early American political thought listed above. See Bailyn (1967, 22–30), Kaye (1992, 729–34), May (1976), Miller (1991), Pocock (1975, ch. 15), Shain (1994, esp. introduction), Wills (1978, esp. prologue), and Wood (1969, pt. 1). Many of these scholars note the simultaneous influences of two or more intellectual traditions.

11. On the radical rethinking that took place between the Revolution and national founding, see Agresto (1977), Conkin (1974, 177), Lutz (1988, 5–6), Pocock (1975, 544–45), Shain (1994, 320–22), and Wood (1969, 606–12). Of course, these and other scholars may debate just how liberal-minded the writers of the national document actually were. After all, the original document enumerated few rights, and some supporters declared it a document of popular will, reliant on virtue. However, whether the proper adjective is *liberal* or not, there exists substantial evidence that the document and *Publius*—the alias for its most famous defenders—endorsed a new science of politics, which reduced the status of popular sovereignty so as to protect rights in the face of the unreliability of selfless virtue. On this last point, see Appleby (1992, 218–19), Diggins (1984, 61–62, 67), Hartz (1955, ch. 3), Hofstadter (1973, ch. 1), Kerber (1980, 195–200), and Pangle (1988, ch. 12).

12. This excerpt was taken from Missouri's 1820 constitution (Poore 1898, pt. 2, 1104). A total of twenty-one states contained a proclamation of this sort.

13. During the antebellum period governors gained veto power and took over various officer appointments from the legislature. Judges gained the power of judicial review. At the same time, states provided for the popular election of governors, and many also made appellate, supreme, and district court judges popularly elected. For an analysis of how increased judicial power interacted with new electoral provisions, see Hall (1983).

14. There is no debating that America does not deserve the democratic label its nineteenth-century politicians gave themselves. Then, only four states granted suffrage rights to Americans of African descent. Though many states debated the issue, it was not a broadly supported policy, even in the late 1870s, after the Fifteenth Amendment was passed. See Olbrich (1912, conclusion). States began debating the enfranchisement

of women during the 1850s. By 1900 only four states granted full female suffrage, though nineteen granted women limited voting privileges. The question remained a political issue so that by the time the Nineteenth Amendment became part of the U.S. Constitution, twenty states granted women full voting privileges, and several others had only narrowly defeated the cause. See Flexner (1972, esp. chs. 12, 23). On the problem of franchise restrictions throughout much of U.S. history, see Smith (1988, 1989).

15. The ideology described in the book should be thought of as the admissible public language, not necessarily the whole picture. After all, delegates knew that observers sat in convention halls, that newspapers would reproduce some speeches, and that their state would ultimately record proceedings for posterity. Thus, just as congressional members avoid certain topics in order to avoid political criticism, so might these speakers have done.

16. These are later, twentieth-century visions of what constitutes American liberalism, and in fact partially conflict with the aspects of the liberal tradition that were stressed then.

17. On the inherent importance of virtue and participation in the republican tradition see, for example, Pocock (1975, ch. 3) or Yarbrough (1979a, 64–66). On the ongoing importance of virtue and political participation for early nineteenth-century politicians, see Banning (1978, 1986), Ketcham (1984, ch. 6–7), and Shalhope (1976). None of these authors sees republican rhetoric as the dominant or sole voice in America at this time.

18. On the role of the Bible, religion, and Protestantism in the early nineteenth century, see Cooke (1986) or Jaenicke (1981). More recently, scholars emphasize how these traditions interacted with liberalism and with one another, in the late eighteenth century and beyond. For examples, see Dworetz (1990), Ellis (1993), Sinopoli (1992), and Smith (1993).

19. See Smith (1997). There is some extent to which the kind of illiberal ideas that Smith uncovers are actually present in some state constitutional discussions regarding electoral reform. See Scalia (1998).

20. Examples of these democratic theorists include Barber (1984, pt. 1), Braybrooke (1983), Levine (1981, esp. ch. 1), Macpherson (1972, ch. 1), Pateman (1970, ch. 1), and Walzer (1984).

21. Those who fought electoral reform are said to have stressed the destructive ends that would follow suffrage expansion. Those who supported reform are said to have argued that the people would safely protect their rights from government abuse. Few scholars argue that partisans endorsed expansion because of the intrinsic value of active participation and popular virtue. Most would agree that, to the extent republican ideology had any rhetorical force after 1820, it had resonance among those Whigs fighting against a broader interpretation of America's commitment to popular sovereignty. Jacksonian Democrats supposedly emphasized that extension would limit the power of "aristocratic" influences and grant influence to the interests of common man. See Ashworth (1983, 10–12, 56–57), Howe (1979, 81–86, 236), Remini (1981, ch. 2), and Welter (1975, ch. 7).

22. Ericson (1993) looks at debates over ratification, nullification, and slavery and stresses liberal disputes over pluralism versus the common good, and private rights versus participation. Greenstone (1993) focuses on debates over slavery and outlines the reigning liberal dispute over whether government was an interest-provider or a human-developer. Smith (1985) examines Supreme Court decisions over a two-hundred-year period and describes an evolutionary conception of the good state.

INTRODUCTION

1. All of the above quotations, with the exception of the last, were taken from Madison's letter to Jefferson, dated February 4, 1790, reproduced in Nichols and Nichols (1996, 377–79). Richards (1989, 132–38) discusses this letter and Madison's general hostility to frequent constitutional revision. The last quote regarding the importance of property was taken from *Federalist* essay no. 10. For a discussion of Madison's views on the importance of rights, especially property rights, see Nedelsky (1990, ch. 2).

2. Quotations are from Jefferson's letter to Samuel Kercheval dated July 12, 1816, and reproduced in Pate (1932, 28–29). Jefferson lays out a similar argument on the importance of frequent popular revision of laws, in a letter to James Madison, dated September 6, 1787. On Jefferson's faith in the progress of the human mind, see Peterson (1962, 11) and Sheldon (1991, 59–70). On Jefferson's advocacy of self-government, see Parrington (1927, 347–62). On his advocacy, together with the limits of calling Jefferson a democrat, see Hofstadter (1973, 32–40).

3. After the addition of the Bill of Rights, there have been only seventeen amendments to the national Constitution. Although judicial opinions have radically changed the document, the relative stability of its words is remarkable, especially in contrast to the history of state constitutional development, the topic of this book.

4. See Appleby (1992, 228) and Graglia (1991, 97–101).

5. See for example the comments of democratic critics such as Barber (1991, 25–27) and Miller (1988) or of scholars of constitutional and American political thought such as Nedelsky (1990, 1) and Smith (1966).

6. By the close of the antebellum period, nearly every state had held at least one constitutional convention to revise its foundational document, with many holding two or three. Seventeen other conventions were held to write first-time constitutions.

7. During the early nineteenth century and antebellum period ten constitutions—a little over a quarter of those written during this period—were *not* subject to popular approval. By the mid-1830s nearly every constitution stipulated that both legislative and popular approval were required prior to amendment. Sturm (1982, 57–58) gives a list of these provisions.

8. Scholars debate how inclusive early provisions were. Bailyn (1968, 87) argues that by 1787 between 50 and 75 percent of the adult white male population could vote. West (1997, 71, 113–15) estimates eligibility at closer to 90 percent. Better accuracy would account for variances within and between states. For example, Williamson (1960) shows that in 1800 Pennsylvania allowed as much as 90 percent of the adult white male

population to vote in all elections, whereas New York allowed only about 33 percent to vote in state senatorial elections. Bruce (1982, 2–3) describes voter eligibility in Virginia across counties and finds that, in 1829, 73 percent of the adult white male population could vote in the eastern part of the state, 56 percent in the western part, and 51 percent in the Shenandoah valley.

9. Despite "color blind" provisions, few blacks voted. Most lacked sufficient property. Other, silent taboos and obstructions may have simultaneously prevailed as they did in the case of women. Despite voting requirements that were gender neutral, women never voted except for isolated cases in revolutionary Virginia and New Jersey (Flexner 1972, 143).

10. For a study of negro suffrage and the various political pressures accompanying early restrictions and later expansions, see Olbrich (1912).

11. Democratic practice evaded states for generations to come, with universal black suffrage waiting until 1964 and the passage of the Twenty-Fourth Amendment.

12. Progressive historians like Beard (1986) claim that these exclusions make early America elitist. Recently Smith (1989, 1993) has reminded us of the ways this period was illiberal and undemocratic. Other historians such as Brown (1955, 1956) argue that by "reasonable" calculations, the individual states have been democratic since colonial days. For a critical evaluation of Brown's view and the debate surrounding it, see Murrin (1965). For a history of suffrage laws in the United States, see Porter (1918) or Williamson (1960).

13. Dissatisfaction with districting led many states to hold constitutional conventions during this period. On the role of districting in the South, see Green (1930, ch. 4), in Ohio, see Roseboom and Weisenburger (1956, 163–65), and in North Carolina, see Boyd (1973, 100).

14. In the North, reformers strove to base districts on the population as a whole. In the South, where such a system would give the large slaveholders disproportionate voice, the more egalitarian position was one supporting a voter-population basis.

15. Property remained a factor in districting until the U.S. Supreme Court declared it unconstitutional in 1964. Some see this modern system as equally undemocratic. See Guinier (1994).

16. In compensation, some reduced judicial life tenure to a limited term, thereby making even appointed judges somewhat more publicly accountable for their actions. See Hall (1983, 337 n. 2) and Thorpe (1898, vol. 1, ch. 14).

17. In a way, even in states that enacted these reforms, the democratic consequences were questionable, for they occurred alongside the intentional weakening of the lawmaking branch. See Hall (1983) on the democratic nature of these reforms and the limits to viewing these reforms strictly in this light. Of interest, close to half the states still do not popularly elect important judicial figures or various low-level officers.

18. No state kept a systematic account of its legislative debates until the *late* 1800s, making it impossible to track much of the ideological development underlying America's first reform movement. Of the over sixty constitutional conventions held,

there remain records for twenty, all held after 1820. See Shearer (1915) for a list of the documentary material available.

19. On the economic and political character of the region, see Turner (1950, ch. 3). For a brief description of New England's constitutional tradition, see Elazar (1982, 13, 18–19).

20. On the strong Whig influence in Massachusetts, see Schlesinger (1950, ch. 12). On the various strands within the state's culture, including abolitionists and religiosity, see Formisano (1983, esp. ch. 14).

21. The document has been amended ninety-one times, a relatively low amount compared to other constitutions, even those in existence half the time. See Sturm (1970, 7–9) for a tabulation.

22. The mandated popular referendum of 1795 revealed no sentiment for revision.

23. Only a few delegates argued to retain a property qualification. These proponents were generally leading Federalists like Josiah Quincy. See Formisano (1983, 137).

24. On the importance of religion in Massachusetts politics and its influence at the convention, see Glasser (1930, 8–14) and Stokes (1950, 425). For further details on the politics and history leading up to the 1820–1821 convention, see Glasser (1930, 1–5).

25. On the constitutional traditions of the Mid-Atlantic states, see Elazar (1982, 19–20). On the features of the region, see Turner (1950, ch. 4).

26. For example, New York Democrats split on the issue of extending slavery into the territories. On the weak party system in New York and the fractures in the Democratic party, see Berger (1973, ch. 1), Fox (1919), Kass (1965), Schlesinger (1950, ch. 14–15), and Turner (1950, 121–27).

27. Although at the time not many African Americans enjoyed a free status, New York City contained a sizable population of blacks. Given their Whig leaning, city Democrats insisted that free men of color hold $250 worth of property before voting. By at least one estimate, this restriction notably limited their political power, denying some ten thousand city dwellers the chance to vote in the 1844 presidential election. According to Howe (1979, 17), this exclusion prevented Henry Clay from winning the state and ultimately the election.

28. Whigs sometimes favored the popular election of judges. On the political positions of liberal Whigs regarding suffrage reform, see Ashworth (1983, 225–28). On the positions of New York Federalists, see Fox (1919) and Kass (1965, ch. 5). On the Whig endorsement of popularly elected judges, see Thorpe (1898, vol. 1, ch. 2).

29. On the role these other forces played in New York, see Wyatt-Brown (1969) and Sorin (1971). For the importance of these forces not only in New York, but elsewhere in the United States, see Howe (1990), Sorin (1972), Stokes (1950, 833–35), and Swierenga (1990).

30. Blacks generally supported Whigs and new immigrants generally supported Democrats, so coalitions regarding their empowerment were usually partisan. On the tensions and conflicts over questions of immigrants in the state, especially regarding party politics after 1840, see Berger (1973, chs. 1, 8, 13). On the party politics surround-

ing judiciary reform, see Hall (1983, 342–53) and Henretta (1989, 390–93). For a general discussion of the partisan influences at the 1821 convention, see Kass (1965, 45–50, 84–90), and at the 1846 convention, see Gunn (1979, 293) and Turner (1950, 127–29).

31. See Grisby's 1853 on-hand account, reproduced by Da Capo Press (1969, 45).

32. See Bruce (1982, ch. 1) and Green (1930, ch. 4).

33. The new constitution contained a detailed list with all counties and newly defined senatorial districts as well as the number of representatives to be granted to each unit. Virginia still avoided basing representation for either house on a "region-blind" principle of voter population or some balance between voters and the property held or taxes paid. The constitution did include a provision to open this question to voters in the year 1865.

34. On the politics and results of this later convention, see Pate (1932, 41–43).

35. On North Carolina's party politics during the period, see Rankin (1955, 24–26) and Kruman (1983, 6–14). On various characteristics of general state politics at the time, see Turner (1950, ch. 5).

36. The only other southern state without an explicit declaration of its commitment to popular sovereignty was Georgia.

37. Whigs managed to overturn this representation system in 1852. The new system ensured apportionment by total population, instead of by white population. Democratic as this may sound, it actually meant that a few slaveholders and their disenfranchised slaves had as many representatives as a large number of small farmers and city-dwelling freemen. On the party politics surrounding this issue at both conventions, see Adams (1973, 147–50).

38. It also reduced the number of years for a company to incorporate itself. For a history of the issues influencing Louisiana politics at the time, see Gayarré (1965, 643–71).

39. On the economic and political character of this region of the country, see Turner (1950, ch. 7). Elazar (1972, 106–7) characterizes most western states as having "mixed" cultural traditions, one of which is always individualistic.

40. Since neither of the major parties held a majority in the state legislature and the Free Soilers had a sufficient following, few decisions could be reached without their support. See Smith (1967, ch. 10–12). Also see Roseboom and Weisenburger (1956).

41. See Turner (1950, 263).

42. On Iowa, see ibid., ch. 7. Also see Macy's 1884 account based on the memories of those still living who had experienced territorial life.

43. On Iowa's early constitutional history and the development of its government branches, see Ross (1957, 14–16, 40–46).

44. On the different constitutional cultures and legal traditions, see Elazar (1982).

45. Although nowhere outside the West was it left totally uncriticized, by the 1840s the word *democracy* was politically acceptable to a range of politicians. On the evolving perceptions regarding democracy, see Morantz (1971) and Hanson (1985, ch. 4), both of whom place the 1830s–1850s as the time American politicians began openly to use the word *democracy* to describe their ideals and the realities of government processes.

46. Since most vocal convention participants were those with substantial political careers, in over half the cases something about the speaker's life is known and reported. However, some speeches were made by "unknown" men. Since recorders offer no personal data, in such instances little context is offered. The curious reader who would like to learn more about the various speakers might begin with the *Dictionary of American Biography*, which supplemented much of the information about the delegates offered in the text.

47. Although recorders of Virginia's midcentury convention probably listed participants as they had twenty years earlier, the microfilm that remains lacks this information.

48. Rodgers (1987, 95) also discusses behavior at nineteenth-century conventions and agrees that party allegiance poorly predicts the policy preferences of convention participants. Corwell, Goodman, and Swanson's 1970 analysis of delegates from three state conventions held in the 1960s showed that a participant's view of reform was more useful in the understanding of delegate differences than partisanship.

49. Lutz (1992, ch. 2) justifies studying American political thought in this manner.

Part I. Debates over Defining Rights

1. On Madison's reliance on previous state documents, see Lutz (1992, ch. 3).

2. On similarities between the protection of rights at the national level and at the state level, see Hall (1991, 390–95; 1992, 642), Hutson (1991), Elazar (1982, 14–18), and Rakove (1990, 130). For a close analysis of similarities and differences between the two levels, especially between the U.S. Constitution and California's mid-nineteenth-century constitution, see Fritz (1989, 21–26). For a more general discussion, see Hall (1991, 1992).

3. The states' nineteenth-century practice of incorporating more and more rights into their constitutions may be seen, rather, as a belittling of rights principles. With increasing specificity provisions would require regular revisions, thereby prohibiting them from acquiring long-term revered status. The more the detail, the less power of any general ideal contained. These changes may thus have unintentionally decreased the liberal ideals.

1. The Origin of Rights

1. Some of the same issues were discussed at New York's constitutional convention held the following year. This was the time when the nativist party was gaining sympathy across the nation, especially in areas hard hit by European immigration. See Smith (1997, 225–26).

2. Although delegates sometimes explicitly included men and women as bearers of rights, liberties, and economic freedoms, delegates usually referred to the rights and liberties of free men, not free individuals or free men and women. Indeed they often limited rights to free white men. Throughout the book I use the male pronoun when discussing delegates' views as to who should be granted rights, liberties, and political power.

3. At the time of the convention Mr. Benjamin was most famous for his legal work in international law. In 1856 he became a Democrat and later served the Confederacy as Jefferson Davis's secretary of state.

4. If we exclude the Virginia constitution of 1850–1851, the incidence of unsolicited declarations regarding the importance of life, liberty, and property declined after 1830. The same is true regarding most of the themes discussed here (see Conclusion).

5. On the primary importance of freedom of conscience in Revolutionary America, see Miller (1991) and Shain (1994).

6. While this recurrent emphasis clearly shows that these three were deemed of fundamental value, it does not necessarily prove that in the big picture of things all other rights were truly secondary. However, in the small picture of deciding who should govern and how much, the rights of life, liberty, and property were the only rights that mattered or were considered at danger.

7. In his argument for restricting eligibility for governor, Democrat John Grymes explained that laws secured "the most essential privileges." He later explained that Louisiana's laws protected foreigners "in their persons and property as much as American citizens" (LA 1845, 80). Mr. Grymes did not explicitly claim that life and property were essential rights of freemen—he called them privileges. Yet some might say the link is implicit. Throughout this study, whenever counts regarding the incidence of rights declarations are offered, indirect allusions such as this are excluded.

8. See Hartz (1955), Pangle (1988), and Zuckert (1994). There have been many spokesmen of natural law, including Pufendorf, Burlamaqui, Hutchenson, and Blackstone. For scholars who have noted their influence as well, see Haakonssen (1991, 42–52) and White (1978, chs. 4–5, pp. 163–64). There exists significant overlap between the ideas of Locke and Blackstone, say, so the multiple influences on America's allegiance to protecting rights and securing popular sovereignty do not undermine the original claim that early Americans' views of natural law resembled Locke's.

9. Rodgers (1987, ch. 1) claims that Revolutionary Americans turned to utilitarian principles and embraced the right to happiness as inalienable. For the influence of the Scottish Enlightenment on Jefferson and the writing of the Declaration of Independence, see Wills (1978). On the overall influence of the Scottish Enlightenment on revolutionary thought in America, see May (1976).

10. Hutson (1991) and Kaye (1992, 729–34) have emphasized the influence of common law on the American conception of rights. Many scholars note the simultaneous influences of Locke and natural law, the British common law tradition, and the Scottish Enlightenment; see Hutson (1991), Reid (1986), and Sherry (1987, 1992).

11. Locke—as well as other state-of-nature theorists who influenced late eighteenth-century Americans—stressed man's duties and responsibilities in the exercise of rights (Haakonssen 1991). This stress on responsibility is notably absent in nineteenth-century American rhetoric.

12. For the intersection of these three views, see West's call to revolution, reprinted in Hyneman and Lutz (1983, 1: 410–48).

13. Hartz (1955) is the author best known for this understanding of American

political thought. See Pangle (1988) for the relationship between natural law and the founders; see Kramnick (1990, ch. 6) for Locke's influence on these writers. Arieli (1964, 17) and Haakonssen (1991, 47–52) trace this connection back to the Revolution. Lutz (1984, 142–43) discusses how often Locke was quoted during the late eighteenth century; he notes a significant drop from the time of the Revolution to the writing of the national constitution, but in both instances Locke was considered an authority on the basis of good government.

14. Only two speakers, both restrictionists from Virginia, referred to nature in a religious fashion, as the state of man, after the fall. Both saw this as a savage state, wherein men did not live peaceably together. Nature was not the blissful state of Adam and Eve in Eden. Nineteenth-century delegates rarely talked about the laws or duties of nature; instead they emphasized rights. This in itself is a radical departure from Locke's teachings.

15. Winch (1978, 58–59) argues that Adam Smith described rights as postnatural, that is, requiring civil government.

16. Of all the conventions recorded between 1800 and 1850, Virginia's were the most detailed.

17. See Haakonssen (1991, 21, 42–43). The exception may have been in western states, but especially in Iowa since it was populated by young adventurers, seeking economic prosperity. Many delegates of Ohio were born and raised in the East and the various professions for Ohio delegates did not radically differ from other "older" states.

18. The policies these men helped pass stood as a model for much of the South. Since Virginia housed some of America's greatest statesmen of the time, representatives from neighboring states traveled many miles to listen to their deliberations. Norton (1986, ch. 5) notes that southerners used nature as the foundation of rights more often than northerners. Rodgers (1987, ch. 3) makes no distinction.

19. Chapman Johnson may have supported a more egalitarian form of representation but he was against extended suffrage and popularly elected judges. In this sense his skepticism regarding the usefulness of the state-of-nature theory fits the more general dichotomy between reformers and antireformers that is sketched out in this chapter.

20. In a different context, Green (1930, ch. 4) makes a similar observation in his study of the South Atlantic states.

21. Some opponents of reform conceded that political voice was a right of nature (see Chapter 2), but none wanted this considered a natural right necessarily sanctioned by government.

22. Half the Virginia delegates who spoke for or against reforming the basis of representation recognized the association between their views and Locke's. Locke is specifically mentioned in eleven speeches, of which two reject his theories as being metaphysical and useless in practical government.

23. Although the Crusoe example was meant to demonstrate the disjuncture between nature and society, both the delegates using it argued also that this story offered a valuable lesson about the natural worth of property. Prior to government men may not have been social, but they coveted their property rights and could—and would—use the

power derived from it to protect their possessions. Life before government still offered an important political lesson: governments must take account of property rights, and such accounting meant giving property a certain amount of power.

24. Mr. Root, who later became a Whig, was among those who believed that the initial contract provided for universal suffrage, but that it did so only for "rational" individuals. As he saw it, whites understood contract stipulations and were fully entitled to the natural rights retained by compact. His views on the differences between blacks and whites regarding rights, rationality, and suffrage were shared by others. Henretta (1989, 362) characterizes this as the principle of *Herrenvolk*. Locke too emphasizes rationality as the prerequisite for the free enjoyment of rights and for participating in the compact. On the importance of rationality in Locke's theory of consent, see Grant (1987, ch. 2), as well as his discussion of why children are neither part of the compact nor wholly free (paras. 60, 63).

25. This was an unusual case when delegates discussed the enfranchisement of Americans of African descent. The question of white-only franchise was often supported by Democrats, the same people who rejected other property-based voter restrictions.

26. Townshend meant both men and women. He was the only person, at any convention, to argue seriously in favor of a gender-neutral suffrage.

27. At every convention except North Carolina, there was at least one delegate whose speech indicated he used the concept of natural rights in this way.

28. Michael Zuckert made this argument in a talk given at Loyola University, March 21, 1994. Bailyn (1967, 175–97) also notes that Revolutionary Americans revered rights and understood constitutions as having authority above ordinary legislation and lawmakers.

29. Though these constitutions' provisions meant such rights were neither government grants nor special privileges for the few, all documents did not necessarily make these rights wholly above popular restraint. For example, in every state a jury of peers could force someone to forfeit his or her life. In some states, property could be taken with the consent of the representative body of the people.

30. The silent were likely aware of the philosophical position connecting constitutional principles to the natural rights agreed to in the contract. After all, many of the documents they quoted from—as well as a significant number of fellow convention participants—made the connection explicit. It is only in the states containing this type of declaration that delegates relied on their constitution to bolster the inalienable importance of rights.

31. The views expressed by delegates in this regard are consistent with the interpretation Fritz (1997, 329–38) attributes to constitution writers from the late eighteenth century through much of the nineteenth.

32. Webster spoke against every electoral reform issue raised at this convention.

33. These remarks were made in favor of continuing a propertied franchise.

34. Delegates also occasionally referred to God and earlier statesmen as authorities dictating why Americans were inalienably committed to securing the enjoyment of life, liberty, and property. In comparison with the nature and law, both were discussed

infrequently. Furthermore God was usually an *added* authority, mentioned alongside nature or standing fundamental laws.

35. On the difference between American and British conceptions of rights vis-à-vis principles and tradition, see Bailyn (1967, 175–98).

2. REFORMERS AND POPULAR SOVEREIGNTY

1. This is the liberal view that Hartz (1955) attributed to America.

2. Macpherson (1962, 252–55) strings together evidence to show that Locke meant to enfranchise the propertied. Ashcraft (1986, ch. 11) calls attention to radical aspects and ambiguities and suggests that Locke may not have intended for members of civil society to forfeit the governing privileges they enjoyed in nature. Stevens (1996) seems to agree with Ashcraft's reading and extends his work by discussing the varying levels of participation that Locke justifies. These scholars consider Locke's views about the people's sovereignty to be definitive. See Scalia (1996, 810–12) for a synopsis of the relevant passages in Locke.

3. Most scholars stress these aspects, arguing that Locke offered no explicit provision for popular rule; see Dunn (1971), Grant (1987, ch. 2), Laslett (1988, 108–11).

4. On the influence of the Second Great Awakening on the declining use of Enlightenment rhetoric, see May (1976, pt. 4, ch. 1).

5. On the role of rights rhetoric in the early nineteenth century, and its subsequent decline, see Rodgers (1987, chs. 3–4).

6. Adding together all speeches in favor of extending the franchise beyond its current limits shows that over 60 percent of these speeches described the vote as a right. Out of the approximately sixty speeches put forward in favor of the extension of suffrage, seven intimated the only reason they were for extension was that it brought no harm.

7. As in many speeches in favor of reform, delegates spoke as if they were advocating true democracy: for example, universal suffrage or a perfect system of one person/one vote. However, their preferred policies fell significantly short of that ideal.

8. Another advocate of extending the suffrage, a well-to-do planter who served in public office for forty years, Thomas Bayly followed Thompson's lead and also connected political power to liberty, and the lack of voice to slavery: any "free man who is willing to be governed by laws and . . . prefers to relinquish to other men the authority to elect the Lawgiver is a slave already" (VA 1829–1830, 373). This argument, though less common than the outright claim that voting was an inalienable natural right, should be construed as liberal as well.

9. Each of these other rationales for glorifying the vote might be considered republican arguments. However, by the nineteenth century, it was individual nonvoters who were considered slaves, even in the midst of a free, independent, self-governing community. This differs from earlier, more communitarian understandings of republican freedom.

10. In Virginia no one even suggested that the vote was a right of nature lost with the compact, although elsewhere this occasionally did form part of the reply.

11. This convention was held prior to great migration of poor Europeans into the state. As most residents had some possessions, the taxation requirement would not disenfranchise many.

12. This rhetorical ploy was especially valuable in Massachusetts where there always existed strong antislavery sentiments and where would soon emerge a forceful abolitionist movement. For examples of early antislavery rhetoric in New England and especially Massachusetts during the founding period, see various essays in the Hyneman and Lutz (1983) reader, especially essays numbers 16, 25, 58. On the antislavery movement in general, see Foner (1970, esp. ch. 4). Of note, Garrison and Frederick Douglass—both strong abolitionists—were based in Massachusetts, as were Emerson and Thoreau. The transcendentalist movement began in the Boston area of the state.

13. At the New York 1821 convention, the equation between rights and self-government was made by Federalists, Whigs, and Democrats.

14. Others who make the same argument include Chancellor Kent (NY 1821, 190) and Rufus King (NY 1821, 192).

15. Restrictionists disagreed with the list of rights but not with the basic premise regarding how to interpret the provisions outlined in article 4, section 2. Chief Justice Spencer disconnected the U.S. Constitution from questions of political rights, arguing that the national document "regards more personal rights, . . . [for example] to purchase property and enjoy all the personal rights" (NY 1821, 195–96). Yet Spencer and the others who made this case indirectly admitted that the national constitutional provision about equal rights and privileges left little discretion to the states. Again, this is a radical departure from the traditional interpretation of this clause and of America's general conception of federalism.

16. Massachusetts was a notable exception. The strength of the abolitionist movement there apparently prevented color qualifications from entering the constitution.

17. This study rarely draws examples from state debates over residency and citizenship requirements. Such requirements were often not debated but were slipped in as a natural change to complement or counteract other reductions. In New York's 1846 constitution a citizen requirement replaced the 1821 one-year residency requirement for taxpayers. In Louisiana we see significant debate and notable differences in alternative residency requirements for citizens. In this southern state, debates over residency and citizen requirements followed the pattern outlined in the next few text paragraphs: they were less emphatically about rights than earlier. There were nonetheless occasional references to the inalienable rights status of the vote.

18. On the specific issue of competence, see the forthcoming chapters in Part 2.

19. In North Carolina no one discussed the natural origin of any right, private or public. They looked to constitutions, at the state and national levels, to make their case.

20. This argument was not apparent in 1821, but in the late 1840s New York's abolitionist movement was gaining strength.

21. In fact Kennedy argued against inserting the word *white* in the New York 1846 constitution as part of the requirements for the franchise. However, he is not an "expansionist" because he clearly wanted to exclude blacks. He simply preferred to do so

through the ordinary legislative process rather than the constitution (NY 1846, 783–84).

22. As in North Carolina, Ohio restrictionists won and took away the black privilege to vote. This is partly because of the increasing black migration to the state and the fears this engendered, especially with inhabitants of Cincinnati, whose population by 1830 was 10 percent black. See Roseboom and Weisenburger (1956, 151–52). There was a strong abolitionist movement afoot in Ohio, which brought intrastate hostility; see Foner (1970, ch. 3).

23. Although Woodbury never specifically called political voice an inalienable right, same as the personal rights, the implication was there, especially when one considers the speech to which he was responding. William Sawyer had just noted that state and national laws may give "equal right to all" but "exclusive privilege" is another matter. He thought the franchise was a privilege that blacks simply did not deserve (OH 1850–1851, 553).

24. The presence of this kind of racism, which Smith (1993) terms ascriptive Americanism, suggests that liberalism was not the only language underlying electoral reform. See Scalia (1998).

25. On the growing role of parties during this period, see McCormick (1966). Questions of party did arise in debates in Ohio over the basis of representation and in Louisiana, New York, and Virginia over the selection of nonlegislative officers. See later in this chapter and Chapter 5.

26. Studies of constitution-making in the 1840s, 1850s, and 1860s (Fritz 1989, 1994; Hall 1983) make no mention of natural law as part of the supporting rhetoric.

27. Ohio, which had long been almost wholly Democratic, began to feel the influence of party opposition in the late 1840s. In 1848 Whigs won an upset gubernatorial victory. The growing strength of an abolitionist movement led to further party divisions. See Roseboom and Weisenburger (1956, 148–54).

28. In New York and Massachusetts where governors were comparatively stronger and had veto power, the vote selected governors and legislators. In most other states examined, the question of franchise usually came up prior to the question of how to select executive or judicial officers. Therefore, debates over suffrage were generally debates over who was going to have the power to select lawmakers.

29. When discussing the great men of the past who sanctioned majority rule, they mostly meant the earlier writers of their state constitution and said so explicitly. Defenders of the national Constitution, most especially *Publius*, did not embrace majority rule with such zeal.

30. Besides Cooke quoted above, four other delegates described equal political power as the very essence of freedom, the very opposite of slavery. Five others emphasized the connection between majority rule and the natural environment people lived in prior to forming the original social compact; three used hypothetical scenarios of how frontiersmen formed government (see Powell's story in Chapter 1). Five referred to Locke and/or his *Second Treatise* as supporting this interpretation. Nine used Virginia's constitution and its rights declaration to justify the inalienability of majority rule.

31. Again, in New York and Massachusetts, governors had significant lawmaking

influence. In those states, therefore, the right to vote was the right to select legislators and the governor.

32. On America's early constitutional views about the primary role of electing legislators and the secondary role of electing governors, see Kruman (1997, ch. 6), Lutz (1980, 87–99), and Wood (1969, 132–43).

33. Their arguments were similar to the national founders' worries regarding the dangers of a directly elected president. See Ceaser (1979, ch. 1).

34. The only other speech at all reminiscent of Hoge's ideas—but certainly not as forceful—was put forward by John Carlile, state senator and soon to be pro-unionist Know Nothing U.S. congressman. He argued that denying the governor reeligibility was equivalent to "depriving the people of that power that naturally belongs to them" (VA 1850–1851, 118).

35. Iowa recorded only a few scattered speeches on this issue and what was said appears to follow this general pattern.

36. Shklar (1991, 39–52) suggests that those favoring the expansion of suffrage made this analogy far more frequently than is revealed by an analysis of these convention debates.

37. This is consistent with Rogers's (1987, ch. 3) argument. Also, prior to 1840, there was little codification of common law (Hall 1989, 126–27). This might explain why, in the 1820s and 1830s, principle was deemed more important than law; the laws had yet to be written.

38. See Ashcraft (1986, ch. 11) and Stevens (1996).

39. Obviously some revolutionaries and late eighteenth-century statesmen declared self-government an inalienable right (Paine, for example). Kruman (1997, ch. 5) quotes from some revolutionary constitution writers who made this case. Nedelsky (1990, 113) describes James Wilson, an influential participant at the nation's constitutional convention, as also sharing this view. What makes the nineteenth-century arguments so striking is their elaborate Lockean-like explanations as to why self-government should be considered a right.

40. See Barber (1991, 25–27), Beard (1986, 324–25), Hartz (1955, ch. 1), and Miller (1988).

3. Antireformers and Property

1. Scholars of Locke who claim he gave equal preference to all three aims include Laslett (1988, 102–3), Grant (1987, ch. 2), and Zuckert (1994, ch. 9). Those who see him as especially bourgeois and stressing material possessions above all other rights include Macpherson (1962, 197–99) and perhaps Strauss (1950, 245–48).

2. McDonald (1985, 152) describes America's allegiance to private property as originating from Locke.

3. Some of the arguments in Paine's *Common Sense* are devoted to these issues. See his essay, especially the Library of Liberal Arts edition, pp. 20–24, 39–40.

4. On Hamilton's capitalist biases, see McCoy (1980, 134, 152–56). On Madison's

view of property, see Nedelsky (1990, ch. 2). On the general importance of economic development to the nation's constitution writers, see Beard (1986) or Matson and Onuf (1990), who agree that economic considerations mattered greatly, yet whose approaches and conclusions differ radically.

5. On these concerns during the founding era, see Epstein (1984, 82–87), Nedelsky (1990, 35), and Pangle (1988, 94). On the importance of property in nineteenth-century America, see Hurst (1956) and Welter (1975). On the effects of banks and national economic planning on American development away from an agrarian economy, see Hammond (1957).

6. Praises of property were visibly absent from western states. In every case where property was praised, delegates meant material possessions. Their accolades belittled the importance of day laborers and those not self-employed, an argument Macpherson (1962, 197–222) attributes to Locke. Matson and Onuf (1990, 21–22) note this same Lockean aspect in Revolutionary America.

7. This concern was one that Nedelsky (1990, 27–28) describes as troubling Madison and as illustrative of the special value Madison gave material possessions.

8. On the political turmoils in New York at this time, see Wilentz (1984).

9. This was one of the few instances when delegates went out of their way to praise a particular speaker and endorse their allegiance to his perspectives, knowing that he was a well-respected statesman.

10. This latter argument is embedded in a larger argument about human nature (see Chapter 5).

11. There were a few others that defy easy categorization. Morgan Taylor of Louisiana, for example, made the case for a senatorial district system by county as a means to encourage movement to the unpopulated regions of the state. Then, "in a few years, the fertile districts will be filled up" (LA 1845, 565–66). This he saw as a great advantage to the state and its prosperity.

12. As with Justice Story, the contributions applauded were often those made outside of government, that is, philanthropic contributions to church and school building.

13. At the outset Americans tied the public good to agriculture and landed property. Later the public good became more closely aligned with personal property and capital accumulation. On the relationship between economic landed interests and the common good, see Adams (1980, 224–26) and DeGeorge (1988, 11–12). On the importance of property in nineteenth-century America, see Hurst (1956) and Welter (1975).

14. Nedelsky (1990, 207–8) makes the case that Madison too thought that without secured property there could be no secured life or liberty.

15. See Calhoun's *Disquisition on Government*, particularly the 1953 Macmillan edition, pp. 12–19.

16. This is Macpherson's understanding of Hobbes's state of nature. See his introduction to *The Leviathan*, in the Penguin 1985 edition. On this point, also, see Simmons (1992).

17. On this aspect of Locke, clearly not an uncontroversial one, see Macpherson (1962). On the importance of prosperity in Locke's theory, see Strauss (1950, 236–51).

18. Schlesinger (1950, 308–14) notes that Jacksonian Democrats often deemphasized property rights in relation to other rights, most especially liberty. If reform delegates ever emphasized any right it was liberty, and this was mostly in New York in arguments favoring black suffrage. These proponents were often Whigs, which suggests that the phenomenon noted by Schlesinger crossed party lines.

19. See Macpherson (1962).

20. They might be said to represent the Lockes of Ashcraft (1986), Hartz (1955), and Macpherson (1962), respectively.

PART II. DEBATES OVER PROTECTING RIGHTS

1. See *Federalist Essays* especially 10, 47–51, 62–63 (Hamilton et al. 1982). Several have argued that procedures and institutional mechanisms were put in place largely in response to the realization that self-interest was the dominant force driving human behavior. "They innovatively wrote tactics for checking power abuses, . . . relying on the self-interest of individual officeholders to preserve the boundaries among the legislature, the executive and the judiciary. . . . Self interest was accepted as a functional equivalent to civic virtue" (Appleby 1992, 218–19). "The framers saw themselves as enlightened architects working with forces and weights to erect a government primarily of mechanisms rather than of men" (Diggins 1984, 67). Both these authors admit that the rhetoric of virtue continued but that the founders recognized it had no real chance of guiding government. See Appleby (1992, 215–18) and Diggins (1984, ch. 3). Others who insist on the founders' newfound reliance on self-interest include Hartz (1955, ch. 3), Hofstadter (1973, 3), Kerber (1980, 195–200), and Wood (1969, 611–12). There are some who note that these designers in fact still believed virtue to be an essential component of the good state. See Epstein (1984, 22–26), Gill (1988, 37), Lutz (1988, 86–89), McDonald (1985, 189–99), and Sinopoli (1992, 19). Pangle (1988, 71–73; 1991, 118) makes the case that, while the founders worked to harness both as best they could, in fact the virtue they spoke about was certainly less noble than the classic one. In this sense, Pangle's view approaches that of Appleby and Diggins.

2. For a discussion of these institutional features and the theory underlying them, see Adams (1980, ch. 12), Hall (1991, 396), Kruman (1997, chs. 4–5), Main (1973, 151–200), Nevins (1969, ch. 4), Sturm (1982, 61), and Wood (1969, ch. 5).

3. See Kruman (1997, ch. 3).

4. Every initial constitution contained pecuniary restrictions on who had political influence. Thus, original designers may have relied on popular virtue, but they recognized that not all citizens had the disposition necessary to live up to the protective role laid out for them. For a discussion of state constitutional writers' concerns with government abuse as well as an overall analysis of the relationship between initial constitutional designs and questions of popular virtue versus popular tyranny, see Lutz (1980, esp. ch. 1) or Wood (1969, pt. 2).

5. See various essays in Hyneman and Lutz (1983, vol. 1), such as essays 4, 5, 10, 37, 44, 47. See also Appleby (1984), Dworetz (1990, ch. 1), Ketcham (1984, 76–85),

Kloppenberg (1987), Pocock (1975, ch. 15), and Wood (1969, 65–70).

6. For a discussion of the religions provisions in early state constitutions, see Levy (1986) and Wald (1987, 36–38). The political intent of these provisions were sometimes discussed by contemporary preachers and statesmen, who stressed the importance of godly selfless behavior, not just as a means to acquire individual salvation but also to foster good citizenship. See Hyneman and Lutz (1983, 1: 658–74), Sandoz (1991, 627–56), and Shain (1994, 38–41, 132). Nineteenth-century constitutional debates over whether to lift these restrictions include discussions of how these initial requirements were useful in the production of the moral citizens that republican government relied upon. For an analysis of these discussions, see Scalia (1997).

7. There remains widespread agreement that the political philosophy of John Locke and the liberal tradition he inspired have influenced American political thought, especially in the late eighteenth century. See Diggins (1984), Hartz (1955), Pangle (1988), Smith (1985), Zuckert (1994, 18–25), or nearly any essay in Licht (1991). At the same time many have discussed other, non-Lockean, religious and secular sources of early American political thought. See Bailyn (1967, 22–30), May (1976), Miller (1991), Pocock (1975, ch. 15), Shain (1994, esp. intro.), Wills (1978, esp. prologue), and Wood (1969, pt. 1). Many of these scholars note the simultaneous influences of two or more intellectual traditions.

8. While no longer legally precluded, atheism was still socially taboo. The belief that good men were God-fearing, God-respecting men remained unquestioned throughout the time period studied. On the prevalence of religious sentiments and ideals in early nineteenth-century American thought, see Cooke (1986), who studies the concept of liberty and its connection to notions of religious freedom. In fact, there exists much evidence that many Americans believed religiosity the key not only to the private life but also to the operations of the good state. Debates in Massachusetts and North Carolina on the lifting of religious restrictions clearly illustrate their belief in the ongoing importance of moral virtue. On American thought regarding the need of Christian values to support democracy, see Clarke (1958). On this same point, see also Jaenicke (1981), who discusses the widespread role of religion in early nineteenth-century rhetoric regarding the individual, the community, and party politics. Finally, on the importance of religion in the good state according to Whig ideology, see Howe (1979, ch. 7) or Schlesinger (1950, ch. 27). Nonetheless, these ideas did not manifest themselves in the law since legal sanctions to enforce religious obligation, even at the local level, basically disappeared by the early nineteenth century. On the changing local legal provisions, see Lutz (1980, 167–70).

9. See Thorpe (1898, 2: 423–25). Because executive changes began prior to the U.S. Constitution, some say the Federalists followed state cues. On this point, see Lutz (1988, 108), Nevins (1969, 172–73), and Wood (1969, ch. 11). Although defenders of the national Constitution certainly wanted to make the case that the president was no different from state governors, in fact the former was far more powerful and people of the time knew it—as certain defensive arguments in the *Federalist Papers* (67–73, for example) make clear.

10. See Thorpe (1898, vol. 2, ch. 14) and Wood (1993, 323–25). Judicial changes began occurring after the passage of the national Constitution. State judges continued gaining power throughout the 1860s (see Hall 1983).

4. VIRTUE AND GOVERNMENT

1. Yarbrough (1979b) discusses many of these aspects as part of *The Federalist*'s view of representation. Anderson (1993, 170) also describes this filtering argument. He sees Madison's argument as an elitist attempt to reduce the political influence of the general public.

2. Ohio's 1802 constitution had judges selected by the house. No one spoke in favor of perpetuating this practice. Instead, it was a question of how extended the territory per selecting district should be.

3. The speech of King at the Ohio convention (OH 1850–1851, 146–48) is an example of one of these isolated incidents.

4. In some states, such as Virginia, delegates preferred to make the house of delegates the more deliberative branch and to use it to check the senate.

5. Convention participants aimed to design a government that protected rights and ensured prosperity. On the general importance of economic prosperity and its relation to nineteenth-century conceptions of the common good, see Hurst (1956) and Nelson (1987). On the relationship between rights and the common good, see DeGeorge (1988, 11–12) and Rodgers (1987, ch. 3). For a detailed description of what delegates meant by virtue and good citizenship, see Chapter 5.

6. Those in Virginia blamed political uprisings in New York on the state's policy of universal suffrage. On the economic upheavals in New York at this time, see Wilentz (1984).

7. The word *virtue* is used broadly throughout the next two subsections. For a detailed explanation of what delegates meant by this term, see Chapter 5.

8. Williams compared his argument to Jefferson's, arguing that he had this great American founder on his side.

9. It was only in debates over whether to make previously appointed officers popularly elected that questions of party influence were consistently and visibly present.

10. Although Van Buren was not one of the delegates who demanded suffrage expansion because he thought the vote was an inalienable right of nature, others making this connection were against electing justices of the peace. Compare John Cramer's speech about these judges and his rationale for suffrage expansion (NY 1821, 324, 335–39). Holding both views is not necessarily inconsistent, however (see Chapter 2). Although voting for lawmakers was deemed an essential right, voting for nonlegislative officers was not.

11. Dorr's rebellion might serve as a good example here. Men without political power were able to stage an uprising and bring havoc to Rhode Island. Of course, given the cause, expansionists might not have portrayed this situation as one of corruption. Given the outcome of the rebellion, however, expansionists would probably not have

used this case as an example of the powerlessness of a propertied senate.

12. Hall (1983) describes the same general features but uses them to illustrate a different point.

13. These words were taken from Virginia's 1776 constitution, though at the time, the declaration had less practical meaning than it had by 1850. For every state constitution examined, both new and old constitutions had similar declarations.

14. On the important instrumental role of virtue within the liberal tradition and among the national founders, see Diggins (1984, chs. 2–3), Kloppenberg (1987), and Pangle (1988, 71–73).

15. Though radically different from the views of *Publius*, nineteenth-century accounts of how checks and balances operate in some sense resemble those of James Wilson, who never expected designs to be able to prevent the legislature from implementing the will of the people, even if their will was unwise or unjust. See Nedelsky (1990, 133).

5. HUMAN NATURE AND GOOD CITIZENSHIP

1. On the consequences of the liberal emphasis on interests as the basis of behavior and its embrace of limited government mediation in morality, see various essays in Rosenblum (1989). For an extended discussion on this liberal conception of virtue and how it differs from other intellectual traditions, see Galston (1988).

2. Revolutionary Americans and the nation's state builders are said to have made similar arguments, recognizing that acquisitiveness brought the very prosperity and distributive justice that Locke acclaimed (Pangle 1988, 92–93; Rahe 1992, 560–63). These late eighteenth-century Americans are said to have built on this and other Lockean principles regarding the origins of government by noting that people who cared primarily about their own economic advancement would seek government mainly to protect rights, especially their property holdings (Diggins 1984, 7; Pangle 1988, 97–98). This independent connection to Lockean ideas does not necessarily indicate defiance of the first view, for there exist clear connections between the economic views of Hobbes and Locke on one hand and Smith and Hume on the other. On this point, see Grampp (1965, 11–12, 16, 20–22, 42–44).

3. On a similar theory of human motivation in Hobbes, see Shapiro (1986, 57–59), and in Hobbes and Locke, see Macpherson (1962, 41–46, 232–35). Both Shapiro and Macpherson emphasize the connection between one's interest in property and one's interest to acquire power.

4. Adams (1980, 211–12) briefly discusses a similar perspective among state constitution writers in the late eighteenth century.

5. Whenever I refer to this particular aspect of good citizenship, I use the word *private* in quotes.

6. This is consistent with the Protestant view sometimes attributed to Locke and early Americans. In this case, Locke is recognized as a Calvinist, who connected the fruits of labor and industry to God's will and perhaps salvation (Diggins 1984, 7–9; Dworetz 1990, ch. 4, esp. p. 133). Some scholars question Locke's connection to Calvin-

ism per se, but not to Protestant values in general (Dunn 1971; Rahe 1992, 489). According to this reading of Locke and of Americans who followed the ideas associated with it, "private" virtue is valued because it marks godly honor (Diggins 1984, 7–9; Dworetz 1990, ch. 4; Greenstone 1986).

7. This is consistent with the more economically interested Locke. It is actually difficult, if not impossible, to separate secular liberal virtues from those Protestant virtues that were supposed to lead to salvation (Appleby 1992, 182). These ideals—regardless of why individuals seek them—still have the same de facto outcome, namely, to encourage work instead of dangerous political demands.

8. Josiah Quincy was speaker of the state house at the time and later became Boston mayor and then president of Harvard.

9. John Adams is well known for his belief that power holders consult only their own narrow self-interests when acting in political matters. Virtue was not a trustworthy foundation for government. See the selection from his *Defense of the Constitution of Government of the U.S.* against the attack of M. Trugot, reproduced in *The People Shall Judge*, 208–13. On this point, see also Appleby (1992, ch. 7, esp. 196) and Diggins (1984, ch. 3).

10. This is the view attributed to the founders. See Appleby (1992, ch. 8, esp. 215–18) and Diggins (1984, 54–55).

11. McCoy (1980, 68) discusses a similar argument at the national level. As he depicts it, Americans connected independence to property, with this connection being part of the idea that property ownership led to responsible citizenship.

12. Cooke (1986) connects the underlying assumption of black irrationality to America's religious beliefs. Henretta (1989, 362), who studies other aspects of constitutional reform during the antebellum period, describes this as a common perspective shared by politicians at the time; he characterizes this as the principle of *Herrenvolk*. See also Smith (1988, 235). On the illiberal underpinnings of American views toward blacks, see Smith (1993) and Scalia (1998, esp. 357–62).

13. See Madison's letter to the *National Gazette*, reproduced in Meyers (1981, 246–48). On Jefferson's views, see the selections from his *Anas* reproduced in *The People Shall Judge* (1949, 395–400). For Hamilton's perspective, see his letter to Edward Carrington of May 26, 1792 (Frisch 1984).

14. On early party skepticism, see Hofstadter (1969, esp. chs. 1–2). On America's continuing negative evaluation of party politics, see Howe (1979, 51–54), McCormick (1986, 159–60), and Meyers (1957, 242–45).

15. See Pangle (1988, 168–69) and Rahe (1992, 514–18, 560–63).

16. One Virginia reformer talked about the "private" virtues and the role they played in good government; he did this only vaguely and indirectly. According to Richard Henderson, voters required a "prevailing and discriminating common sense . . . to select their public functionaries with judgment." For Henderson it was work not property that brought this kind of good character: "moderate labor inspires sound sense." At the same time, he echoed the sentiments repeatedly noted by his expansionist colleagues: "Sacred love of country [and] ineffable attachment" cannot be purchased with gold, he believed. A freeholder has no "more enduring attachment to his country,

than" a member of the peasant class. "A man without property stakes his liberty, his life, his reputation, his happiness and *his right to acquire property*." One need not have a personal stake in something in order to protect it (VA 1829–1830, 357).

17. Embedded in his argument was an allusion to the importance of Christian virtue. There is good evidence to suggest that this conception underlay the positions of many. Earlier constitutions contained elaborate provisions and declarations aimed at encouraging Christianity, and when delegates in Massachusetts and North Carolina debated whether the state should encourage religious faith among its citizens and leaders, delegates made it clear they believed that Christian morality and piety lay at the foundation of the good state. At the same time, their speeches suggest they saw Christian virtue not only as connected to "private" virtue but also as sharing characteristics with it. People cultivated Christian virtue for a private purpose, this time for salvation rather than personal gain. The benefits that accrued to the state were inadvertent. Because the people desired salvation (a private interest), they would act more justly toward their fellow citizens. On this subject, see Scalia (1997). For the ongoing influence of religion in nineteenth-century political conceptions of and protections for liberty, see Cooke (1986).

18. Nash's position is an unusual one. Across all conventions, only three other speeches favoring the extension of political power explicitly discussed political virtue in such self-sacrificing terms.

19. This was one of the few cases outside Virginia that delegates continued to discuss virtue. However, in this case virtuousness was equated with behavior in the economy, and this equation was made by expansionists. Although it was often Whigs who favored this policy, party alone does not explain this crossover in rhetoric.

20. Prior to this convention Willey had served on the state's house of delegates for many years; he soon went on to the state senate. He later represented the state in the U.S. Senate as a vocal Unionist.

21. On the connection between these sentiments and the republican tradition, see Banning (1978, 11–12) or Pocock (1975, esp. ch. 3), who both believe these values influenced American thinking of the good state. Many others discuss this connection but are skeptical of its influence in America (see Diggins 1984, 9–11).

22. Wilson too had a sense that individuals naturally had moral and social sensibilities, that they saw themselves as responsible to their communities. Nedelsky (1990, ch. 4, esp. 97–99) discusses his perspective and its intellectual debt to Scottish Enlightenment thinkers.

23. This does not mean there were not other significant ideological influences in American political thought during this time, only that these other influences did not appear to guide their visions of human nature and minimal good citizenship, particularly in connection with white men.

CONCLUSION

1. Levinson (1990, 2443–44), Murphy (1988, 63–64), and Richards (1989, 132–38) discuss Madison's hostility to frequent constitutional revision. Kammen (1988,

ch. 1, esp. 29) and Nedelsky (1990, 154–63) stress the antidemocratic features of this and other designs that Madison advocated.

2. Hofstadter (1973, 32–40) and Murphy (1988, 62, 64) discuss Jefferson's principled commitment to frequent constitutional revision and the consequences he feared should such freedom be stifled. Peterson (1962, 11) and Sheldon (1991, 59–70) discuss Jefferson's enlightenment understanding and his faith in the progress of the human mind, and how these views account for his predictions regarding the consequences of popular influence.

3. Lutz (1994) claims that the size of any constitution is the most important determinant of the stability of its contents. Neither the available means for its alteration nor its cultural traditions regarding popular sovereignty substantially account for the frequency of constitutional revision. Although there is good evidence for his case, there remains the question of what caused the initial length, especially in the American case where some of the very constitutions that began as short, concise documents—under ten pages long—are now three or four times that size.

4. On the statutory features of state constitutions and their potential consequences, see Hall (1991).

5. James Bryce recognized that state constitutions contained two kinds of laws: statutory regulations and fundamental principles. See Bryce 1899, vol. 1, ch. 37 (quotations pp. 436, 437).

6. On the general population's lack of knowledge about state constitutions, see Kincaid (1988, 163, 169). See Sturm (1982) for a historical account of the development of American state constitutions, including the frequency of revision. Sturm calculates the frequency of constitutional amendments from 1776 to 1979 (78–79).

7. Colorado's recent attempt to discredit homosexuals as a legitimate minority, able to litigate against discrimination, is a case in point. The amendment—entitled "No Protected Status Based on Homosexual, Lesbian, or Bisexual Orientation"—forbade the state or any of its branches or agencies to adopt or enforce any statute that entitled homosexuals, lesbians, or bisexuals to claim minority or protected status or discrimination. See Koppelman (1997, 93) for a full text of the amendment.

8. Bryce uses this as an example to make his case—that despite statutory features, constitutions retain their status as fundamental law. See Bryce (1899, vol. 1, ch. 37). Of course, the actions of lawmakers are sometimes contested and deemed unconstitutional, but this only underlines the point that state constitutions remain important guides.

9. It was this kind of analysis that supported the overturning of Colorado's "antidiscrimination" amendment. See the U.S. Supreme Court decision *Roemer v. Evans* 116 U.S. 1996. Koppelman (1997), who discusses the decision in detail, argues that the main rationale for the court's decision was the perceived intent of the amendment to harm the rights of a certain group of individuals. It was determined that anti-right features were inconsistent with the meaning and purpose of state constitutions.

10. The concern with religion, rights, and popular sovereignty is probably best illustrated by reading the documents themselves. For a discussion on the influence of consent and the popular sovereignty doctrine on colonial thinking and charter

development, see Lutz (1988, 38–63). On how their perceptions of human nature influenced government design, see Lutz (1988, 23–31) and Wald (1987, 36–38). On the role of religion and its covenantal tradition on the writing of these documents, see Elazar (1994, chs. 1, 2, 5) and Lutz (1988, 25–27, 38). On the role of the common law tradition on colonial constitutions, see Kaye (1992, 730–32).

11. Although, during this period, no state kept a record of the precise issues concerning its constitutional design, Handlin and Handlin (1966) have reconstructed a record of local Massachusetts responses to its first constitution. The views recorded are informative and show an active concern with human nature, rights protection, and popular sovereignty (see Scalia 1997). On the importance of popular sovereignty to revolutionary constitution writers, see Kruman (1997, ch. 4), Lutz (1988, 101–8), and Wood (1969, chs. 5, 9). On the inalienable importance these individuals placed on rights, see Kruman (1997, 37–49). On their views about human nature and the need for virtue, coupled with republican influences, see Wood (1969, 65–70, 93–97, 107–24). On the various traditions affecting American political thought during the founding era, see Appleby (1992, ch. 5), and Bailyn (1967, ch. 2).

12. On changing views regarding the potential for virtue and how these contributed to new ideas, regarding the priority of rights over popular sovereignty, see Agresto (1977), Conkin (1974, 177), Diggins (1984, 61–62), Kammen (1988, ch. 1, esp. 29), Lutz (1988, 5–6), Pangle (1988, ch. 12), Wood (1969, 475–524), and Yarbrough (1979a, b). On the specific connections between liberal ideology and the thinking of the national Constitution writers, especially *Publius*, see Appleby (1992, ch. 8, 337), Nedelsky (1990, 175, 181–82), and Kramnick (1982, esp. 662).

13. Fritz (1997, 322–29), Kruman (1997, ch. 2), and Rodgers (1987, 94–101) speak of constitutional conventions as suspending all power and authority except those of the people. On occasion, antebellum delegates too spoke of themselves as purely popular delegates, joined together to form a new social contract.

14. Black enfranchisement was in some sense a special case (see Chapters 2, 5, and Scalia 1998). Debates over this issue did not engender the liberal rhetoric that other issues so definitively encouraged.

15. Banning (1986, 11–12) nicely contrasts what he and others take to be the views embodying liberalism and republicanism. In addition to Appleby and Kramnick, whom Banning mentions, Diggins (1984, ch. 1) and Hofstadter (1973, ch. 1) also describe American liberalism in the narrow Lockean terms described in the text. Also, in addition to Banning himself and Pocock, whom he cites in this contrast, Yarbrough (1979a, 64–66) describes civic virtue and the intrinsic commitment to popular participation as essential elements of American adaptation of republican theory.

Of note, most of these individuals do not claim that just one ideological tradition held full and complete sway over eighteenth-century Americans. In addition to Lockean liberalism and classical and Renaissance republicanism, some of the other traditions thought to influence eighteenth-century American political thought include British Common Law, the Scottish Enlightenment, and Puritanism. See Bailyn (1967, 22–30), Dworetz (1990, ch. 1, 191), Kramnick (1988), May (1976), Miller (1991), Shain (1994, esp. intro.), Wills (1978, esp. prologue), and Wood (1969, pt. 1). Most of these scholars note the simultaneous influence of two or more of these intellectual traditions.

16. That Americans translated concepts of virtue into modern liberal language is not a new finding. See Appleby (1992, ch. 13), Ashworth (1984), McCoy (1980, 72–77), Shalhope (1982, 350–52), and Yarbrough (1979a, 70–72). The point here is much broader. By now, multiple meanings of a liberal interpretation of natural virtue had prominent voice. One of these interpretations—the newfound view that social sentiments were a *reliable* basis upon which to build government designs—was for the first time granted a constitutional place of consequence.

17. These very ideas would undergo reformulation again in the years following. In response to demands to alleviate the ills of monopoly power and later depression woes, for example, economic rights such as the right to a job and fair wages would be added to the liberal language of rights. Political rhetoric would learn to accept a new kind of natural human phenomenon, that of economic helplessness. These views would then find their way into twentieth-century state constitutions. Debates among laissez-faire economists and advocates of government intervention each strove to use the language of liberalism to support their position. See the excerpts in Dolbeare (1996, 482–516) and Levy (1992, 395–435). Neither side definitively won this ideological battle. On the use and abuse of liberal ideology throughout America's political tradition, see Rotunda (1986) and Young (1996).

18. This was especially the case of the speeches of the most celebrated speakers. On this point and the general public's interest in convention debates, see Rodgers (1987, 94).

19. This dialectic has been suggested before; see the works of Rogers M. Smith and of Terence Ball and J. A. G. Pocock. For these authors, the U.S. Constitution—a document of foundational values—naturally encouraged writers and interpreters to fit their vision of the American system into actual policies, thereby contributing to changing perceptions of the American ideal. See the introductions to Smith (1985) and to Ball and Pocock (1988). Rodgers (1987, 212–25) makes a similar claim when describing how the meanings of key words change over time.

20. See Ericson (1993, 73–113).

21. On the republican features of political economy debates, see McCoy (1980, chs. 7–9). On the role of religion on nineteenth-century understandings of liberty, see Cooke (1986, ch. 3). On the role of ethnocentric prejudices (termed Ascriptivism) on immigration policy, see Smith (1997, chs. 7–8, 10–11).

References

Adams, Ephraim Douglass. 1913. *The Power of Ideals in American History.* New Haven: Yale University Press.

Adams, William H. 1973. *The Whig Party of Louisiana.* Lafayette: University of Southwestern Louisiana.

Adams, Willi Paul. 1980. *The First American Constitutions: Republican Ideology and the Making of the State Constitutions in the Revolutionary Era.* Translated by Rita and Robert Kimber. Chapel Hill: University of North Carolina Press.

Agresto, John T. 1977. "Liberty, Virtue and Republicanism, 1776–1787." *Review of Politics* 39, no. 4 (October): 473–504.

Amar, Ahkil Reed. 1988. "Philadelphia Revisited: Amending the Constitution outside Article V." *University of Chicago Law Review* 55, no. 4 (fall): 1043–104.

Anderson, Thornton. 1993. *Creating the Constitution: The Convention of 1787 and the First Congress.* University Park: Pennsylvania State University Press.

Appleby, Joyce. 1984. *Capitalism and a New Social Order: The Republican Vision of the 1790s.* New York: New York University Press.

———. 1992. *Liberalism and Republicanism in the Historical Imagination.* Cambridge, Mass.: Harvard University Press.

Aptheker, Herbert. 1970. *American Negro Slave Revolts.* 1943. Reprint, New York: International Publishers.

Arieli, Yehoshua. 1964. *Individualism and Nationalism in American Ideology.* Cambridge, Mass.: Harvard University Press.

Ashcraft, Richard. 1986. *Revolutionary Politics and Locke's Two Treatises of Government.* Princeton, N.J.: Princeton University Press.

Ashworth, John. 1983. *Agrarians and Aristocrats: Party Political Ideology in the United States, 1837–1846.* London: Swift Printers.

———. 1984. "The Jeffersonians: Classical Republicans or Liberal Capitalists?" *Journal of American Studies* 18, no. 3 (December): 425–35.

Bailyn, Bernard, 1967. *The Ideological Origins of the American Revolution.* Cambridge. Mass.: Harvard University Press.

———. 1968. *The Origins of American Politics.* New York: Vintage Books.

Baker, Lynn A. 1995. "Constitutional Change and Direct Democracy." *University of Colorado Law Review* 66, no. 1 (winter): 143–58.

Ball, Terence, and J. G. A. Pocock. 1988. *Conceptual Change and the Constitution*. Lawrence: University Press of Kansas.

Banning, Lance. 1978. *The Jeffersonian Persuasion: Evolution of a Party Ideology*. Ithaca: Cornell University Press.

———. 1986. "Jefferson Ideology Revisited: Liberal and Classical Ideas in the New American Republic." *William and Mary Quarterly* 43, no. 1 (January): 3–19.

Barber, Benjamin. 1984. *Strong Democracy: Participatory Politics for a New Age*. Berkeley and Los Angeles: University of California Press.

———. 1991. "Constitutional Rights: Democratic Instrument or Democratic Obstacle?" In *The Framers and Fundamental Rights*, edited by Robert A. Licht, 23–36. Washington, D.C.: AEI Press.

Bartlett, Irving H. 1982. *The American Mind in the Mid-Nineteenth Century*. Arlington Heights, Ill.: Harlan Davidson.

Beard, Charles A. 1986. *An Economic Interpretation of the Constitution of the United States*. 1913. Revised edition. New York: Free Press.

Beckel, Alexander. 1962. *The Least Dangerous Branch: The Supreme Court and the Bar of Politics*. New Haven: Yale University Press.

Benson, Lee. 1961. *The Concept of Jacksonian Democracy: New York as a Test Case*. Princeton, N.J.: Princeton University Press.

Berger, Mark L. 1973. *The Revolution in the New York Party Systems, 1840–1860*. Port Washington, N.Y.: Kennikat Press.

Bloom, Allan, ed. 1990. *Confronting the Constitution*. Washington, D.C.: AEI Press.

Boyd, William K. 1973. *History of North Carolina*. Vol. 2 of *The Federal Period, 1783–1860*. 1919. Reprint, Spartanburg, S.C.: Reprint Company.

Braybrooke, David. 1983. "Can Democracy Be Combined with Federalism or with Liberalism?" In *Liberal Democracy: Nomos XXV*, edited by J. Ronald Pennock and John W. Chapman, 109–18. New York: New York University Press.

Brown, Robert E. 1955. *Middle-Class Democracy and the Revolution in Massachusetts, 1691–1780*. Ithaca: Cornell University Press.

———. 1956. *Charles Beard and the Constitution: A Critical Analysis of "An Economic Interpretation of the Constitution."* Princeton, N.J.: Princeton University Press.

Bruce, Dickson D., Jr. 1982. *The Rhetoric of Conservatism: The Virginia Convention of 1829–1830 and the Conservative Tradition in the South*. San Marino, Calif.: Huntington Library.

Bryce, James. 1899. *The American Commonwealth*. 2 vols. New York: Macmillan.

Burns, Edward McNall. 1968. *James Madison, Philosopher of the Constitution*. New York: Octagon Books.

Calhoun, John C. 1953. *A Disquisition on Government and Selections from the Discourse*. Edited, with an introduction by C. Gordon Post. 1848. Reprint, New York: Macmillan.

Carey, George W. 1995. *In Defense of the Constitution*. 1987. Revised and expanded edition. Indianapolis: Liberty Press.

Ceaser, James. 1979. *Presidential Selection*. Cambridge, Mass.: Harvard University Press.

Clarke, J. E. 1958. "The American Critique of the Democratic Idea, 1919–1929." Ph.D. dissertation, Stanford University, Stanford, Calif.

Colantuono, Michael G. 1987. "The Revision of American State Constitutions: Legislative Power, Popular Sovereignty and Constitutional Changes." *California Law Review* 75, no. 4 (July): 1473–512.

Conkin, Paul K. 1974. *Self-Evident Truths: A Discourse on the Origins and Development of the First Principles of American Government—Popular Sovereignty, Natural Rights and Separation of Powers.* Bloomington: Indiana University Press.

Cooke, J. W. 1986. *The American Tradition of Liberty, 1800–1860: From Jefferson to Lincoln.* Vol. 1 of *Studies in Social and Political Theory.* Lewiston, N.Y.: Edwin Mellen.

Corwell, Elmer E. Jr., Jay S. Goodman, and Wayne R. Swanson. 1970. "State Constitutional Conventions: Delegates, Roll Calls and Issues." *Midwest Journal of Political Science,* no. 1 (February): 105–30.

Croly, Herbert. 1911. *The Promise of American Life.* New York: Macmillan.

Cronin, Thomas E. 1989. *Direct Democracy: The Politics of Initiative, Referendum, and Recall.* Cambridge, Mass.: Harvard University Press.

DeGeorge, Richard T. 1988. "Introduction: The Philosophical Foundations of the U.S. Constitution." In *Philosophical Dimensions of the Constitution,* edited by Diana T. Meyers and Kenneth Kipnis, 1–14. Boulder, Colo.: Westview Press.

Dethloff, Henry C., ed. 1971. *Thomas Jefferson and American Democracy.* Lexington, Mass.: D. C. Heath.

Dietze, Gottfried. 1960. The Federalist: *A Classic of Federalism and Free Government.* Baltimore: Johns Hopkins University Press.

Diggins, John P. 1984. *The Lost Soul of American Politics.* Chicago: University of Chicago Press.

Dolbeare, Kenneth M. 1996. *American Political Thought.* 3d edition. Chatham, N.J.: Chatham House.

Dunn, John. 1971. "Consent in the Political Theory of John Locke." In *Life, Liberty and Property: Essays on Locke's Political Ideas,* edited by Gordon J. Schochet, 129–61. Belmont, Calif.: Wadsworth.

Dworetz, Steven M. 1990. *The Unvarnished Doctrine: Locke, Liberalism, and the American Revolution.* Durham, N.C.: Duke University Press.

Elazar, Daniel J. 1972. *American Federalism: A View from the States.* New York: Thomas Y. Crowell.

———. 1982. "The Principles and Traditions Underlying State Constitutions." *Publius: The Journal of Federalism* 12 (winter): 11–25.

Elazar, Daniel, ed. 1994. *Covenant in the Nineteenth Century: The Decline of an American Political Tradition.* Lanham, Md.: Rowman and Littlefield.

Ellis, Richard E. 1987. *The Union at Risk: Jacksonian Democracy, States' Rights and the Nullification Crisis.* New York: Oxford University Press.

Ellis, Richard J. 1992. "Radical Lockeanism in American Political Culture." *Western Political Quarterly* 45, no. 4 (December): 825–49.

———. 1993. *American Political Cultures.* New York: Oxford University Press.

Epstein, David F. 1984. *The Political Theory of* The Federalist. Chicago: University of Chicago Press.

Ericson, David F. 1993. *The Shaping of American Liberalism: The Debates over Ratification, Nullification and Slavery*. Chicago: University of Chicago Press.

Flexner, Eleanor. 1972. *Century of Struggle: The Woman's Rights Movement in the United States*. Cambridge, Mass.: Harvard University Press.

Foner, Eric. 1970. *Free Soil, Free Labor, Free Men: The Ideology of the Republican Party before the Civil War*. Oxford: Oxford University Press.

Formisano, Ronald P. 1983. *The Transformation of Political Culture: Massachusetts Parties, 1790s–1840s*. New York: Oxford University Press.

Fox, Dixon Ryan. 1919. *The Decline of Aristocracy in the Politics of New York*. London: P. S. King and Son.

Frisch, Morton J., ed. 1984. *Selected Writings and Speeches of Alexander Hamilton*. Washington, D.C.: American Enterprise Institute for Public Policy Research.

Fritz, Christian G. 1989. "More than 'Shreds and Patches': California's First Bill of Rights." *Hastings Constitutional Law Quarterly* 17, no. 1 (fall): 13–34.

———. 1994. "State-Constitution Making in the Nineteenth-Century West." *Rutger's Law Journal* 25, no. 4 (summer): 945–98.

———. 1997. "Alternative Visions of American Constitutionalism: Popular Sovereignty in the Early American Constitutional Debate." *Hastings Constitutional Law Quarterly* 24, no. 2: 287–357.

Galston, William. 1988. "Liberal Virtues." *American Political Science Review* 82, no. 4: 1277–90.

Garry, Patrick. 1992. *Liberalism and American Ideology*. Kent: Kent State University Press.

Gayarré, Charles. 1965. *History of Louisiana*. Vol. 4. New Orleans: Pelican.

Gill, Emily R. 1988. "Virtue, the Public Good, and Publius." In *Philosophical Dimensions of the Constitution*, edited by Diana T. Meyers and Kenneth Kipnis, 19–39. Boulder, Colo.: Westview Press.

Glasser, Eli A. 1930. "Government and the Constitution." In *Commonwealth History of Massachusetts*, vol. 4, edited by Albert Bushnell Hart, 1–34. New York: The States History Company.

Goldston, Robert. 1968. *The Negro Revolution*. New York: Macmillan.

Graglia, Lino A. 1991. "The Constitution and 'Fundamental Rights.'" In *The Framers and Fundamental Rights*, edited by Robert A. Licht, 86–101. Washington, D.C.: AEI Press.

Grampp, William D. 1965. *Economic Liberalism*. Vol. 2. New York: Random House.

Grant, Ruth W. 1987. *John Locke's Liberalism*. Chicago: University of Chicago Press.

Green, Fletcher M. 1930. *Constitutional Development in the South Atlantic States, 1776–1860: A Study in the Evolution of Democracy*. Chapel Hill: University of North Carolina Press.

Greenstone, J. David. 1986. "Political Culture and American Political Development: Liberty, Union and the Liberal Bipolarity." In *Studies in American Political Development*, edited by Karen Orren and Stephen Skowronek, 1: 1–49. New Haven: Yale University Press.

———. 1993. *The Lincoln Persuasion: Remaking American Liberalism.* Princeton, N.J.: Princeton University Press.

Griffin, Clifford S. 1957. "Religious Benevolence as Social Control, 1815–1860." *Mississippi Valley Historical Review* 44 (December): 423–44.

———. 1960. *Their Brothers' Keepers: Moral Stewardship in the United States, 1800–1865.* New Brunswick, N.J.: Rutgers University Press.

Grisby, Hugh Blair. 1853. *The Virginia Convention of 1829–1830.* New York: Da Capo Press, 1969.

Guinier, Lani. 1994. *The Tyranny of the Majority: Fundamental Fairness in a Representative Democracy.* New York: Free Press.

Gunn, L. Ray. 1979. "The Crisis of Authority in the Antebellum States: New York, 1820–1860." *Review of Politics* 41, no. 2 (April): 273–97.

Haakonssen, Knud. 1991. "From Natural Law to the Rights of Man: A European Perspective on American Debates." In *A Culture of Rights*, edited by Michael J. Lacey and Knud Haakonssen, 19–61. Cambridge, England: Cambridge University Press.

Hall, Kermit L. 1983. "The Judiciary on Trial: State Constitution Reform and the Rise of an Elected Judiciary." *Historian* 44: 337–54.

———. 1989. *The Magic Mirror: Law in American History.* New York: Oxford University Press.

———. 1991. "Mostly Anchor and Little Sail: The Evolution of American State Constitutions." In *Toward a Useable Past: Liberty under State Constitutions*, edited by Paul Finkelman and Stephen E. Gottlieb, 388–417. Athens: University of Georgia Press.

———. 1992. "Of Floors and Ceilings: The New Federalism and State Bills of Rights." *Florida Law Review* 44, no. 4 (September): 637–60.

Hamilton, Alexander, et al. 1982. *The Federalist Papers.* New York: Bantam Books.

Hammond, Bray. 1957. *Banks and Politics in America.* Princeton, N.J.: Princeton University Press.

Handlin, Oscar, and Mary Handlin, eds. 1966. *The Popular Sources of Political Authority: Documents on the Massachusetts Constitution of 1780.* Cambridge, Mass.: Belknap Press of Harvard University Press.

Hanson, Russell. 1985. *The Democratic Imagination in America.* Princeton, N.J.: Princeton University Press.

Hartz, Louis. 1955. *The Liberal Tradition in America.* New York: Harcourt Brace Jovanovich.

Henretta, James A. 1989. "The Rise and Decline of 'Democratic Republicanism': Political Rights in New York and the Several States, 1800–1915." *Albany Law Review* 53: 357–401.

Hofstadter, Richard. 1969. *The Idea of a Party System: The Rise of Legitimate Opposition in the United States, 1780–1840.* Berkeley and Los Angeles: University of California Press.

———. 1973. *The American Political Tradition and the Men Who Made It.* 1948. Reprint, New York: Vintage Books.

Horne, Thomas A. 1981. "Envy and Commercial Society: Mandeville and Smith on 'Private Vices, Public Benefits.'" *Political Theory* 9, no. 4: 551–69.

Horowitz, Robert H., ed. 1986. *The Moral Foundations of the American Republic.* 3d edition. Charlottesville: University Press of Virginia.

Howe, Daniel Walker. 1979. *The Political Culture of the American Whigs.* Chicago: University of Chicago Press.

———. 1990. "Religion and Politics in the Antebellum North." In *Religion and American Politics from the Colonial Period to the 1980s,* edited by Mark A. Noll, 121–45. New York: Oxford University Press.

Huntington, Samuel. 1981. *American Politics: The Promise of Disharmony.* Cambridge, Mass.: Harvard University Press.

Hurst, J. W. 1956. *Law and the Conditions of Freedom in Nineteenth-Century United States.* Madison: Wisconsin University Press.

Hutson, James H. 1991. "The Bill of Rights and the American Revolutionary Experience." In *A Culture of Rights,* edited by Michael J. Lacey and Knud Haakonssen, 62–97. Cambridge, England: Cambridge University Press.

Hyneman, Charles S., and Donald S. Lutz, eds. 1983. *American Political Writing during the Founding Era, 1760–1805.* Vols. 1 and 2. Indianapolis: Liberty Press.

Jaenicke, Douglas Walter. 1981. "American Ideas of Political Party as Theories of Politics: Competing Ideas of Liberty and Community." Ph.D. dissertation, Cornell University, Ithaca, N.Y.

Kammen, Michael. 1988. *Sovereignty and Liberty: Constitutional Discourse in American Culture.* Madison: University of Wisconsin Press.

Kass, Alvin, 1965. *Politics in New York State, 1800–1830.* Syracuse, N.Y.: Syracuse University Press.

Kaye, Judith S. 1992. "Foreword: The Common Law and State Constitutional Law as Full Partners in the Protection of Individual Rights." *Rutgers Law Journal* 23, no. 4 (summer): 727–52.

Kendall, Willmoore, and George W. Carey. 1970. *The Basic Symbols of the American Political Tradition.* Baton Rouge: Louisiana State University Press.

Kerber, Linda D. 1980. *Women of the Republic: Intellect and Ideology in Revolutionary America.* Chapel Hill: University of North Carolina Press.

Ketcham, Ralph. 1984. *Presidents above Party: The First American Presidency, 1789–1829.* Chapel Hill: University of North Carolina Press.

Ketcham, Ralph, ed. 1986. *The Anti-Federalist Papers and the Constitutional Convention Debates.* New York: New American Library.

Kincaid, John. 1988. "State Court Protections of Individual Rights under State Constitutions: The New Judicial Federalism." *Journal of State Government* 61, no. 5: 163–69.

Kincaid, John, ed. 1982. *Political Culture, Public Policy and the American States.* Philadelphia, Pa.: Institute for the Study of Human Issues.

Kloppenberg, James T. 1987. "The Virtues of Liberalism: Christianity, Republicanism and Ethics in Early American Political Discourse." *Journal of American History* 74, no. 1 (June): 9–33.

Koppelman, Andrew. 1997. "*Romer v. Evans* and Invidious Intent." *William and Mary Bill of Rights Journal* 6, no. 1 (winter): 89–146.

Kramnick, Issac. 1982. "Republican Revisionism Revisited." *American Historical Review* 87 (June): 629–64.

———. 1988. "The 'Great National Discussion': The Discourse of Politics in 1787." *William and Mary Quarterly* 45, no. 1 (January): 3–32.

———. 1990. *Republicanism and Bourgeois Radicalism: Political Ideology in Late Eighteenth-Century England and America*. Ithaca: Cornell University Press.

Kruman, Marc W. 1983. *Parties and Politics in North Carolina, 1836–1865*. Baton Rouge: Louisiana State University Press.

———. 1997. *Between Authority and Liberty: State Constitution Making in Revolutionary America*. Chapel Hill: University of North Carolina Press.

Larkin, Jack. 1988. *The Reshaping of Everyday Life, 1790–1840*. New York: Harper and Row.

Laslett, Peter. 1988. "Introduction." In *Two Treatises of Government*. Cambridge, England: Cambridge University Press.

Levine, Andrew. 1981. *Liberal Democracy: A Critique of Its Theory*. New York: Columbia University Press.

Levinson, Sandford. 1990. "Veneration and Constitutional Change: James Madison Confronts the Possibility of Constitutional Amendment." *Texas Tech Law Review* 21: 2443–60.

Levy, Leonard W. 1986. *The Establishment Clause: Religion and the First Amendment*. New York: Macmillan.

Levy, Michael B. 1992. *Political Thought in America: An Anthology*. 2d edition. Prospect Heights, Ill.: Waveland Press.

Licht, Robert A., ed. 1991. *The Framers and Fundamental Rights*. Washington, D.C.: AEI Press.

Locke, John. 1988. *Two Treatises of Government*. Edited by Peter Laslett. Cambridge, England: Cambridge University Press.

Lutz, Donald S. 1980. *Popular Consent and Popular Control*. Baton Rouge: Louisiana State University Press.

———. 1984. "The Relative Influence of European Writers on Late Eighteenth-Century American Political Thought." *American Political Science Review* 78: 189–97.

———. 1988. *The Origins of American Constitutionalism*. Baton Rouge: Louisiana State University Press.

———. 1992. *A Preface to American Political Theory*. Lawrence: University Press of Kansas.

———. 1994. "Toward a Theory of Constitutional Amendment." *American Political Science Review* 88, no. 2: 355–70.

Macpherson, C. B. 1962. *The Political Theory of Possessive Individualism: Hobbes to Locke*. Oxford: Oxford University Press.

———. 1972. *The Real World of Democracy*. New York: Oxford University Press.

————. 1977. *The Life and Times of Liberal Democracy*. Oxford: Oxford University Press.

Macy, Jesse. 1884. *Institutional Beginning in a Western State*. Baltimore: Johns Hopkins University.

Main, Jackson Turner. 1973. *The Sovereign States, 1775–1783*. New York: New Viewpoints.

Marshall, Thomas R. 1988. *Public Opinion and the Supreme Court*. Winchester, Mass.: Unwin Hyman.

Matson, Cathy D., and Peter S. Onuf. 1990. *A Union of Interests: Political and Economic Thought in Revolutionary America*. Lawrence: University Press of Kansas.

May, Henry F. 1976. *The Enlightenment in America*. New York: Oxford University Press.

McCormick, Richard P. 1966. *The Second American Party System: Party Formation in the Jacksonian Era*. Chapel Hill: University of North Carolina Press.

————. 1986. *The Party Period and Public Policy: American Politics from the Age of Jackson to the Progressive Era*. New York: Oxford University Press.

McCoy, Drew R. 1980. *The Elusive Republic: Political Economy in Jeffersonian America*. Chapel Hill: University of North Carolina Press.

McDonald, Forrest. 1985. *Novus ordo seclorum: The Intellectual Origins of the Constitution*. Lawrence: University Press of Kansas.

McKay, Robert B. 1983. "Judicial Review in a Liberal Democracy." In *Liberal Democracy: Nomos XXV*, edited by J. Ronald Pennock and John W. Chapman, 121–44. New York: New York University Press.

Meyers, Diana T., and Kenneth Kipnis, eds. 1988. *Philosophical Dimensions of the Constitution*. Boulder, Colo.: Westview Press.

Meyers, Marvin. 1957. *The Jacksonian Persuasion: Politics and Belief*. Stanford: Stanford University Press.

Meyers, Marvin, ed. 1981. *The Mind of the Founder: Sources of the Political Thought of James Madison*. New York: Bobs-Merrill.

Miller, Joshua. 1988. "The Ghostly Body Politic: The Federalist Papers and Popular Sovereignty." *Political Theory* (February): 99–119.

————. 1991. *The Rise and Fall of Democracy in Early America, 1630–1789: The Legacy for Contemporary Politics*. University Park: Pennsylvania State University Press.

Morantz, R. A. M. 1971. "'Democracy' and 'Republic' in American Ideology, 1787–1840." Ph.D. dissertation, Columbia University, New York.

Morgan, Edmund S. 1987. "Popular Fiction." *New Republic*, 29 June 1987, pp. 25–36.

————. 1988. *Inventing the People: The Rise of Popular Sovereignty in England and America*. New York: W. W. Norton.

Murphy, Cornelius F., Jr. 1988. "Constitutional Revision." In *Philosophical Dimensions of the Constitution*, edited by Diana T. Meyers and Kenneth Kipnis, 60–74. Boulder, Colo.: Westview Press.

Murrin, John R. 1965. "The Myths of Colonial Democracy and Royal Decline in Eighteenth-Century America: A Review Essay." *Cithara* 5: 53–69.

Nagel, Robert F. 1983. "Interpretation and Importance in Constitutional Law: A Reassessment of Judicial Restraint." In *Liberal Democracy: Nomos XXV*, edited by J.

Ronald Pennock and John W. Chapman, 181–207. New York: New York University Press.

Nedelsky, Jennifer. 1990. *Private Property and the Limits of American Constitutionalism: The Madisonian Framework and Its Legacy.* Chicago: University of Chicago Press.

Nelson, John R., Jr. 1987. *Liberty and Property: Political Economy and Policy Making in the New Nation, 1789–1812.* Baltimore: Johns Hopkins University Press.

Nevins, Allan. 1969. *The American States during and after the Revolution, 1775–1789.* New York: Augustus Kelley.

Nichols, Mary P., and David K. Nichols. 1996. *Readings in American Government, Fifth Edition.* Dubuque: Kendall/Hunt Publishing Company.

Norton, Anne. 1986. *Alternative Americas: A Reading of Antebellum Political Culture.* Chicago: University of Chicago Press.

Olbrich, Emil. 1912. *The Development of Sentiment on Negro Suffrage to 1860.* Madison: University of Wisconsin.

Oliver, Frederick Scott. 1921. *Alexander Hamilton: An Essay on American Union.* New York: G. P. Putnam's Sons.

Paine, Thomas. 1953. *Common Sense and Other Political Writings.* Edited with introduction by Nelson F. Adkins. 1776. Reprint, New York: Bobbs-Merrill.

Pangle, Thomas. 1988. *The Spirit of Modern Republicanism.* Chicago: University of Chicago Press.

———. 1991. "Republicanism and Rights." In *The Framers and Fundamental Rights,* edited by Robert A. Licht, 102–20. Washington, D.C.: AEI Press.

Parrington, Vernon L. 1927. *Main Currents in American Thought.* Vol. 1. New York: Harcourt, Brace and World.

Pate, James E. 1932. *State Government in Virginia.* Richmond: The Appeals Press.

Pateman, Carole. 1970. *Participation and Democratic Theory.* Cambridge, England: Cambridge University Press.

The People Shall Judge. 1949. Selected and edited by the staff of Social Sciences 1, College of the University of Chicago. Chicago: University of Chicago Press.

Pessen, Edward. 1969. *Jacksonian America: Society, Personality and Politics.* Homewood, Ill.: Dorsey Press.

Peters, Ronald M., Jr. 1978. *The Massachusetts Convention of 1780: A Social Compact.* Amherst: University of Massachusetts Press.

Peterson, Merill D. 1962. *The Jefferson Image in the American Mind.* New York: Oxford University Press.

Peterson, Merill D., ed. 1986. *The Portable Thomas Jefferson.* 1975. Reprint, New York: Penguin Books.

Pocock, J. A. G. 1975. *The Machiavellian Moment.* Princeton, N.J.: Princeton University Press.

Pole, Jack Richon. 1957. "Suffrage and Representation in Massachusetts: A Statistical Note." *William and Mary Quarterly* 14: 561–92.

———. 1966. *Political Representation in England and the Origins of the American Republic.* London: Macmillan.

Poore, Ben Perley, comp. 1878. *The Federal and State Constitutions, Colonial Charters and other Organic Laws of the United States, Part One and Two.* Washington, D.C.: Government Printing Office.

Porter, Kirk Harold. 1918. *A History of Suffrage in the United States.* Chicago: University of Chicago Press.

Presser, Stephen B., and Jamil S. Zainaldin. 1989. *Law and Jurisprudence in American History: Cases and Materials, Second Edition.* St. Paul: West Publishing Company.

Rahe, Paul. 1992. *Republics: Ancient and Modern.* Chapel Hill: University Press of North Carolina.

Rakove, Jack N. 1990. *Interpreting the Constitution: The Debates over Original Intention.* Boston: Northeastern University Press.

Rankin, Robert S. 1955. *The Government and Administration of North Carolina.* New York: Thomas Y. Crowell.

Reid, John Phillip. 1986. *The Constitutional History of the American Revolution: The Authority of Rights.* Madison: University of Wisconsin Press.

———. 1989. *The Concept of Representation in the Age of the American Revolution.* Chicago: University of Chicago Press.

Remini, Robert V. 1981. *Andrew Jackson and the Course of American Freedom, 1822–1832.* Vol. 2. New York: Harper and Row.

———. 1987. *The Revolutionary Age of Andrew Jackson.* 1976. Reprint, New York: Harper and Row.

———. 1989. *The Jacksonian Era.* Arlington Heights, Ill.: Harlan Davidson.

Richards, David A. J. 1989. *Foundations of American Constitutionalism.* New York: Oxford University Press.

Richardson, William D. 1984. "Thomas Jefferson and Race: The Declaration and *Notes on the State of Virginia.*" *Polity* (spring): 447–66.

Riemer, Neal. 1967. *The Democratic Experiment: American Political Theory.* Vol. 1. Princeton: D. Van Nostrand.

Rodgers, Daniel T. 1987. *Contested Truths: Keywords in American Politics since Independence.* New York: Basic Books.

Rogin, Michael P. 1975. *Andrew Jackson and the Subjugation of the American Indian.* New York: Knopf.

Roper, Jon. 1989. *Democracy and Its Critics: Anglo-American Democratic Thought in the Nineteenth Century.* London: Unwin Hyman.

Roseboom, Eugene H., and Francis P. Weisenburger. 1956. *A History of Ohio.* Columbus: Ohio State Archaeological and Historical Society.

Rosenberg, Gerald N. 1990. *The Hollow Hope: Can Courts Bring About Social Change?* Chicago: University of Chicago Press.

Rosenblum, Nancy L., ed. 1989. *Liberalism and the Moral Life.* Cambridge, Mass.: Harvard University Press.

Ross, Russell M. 1957. *The Government and Administration of Iowa.* New York: Thomas Y. Crowell.

Rotunda, Ronald D. 1986. *The Politics of Language: Liberalism as Word and Symbol.* Iowa City: University of Iowa Press.

Sandoz, Ellis, ed. 1991. *Political Sermons of the Founding Era, 1730–1805.* Indianapolis: Liberty Fund.

Satz, Ronald N. 1975. *American Indian Policy in the Jacksonian Era.* Lincoln: University of Nebraska Press.

Scalia, Laura J. 1996. "The Many Faces of Locke in America's Early Nineteenth-Century Democratic Philosophy." *Political Research Quarterly* 49, no. 4: 807–36.

———. 1997. "Constitutions as Constituting People: The Interaction of Good Laws and Good Men, with Massachusetts as a Case Study, 1641–1853." Paper presented at the 1997 annual meeting of the American Political Science Association.

———. 1998. "Who Deserves Political Influence? How Liberal Ideals Helped Justify Mid-Nineteenth-Century Exclusionary Policies." *American Journal of Political Science* 42, no. 2: 349–76.

Schambra, William A. 1982. "The Roots of the American Public Philosophy." *The Public Interest* 67 (spring): 36–48.

Schlesinger, Arthur M., Jr. 1950. *The Age of Jackson.* Boston: Little, Brown.

Schultz, Stanley K. 1973. *The Culture Factory: Boston Public Schools, 1789–1860.* New York: Oxford University Press.

Shain, Barry Alan. 1994. *The Myth of American Individualism: The Protestant Origins of American Political Thought.* Princeton, N.J.: Princeton University Press.

Shalhope, Robert E. 1976. "Thomas Jefferson's Republicanism and Antebellum Southern Thought." *Journal of Southern History* 42, no. 4 (November): 529–56.

———. 1982. "Republicanism and Early American Historiography." *William and Mary Quarterly* 39, no. 2 (April): 334–56.

———. 1990. *The Roots of Democracy: American Thought and Culture, 1760–1800.* Boston: Twayne Publishers.

Shapiro, Ian. 1986. *The Evolution of Rights in Liberal Theory.* Cambridge, England: Cambridge University Press.

Shearer, Augustus Hunt. 1915. *A List of Documentary Material Relating to State Constitutional Conventions, 1776–1912.* Chicago: The Newberry Library, Bulletin No. 4.

Sheldon, Garrett Ward. 1991. *The Political Philosophy of Thomas Jefferson.* Baltimore: Johns Hopkins University Press.

Sherry, Suzanna. 1987. "The Founders' Unwritten Constitution." *University of Chicago Law Review* 54: 1120–47.

———. 1992. "Natural Law in the States." *University of Cincinnati Law Review* 61, no. 1: 171–222.

Shklar, Judith N. 1991. *American Citizenship: The Quest for Inclusion.* Cambridge, Mass.: Harvard University Press.

Simmons, A. J. 1992. *The Lockean Theory of Rights.* Princeton, N.J.: Princeton University Press.

Sinopoli, Robert C. 1992. *The Foundations of American Citizenship: Liberalism, the Constitution and Civic Virtue.* New York: Oxford University Press.

Smith, Adam. 1982. *The Theory of Moral Sentiments.* 1759. Reprint, Indianapolis: Liberty Classics.

Smith, David G. 1983. "Liberalism and Judicial Review." In *Liberal Democracy: Nomos*

XXV, edited by J. Ronald Pennock and John W. Chapman, 208–37. New York: New York University Press.

Smith, J. Allen. 1966. "The Constitution: A Reactionary Document." In *Liberalism versus Conservatism: The Continuing Debate in American Government,* edited by Willmore Kendall and George W. Carey, 45–62. Princeton: D. Van Nostrand.

Smith, Rogers M. 1985. *Liberalism and American Constitutional Law.* Cambridge, Mass.: Harvard University Press.

———. 1988. "The 'American Creed' and American Identity: The Limits of Liberal Citizenship in the United States." *Western Political Quarterly* (spring): 225–51.

———. 1989. "'One United People': Second-Class Female Citizenship and the American Quest for Community." *Yale Journal of Law and the Humanities* 1, no. 2 (May): 229–93.

———. 1993. "Beyond Tocqueville, Myrdal, and Hartz: The Multiple Traditions in America." *American Political Science Review* 87, no. 3 (September): 549–66.

———. 1997. *Civic Ideals: Conflicting Visions of Citizenship in U.S. History.* New Haven: Yale University Press.

Smith, Theodore Clarke. 1967. *The Liberty and Free Soil Parties in the Northwest.* 1897. Reissue, New York: Russell and Russell.

Sorin, Gerald. 1971. *The New York Abolitionists.* Westport, Conn.: Greenwood Press.

———. 1972. *Abolitionism: A New Perspective.* New York: Praeger.

Stevens, Harry R. 1957. *The Early Jackson Party in Ohio.* Durham, N.C.: Duke University Press.

Stevens, Jacqueline. 1996. "The Reasonableness of John Locke's Majority: Property Rights, Consent, and Resistance in the *Second Treatise.*" *Political Theory* 24, no. 3 (August): 423–63.

Stokes, Anson Phelps. 1950. *Church and State in the United States.* Vol 1. New York: Harper and Brothers.

Storing, Herbert J. 1981. *What the Anti-Federalists Were For.* Chicago: University of Chicago Press.

Strauss, Leo. 1950. *Natural Right and History.* Chicago: University of Chicago Press.

Sturm, Albert L. 1970. *Thirty Years of State Constitution-Making, 1938–1968.* New York: National Municipal League.

———. 1982. "The Development of American State Constitutions." *Publius: The Journal of Federalism* 12, no. 1: 57–98.

Swierenga, Robert P. 1990. "Ethnoreligious Political Behavior in the Mid–Nineteenth Century: Voting Values and Cultures." In *Religion and American Politics from the Colonial Period to the 1980s,* edited by Mark A. Noll, 146–71. New York: Oxford University Press.

Thorpe, Francis Newton. 1898. *A Constitutional History of the American People, 1776–1850.* Vols. 1 and 2. New York: Harper and Brothers.

Turner, Frederick Jackson. 1950. *The United States, 1830–1850: The Nation and Its Sections.* 1935. Reprint, New York: Peter Smith.

Tushnet, Mark. 1991. "*The Federalist* and the Institutions of Fundamental Rights." In *The Framers and Fundamental Rights*, edited by Robert A. Licht, 121–36. Washington, D.C.: AEI Press.

Wald, Kenneth D. 1987. *Religion and Politics in the United States*. New York: Saint Martins Press.

Walzer, Michael. 1984. "Liberalism and the Art of Separation." *Political Theory* 12, no. 3: 315–30.

Ward, John William. 1953. *Andrew Jackson: Symbol for an Age*. London: Oxford University Press.

Welter, Rush. 1962. *Popular Education and Democratic Thought in America*. New York: Columbia University Press.

———. 1975. *The Mind of America, 1820–1860*. New York: Columbia University Press.

West, Thomas G. 1997. *Vindicating the Founders: Race, Sex, Class & Justice in the Origins of America*. New York: Rowman & Littlefield.

White, Leonard D. 1965. *The Jeffersonians: A Study in Administrative History, 1801–1829*. New York: Free Press.

White, Morton. 1978. *The Philosophy of the American Revolution*. New York: Oxford University Press.

Whitehead, Jaan. 1992. "Reason and Regulation in Economic Theory." In *The Economic Approach to Politics*, edited by Kristen Monroe, 53–73. New York: HarperCollins.

Wiebe, Robert H. 1985. *The Opening of American Society from the Adoption of the Constitution to the Eve of Disunion*. New York: Vintage Books.

Wilentz, Sean. 1982. "On Class and Politics in Jacksonian America." *Reviews in American History* 10, no. 4 (December): 45–63.

———. 1984. *Chants Democratic: New York City and the Rise of the American Working Class, 1788–1850*. New York: Oxford University Press.

Williamson, Chilton. 1960. *American Suffrage from Property to Democracy, 1776–1860*. Princeton, N.J.: Princeton University Press.

Wills, Garry. 1978. *Inventing America: Jefferson's Declaration of Independence*. New York: Vintage Books.

Wilson, Major L. 1987. *Space, Time and Freedom: The Quest for Nationality and the Irrepressible Conflict, 1815–1861*. Westport, Conn.: Greenwood Press.

Winch, D. N. 1978. *Adam Smith's Politics: An Essay in Historiographic Revisions*. Cambridge, England: Cambridge University Press.

Wolin, Sheldon S. 1989. *The Presence of the Past: Essays on the State and the Constitution*. Baltimore: Johns Hopkins University Press.

Wood, Gordon S. 1969. *The Creation of the American Republic, 1776–1787*. New York: W. W. Norton.

———. 1993. *Radicalism and the American Revolution*. New York: Vintage Books.

Wootton, David. 1992. "John Locke and Richard Ashcraft's *Revolutionary Politics*." *Political Studies* 40: 79–98.

Wyatt-Brown, Bevhram. 1969. *Lewis Tappan and the Evangelical War against Slavery.* Cleveland, Ohio: Case Western Reserve.

Yarbrough, Jean. 1979a. "Republicanism Reconsidered: Some Thoughts on the Foundation and Preservation of the American Republic." *Review of Politics* 41, no. 1 (January): 61–95.

———. 1979b. "Thoughts on *The Federalist*'s View of Representation." *Polity* (fall): 65–82.

Young, James P. 1996. *Reconsidering American Liberalism: The Troubled Odyssey of the Liberal Idea.* Boulder, Colo.: Westview Press.

Zuckert, Michael. 1994. *Natural Right and the New Republicanism.* Princeton, N.J.: Princeton University Press.

Index